P299. D46 DIE

DEMONSTRA TIVE

TYPOLOGICAL STUDIES IN LANGUAGE (TSL)

A companion series to the journal "STUDIES IN LANGUAGE"

Honorary Editor: Joseph H. Greenberg
General Editor: Michael Noonan
Assistant Editors: Spike Gildea, Suzanne Kemmer

Editorial Board:

Volumes in this series will be functionally and typologically oriented, covering specific topics in language by collecting together data from a wide variety of languages and language typologies. The orientation of the volumes will be substantive rather than formal, with the aim of investigating universals of human language via as broadly defined a data base as possible, leaning toward cross-linguistic, diachronic, developmental and live-discourse data.

Volume 42

Holger Diessel

Demonstratives
Form, function, and grammaticalization

DEMONSTRATIVES

FORM, FUNCTION, AND GRAMMATICALIZATION

HOLGER DIESSEL

Max Planck Institute for Evolutionary Anthropology

JOHN BENJAMINS PUBLISHING COMPANY
AMSTERDAM/PHILADELPHIA

TM   The paper used in this publication meets the minimum requirements of American National Standard for Information Sciences — Permanence of Paper for Printed Library Materials, ANSI Z39.48-1984.

Library of Congress Cataloging-in-Publication Data

Diessel, Holger.
    Demonstratives : form, function, and grammaticalization / Holger Diessel.
       p. cm. -- (Typological studies in language ISSN 0167-7373 ; v. 42)
    Includes bibliographical references and index.
    1. Grammar, Comparative and general--Demonstratives. I. Title II. Series.

P299.D46 D54 1999
415   99-046743
ISBN 90 272 2942 2 (Eur.) / 1 55619 656 3 (US) (Hb; alk. paper)   CIP
ISBN 90 272 2943 0 (Eur.) / 1 55619 657 1 (US) (Pb; alk. paper)

John Benjamins Publishing Co. • P.O.Box 75577 • 1070 AN Amsterdam • The Netherlands
John Benjamins North America • P.O.Box 27519 • Philadelphia PA 19118-0519 • USA

Table of Contents

Acknowledgments

This book is a revision of my doctoral dissertation, *Demonstratives in Cross-linguistic and Diachronic Perspective*, written at the State University of New York at Buffalo. I would like to thank my thesis advisors, Matthew Dryer, Karin Michelson, Jean-Pierre Koenig, and David Zubin for their guidance and intellectual stimulation. I also would like to acknowledge the support and inspiration that I received from my friends and fellow graduate students David Kemmerer, Martha Islas, Wendy Baldwin, Alissa Melinger, Matthew Davidson, David Houghton, and Cori Grimm. Special thanks goes to Eve Ng, who proofread the entire manuscript. Finally, I am very grateful to Nikolaus Himmelmann and Edith Moravcsik, who provided insightful comments on earlier versions of this book.

Parts of Chapter 4 and Chapter 6 first appeared, in different form, in the following articles and conference papers: "The grammaticalization of demonstratives in crosslinguistic perspective", *Chicago Linguistic Society* 33 (1997); "Predicative Demonstratives", *Berkeley Linguistics Society* 23 (1997) (to appear); "The morphosyntax of demonstratives in synchrony and diachrony", *Linguistic Typology* 3 (1999). I thank the publishers for permission to include revised material from these publications in the present monograph.

Abbreviations

ABL	ablative	DTM	determinative
ABES	abessive	DU	dual
ABS	absolutive	EMPH	emphatic
ACC	accusative	ERG	ergative
ADE	adessive	EXCL	exclamative marker
ADJ	adjective	EXIST	existential marker
ADV	adverbial/adverb	FACT	factive
AFF	affirmative marker	FEM/F	feminine
AGR	agreement marker	FOC	focus
ANA	anaphor	FUT	future
ANIM	animate	GEN	genitive
AOR	aorist	G1s/G2s	noun classes
ART	article	H	hearer
ASS	assertive marker	HAB	habitual aspect
ATT	attribute marker	IDENT	identificational/
BEN	benefactive		identifier
CIRC	circumstantive	ILL	illative
CLASS	classifier	IMP	imperative
COLL	collective	INANIM	inanimate
COM	comitative	INDEF	indefinite
COMP	complementizer	INE	inessive
CONTRF	contrafactive	INSTR	instrumental
COP	copula	INTJEC	interjection
DAT	dative	INVIS	invisible
DEF	definite	LAT	lative
DEIC	deictic	LK	linker
DEM	demonstrative	LOC	locative
DET	determiner	MASC/M	masculine
DIST	distal	MD	modal particle
DP	determiner phrase	MED	medial

N	noun	PRES	present
NC	noun class	PRO	pronominal/pronoun
NEG	negative marker	PROX	proximal
NEUT/N	neuter	PAST	past
NLZ	nominalizer	PURP	purposive
NOM	nominative	Q	question
NONFACT	nonfactive	QNT	quantifier
NONPAST	nonpast	REF	reference
NP	noun phrase	REL	relative marker
NPIP	noun phrase initial position	S	speaker
		SG	singular
NUC	nucleus	SPEC	specific indefinite article
NUM	number		
OBJ	object	SUB	subordinate marker
OBL	oblique	SUBJ	subject
P	preposition	STA	stative aspect
PART	particle	TEMP	temporal
PASS	passive	TNS	tense marker
PERF	perfective aspect	VIS	visible
PF	present perfect	1SG	first person singular
PL	plural	2SG	second person singular
POSS	possessive	3SG	third person singular
PRED	predicative marker	3PL	third person plural

CHAPTER 1

Introduction

1.1 Preliminary remarks

All languages have demonstratives, but their form, meaning and use vary tremendously across the languages of the world. Some languages have only a few demonstrative particles, which they employ in a variety of syntactic contexts for a wide range of semantic and pragmatic functions. Other languages have demonstratives that are morphologically complex (i.e. not merely particles), syntactically restricted, and semantically and pragmatically very specific in function.

This work provides the first large-scale analysis of demonstratives from a crosslinguistic and diachronic perspective. It is based on a sample of 85 languages from a wide range of genetic groups and geographical areas. The first part of this book analyzes demonstratives form a synchronic point of view. It examines their morphological structures, semantic features, syntactic functions, and pragmatic uses. The second part is concerned with diachronic aspects of demonstratives, in particular with their grammaticalization. Across languages, demonstratives provide a common historical source for definite articles, relative and third person pronouns, copulas, sentence connectives, directional preverbs, and many other grammatical items. I describe the different mechanisms by which demonstratives grammaticalize and argue that the evolution of grammatical markers from demonstratives is crucially distinct from other cases of grammaticalization.

The main purpose of this study is to provide a source of reference for both field workers and theoretical linguists who are interested in demonstratives and their grammaticalization. The book provides a systematic overview of all empirical aspects of demonstratives and addresses a number of theoretical issues that are of more general interest in typology, syntax and grammaticalization theory.

This introductory chapter presents a preview of the major results of my investigation and discusses previous work dealing with demonstratives and their grammaticalization. I begin with a brief definition of the notion of demonstrative.

1.2   Towards a definition of demonstratives

There are three criteria that are relevant for the notion of demonstrative that I have used in this study. First, demonstratives are deictic expressions serving specific syntactic functions. Many studies confine the notion of demonstrative to deictic expressions such as English *this* and *that,* which are used either as independent pronouns or as modifiers of a coocurring noun, but the notion that I will use is broader. It subsumes not only demonstratives being used as pronouns or noun modifiers but also locational adverbs such as English *here* and *there.*

Second, demonstratives generally serve specific pragmatic functions. They are primarily used to focus the hearer's attention on objects or locations in the speech situation (often in combination with a pointing gesture), but they may also function to organize the information flow in the ongoing discourse. More specifically, demonstratives are often used to keep track of prior discourse participants and to activate specific shared knowledge. The most basic function of demonstratives is, however, to orient the hearer outside of discourse in the surrounding situation.

Finally, demonstratives are characterized by specific semantic features. All languages have at least two demonstratives that are deictically contrastive: a proximal demonstrative referring to an entity near the deictic center and a distal demonstrative denoting a referent that is located at some distance to the deictic center. There are, however, a few languages in my sample in which some demonstratives are distance-neutral. For instance, though German has three adverbial demonstratives — *hier* 'here', *da* 'there', and *dort* 'there' — it employs a single demonstrative pronoun: *dies* 'this/that' (cf. 3.1.1). Demonstratives such as German *dies* are typologically uncommon and one might argue that they are indistinct from third person pronouns and/or definite articles (cf. Anderson and Keenan 1985: 280), but I will treat them as demonstratives for two reasons: first like distance-marked demonstratives, distance-neutral demonstratives are commonly used to orient the hearer in the surrounding situation, and second they can always be reinforced by demonstratives that are marked for distance if it is necessary to differentiate between two or more referents (see 3.1.1).

1.3   Outline and literature

Demonstratives have been the subject of numerous investigations in linguistics and philosophy.[1] The vast majority of studies concentrates on their pragmatic use and meaning. The scope of the current investigation is broader. It does not only examine their use and meaning, but also their morphological structures, syntactic functions and grammaticalization. One of the major challenges of this work is to integrate the analysis of different aspects of demonstratives into one coherent presentation. This section provides an overview of my investigation, which is organized into five chapters.

Chapter 2 examines the morphology of demonstratives. It is divided into two sections. The first section describes the demonstrative systems of four languages. It illustrates the extent of formal variation among demonstratives in different languages. The second section examines the morphological structures of demonstratives more systematically. It discusses the properties of demonstrative clitics, the inflectional behavior of demonstratives in different syntactic contexts, and the formation of demonstrative stems. There is to my knowledge no previous work on the morphology of demonstratives in typological perspective. The current study is the first investigation in this domain.

Chapter 3 investigates the semantic features of demonstratives. The meaning of demonstratives and other deictics has been studied extensively. The collections of articles edited by Weissenborn and Klein (1982), Jarvella and Klein (1982), and Rauh (1983) present an overview of the research in this domain. Some of the articles in these collections describe the semantic features of demonstratives from a comparative or crosslinguistic perspective (e.g. Fillmore 1982; Ehlich 1983), but most of them concentrate on the demonstratives in one particular language (usually English). There are two studies that are especially important to my investigation: Fillmore (1982) and Anderson and Keenan (1985). Both studies examine the semantic features of demonstratives from a typological perspective. My analysis is inspired by their approach, but it is based on a much larger language sample and distinguishes systematically between semantic features of two different domains: (i) deictic features, which indicate the location of the referent in the speech situation, and (ii) qualitative features, which classify the referent (cf. Lyons 1977; Rauh 1983). The deictic features comprise features that indicate whether the referent is near, away or far away from the deictic center, whether it is visible or out of sight, at a higher or lower elevation, uphill or downhill, or moving toward or away from the deictic center. The qualitative features indicate whether the referent is an object, person or place, whether it is animate or inanimate, human or non-human, female or male, a single entity or a set, or conceptualized as a restricted or extended entity. All of these features are directly encoded by several demonstratives in my sample.

Chapter 4 examines the syntactic properties of demonstratives. It is argued that one has to distinguish between the distribution and the categorial status of demonstratives. The categorial status of a demonstrative is defined by the combination of two features: (i) a certain distribution and (ii) a specific form. Two demonstratives belong to different categories if they are distributionally *and* formally distinguished. I use the attributes pronominal, adnominal, adverbial, and identificational in order to indicate the syntactic context in which demonstratives occur (i.e. their distribution); and I use the nominals (demonstrative) pronoun, determiner, adverb, and identifier in order to indicate their categorial status. Table 1 presents an overview of these terms.

Table 1. *Demonstratives: distribution and category*

Distribution	Category
pronominal demonstrative	demonstrative pronoun
adnominal demonstrative	demonstrative determiner
adverbial demonstrative	demonstrative adverb
identificational demonstrative	demonstrative identifier

The distinction between the distribution and categorial status of demonstratives is crucial because some languages use demonstratives of the same grammatical category in more than one syntactic context, while other languages employ categorially (i.e. formally) distinct demonstratives in each position.

Pronominal demonstratives are independent pronouns in argument position of verbs and adpositions. They are often formally distinguished from adnominal demonstratives, which accompany a cooccurring noun. For instance, French uses the demonstratives *celui, celle, ceux,* and *celles* as independent pronouns and *ce, cette,* and *ces* as modifiers of a subsequent noun. Since pronominal and adnominal demonstratives are formally distinguished in French, I assume that they belong to different categories: *celui, celle, ceux,* and *celles* are demonstrative pronouns, while *ce, cette,* and *ces* are demonstrative determiners.

Unlike French, many languages do not distinguish between demonstrative pronouns and demonstrative determiners. Tuscarora, for instance, has two demonstrative particles, *hè:níkǎ:* 'this/these' and *kyè:níkǎ:* 'that/those', which are either used in isolation as independent pronouns or together with a cooccurring noun. Following Mithun (1987), I assume that pronominal and adnominal demonstratives belong to the same category in Tuscarora. Unlike adnominal demonstratives in French, adnominal demonstratives in Tuscarora do not function as determiners; rather, they are used as independent pronouns that are only loosely adjoined to a coreferential noun in apposition. In other words, Tuscarora does not have demonstrative determiners; it has only demonstrative pronouns that are used in two different syntactic contexts. There are also languages in my sample that do not have a class of demonstrative pronouns. These languages use demonstrative determiners in combination with a third person pronoun or a classifier in contexts where languages such as English employ demonstrative pronouns.

Adverbial demonstratives are usually distinguished from pronominal and adnominal demonstratives. There are only a few languages in my sample in which adverbial demonstratives have the same form as demonstratives that are used as independent pronouns or noun modifiers. For instance, in Ngiyambaa it is possible to refer to a location by a demonstrative pronoun in locative case, as illustrated in (1).

(1)   Ngiyambaa (Donaldson 1980: 317)
       yaba=lugu   **ŋa-ni-la:**   *guri-nja*
       track=3SG.GEN that-LOC-GIVEN lie-PRES
       'His tracks are there.'

The demonstrative in (1) is semantically equivalent to English *there*, but from a morphological and syntactic perspective it can be viewed as a demonstrative pronoun with a locative case marker.

In addition to demonstrative pronouns, determiners and adverbs, there is a fourth demonstrative category, which is almost entirely unknown in the typological literature (but see Himmelmann 1997). Many languages use special demonstrative forms in copular and nonverbal clauses, as in example (2) and (3) from French and Ponapean.

(2)   French
       C'   *est Pascal.*
       this/it is Pascal
       'It/this is Pascal.'

(3)   Ponapean (Rehg 1981: 143)
       Iet   *noumw pinselen.*
       here.is your   pencil
       'Here is your pencil.'

The demonstratives in these examples function to identify a referent in the speech situation. They are usually considered demonstrative pronouns, but many languages distinguish ordinary demonstrative pronouns from demonstratives in copular and nonverbal clauses. Both French and Ponapean employ demonstratives with a different form as independent pronouns in other syntactic contexts. I distinguish therefore between demonstratives in copular and nonverbal clauses and demonstratives that occur in other sentence types. As shown in Table 1, I use

the term identificational demonstrative for demonstratives in copular and nonverbal clauses regardless of their categorial status; and I use the term demonstrative identifier when I refer to demonstratives in copular and nonverbal clauses
that are categorially (i.e. formally) distinguished from demonstratives in other
contexts.

Chapter 5 is concerned with the pragmatic uses of demonstratives. As
pointed out above, demonstratives are primarily used to draw the hearer's
attention to entities in the speech situation, but they may also serve a variety of
other pragmatic functions. Following Halliday and Hasan (1976: 57–76), I use the
notion exophoric for demonstratives that are used with reference to entities in the
surrounding situation, and I use the term endophoric for all other uses. The
endophoric use is subdivided into the (i) anaphoric, (ii) discourse deictic, and (iii)
recognitional uses, as shown in Figure 1.

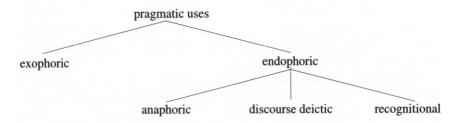

Figure 1. *The pragmatic uses of demonstratives*

The exophoric, anaphoric, and discourse deictic uses are discussed in studies
by Lyons (1977), Levinson (1983), Webber (1991), Fillmore (1997), Himmelmann (1996, 1997), and many others. Exophoric demonstratives refer to non-
linguistic entities in the speech situation; they focus the hearer's attention on
persons, objects or locations in the outside world. Anaphoric demonstratives are
coreferential with a noun phrase in the preceding discourse; they keep track of
prior discourse participants. Discourse deictic demonstratives refer to a chunk of
the surrounding discourse; they express an overt link between two propositions.

In addition to the exophoric, anaphoric and discourse deictic uses, Himmelmann (1996, 1997) describes another usage, which he calls the recognitional use.
In the recognitional use, demonstratives function to indicate that speaker and
hearer are familiar with the referent due to shared experience. The demonstrative
in the following sentence exemplifies this use.

(4)   English
        *Do you still have **that** radio that your aunt gave you for your birthday?*

Although the radio is not present in the speech situation and is mentioned for the first time, it occurs with the distal demonstrative *that*. The speaker uses the demonstrative in order to indicate that the hearer is able to identify the referent based on specific shared knowledge. Aspects of the recognitional use have been described in several recent investigations (cf. Chen 1990; Gundel et al. 1993), but Himmelmann (1996, 1997) provides the only systematic account of this use. His work is especially significant for my treatment of the pragmatic uses in Chapter 5. Though I adopt Himmelmann's distinction of the four pragmatic uses that I have mentioned, I challenge his hypothesis that all four uses have equal status. In accordance with most previous work (cf. Bühler 1934; Lyons 1977), I contend that the exophoric use represents the basic use from which all other uses derive. I support my hypothesis with evidence from language acquisition, markedness theory, and grammaticalization.

The final chapter of this study investigates the diachronic reanalysis of demonstratives as grammatical markers. I argue that the process by which demonstratives grammaticalize is crucially determined by the syntactic context in which the demonstrative occurs. More specifically, I show that pronominal, adnominal, adverbial, and identificational demonstratives provide the source for four different sets of grammatical markers. Pronominal demonstratives are frequently reanalyzed as third person pronouns, relative pronouns, complementizers, sentence connectives, pronominal determinatives, possessive pronouns, and verbal number markers. Adnominal demonstratives may develop into definite articles, linkers, nominal number markers, adnominal determinatives, specific indefinite articles, and boundary markers of postnominal attributes. Adverbial demonstratives provide a common source for temporal adverbs, directional preverbs, and sentence connectives. Finally, identificational demonstratives may evolve into copulas, focus markers, and expletives.

Grammaticalization is a gradual process (Lichtenberk 1991). At the initial stage of this process, grammatical items often have the same form as their historical source. The distinction between demonstratives and grammatical markers such as definite articles is therefore not always immediately obvious. In Chapter 6, I argue that the grammaticalization of demonstratives can be viewed as a cline ranging from exophoric demonstratives used to orient the hearer in the outside world to grammatical markers serving specific syntactic functions. Endophoric demonstratives are somewhere in between the two ends of this cline;

they often mark the initial stage of a grammaticalization process, giving rise to definite articles and many other grammatical items.

The diachronic reanalysis of demonstratives has been the subject of numerous investigations, in both traditional historical linguistics and recent work in grammaticalization. Some of the important older work includes Brugmann (1904), Brugmann and Delbrück (1911), Paul (1920), and Behaghel (1923–1932). These studies are exclusively concerned with the reanalysis of demonstratives in Indo-European languages. More recent studies have shown that the grammaticalization of demonstratives is a common historical process in virtually every language. Heine and Reh (1984), Heine, Claudi and Hünnemeyer (1991a), Hopper and Traugott (1993), Lehmann (1995a), and Harris and Campbell (1995) describe the reanalysis of demonstratives as definite articles, relative and third person pronouns, copulas, and complementizers in a wide variety of languages. Other studies concentrate on the grammaticalization of one particular item. For instance, the reanalysis of demonstratives as definite articles has been described in studies by Christophersen (1939), Heinrichs (1954), Krámský (1972), Ultan (1978a), Harris (1978, 1980), Greenberg (1978, 1991), Lüdtke (1991), Vogel (1993), Cyr (1993a, 1993b, 1996), Leiss (1994), Epstein (1994, 1995), Laury (1995, 1997), and Himmelmann (1997, 1998). There are also several studies that examine the development of copulas from demonstratives: Berman and Grosu (1976), Li and Thompson (1977), Schuh (1983a), Hengeveld (1990), Gildea (1993), and Devitt (1994). Other studies that are relevant to my investigation include Lehmann (1984), who describes the development of relative pronouns in Ancient Greek, Old High German, and several other languages; Sankoff and Brown (1976), who examine the emergence of boundary markers of postnominal attributes in Tok Pisin; Lockwood (1968), who discusses a number of grammatical items that developed from demonstratives in German; and Frajzyngier (1997), who shows that nominal and verbal number markers in many Chadic languages originate from demonstratives. Chapter 6 summarizes much of this work and discusses several other grammaticalization channels that have only been described in reference grammars.

Finally, I consider the question: where do demonstratives come from — what is their historical source? Demonstratives are usually considered grammatical items. Grammaticalization theory claims that all grammatical items are ultimately derived from lexical expressions, but in the case of demonstratives there is no evidence from any language that they developed from a lexical source or any other source, for that matter, that is non-deictic (Himmelmann 1997: 20). Based on this finding, I advance the hypothesis that demonstratives might form a class of deictic expressions that belong to the basic vocabulary of every language (cf. Plank 1979a; Traugott 1982). This would not only explain why demonstratives cannot be traced back to lexical items, it would also account for the fact that demonstratives serve a particular pragmatic function that sets them apart from all other linguistic expressions (cf. Bühler 1934; Peirce 1955; Ehlich 1979, 1982, 1983, 1987). Furthermore, it might explain why demonstratives are among the very few items that exhibit a non-arbitrary relationship between phonetic form and meaning (cf. Woodworth 1991). If demonstratives are not derived from lexical items they would present a second source domain from which grammatical markers may emerge, and that would undermine one of the central assumptions of grammaticalization theory.

1.4 Language sample

My study is based on a sample of 85 languages. The bulk of the data comes from reference grammars and other published sources, supplemented by information obtained from native speakers and language specialists. For each language, I gathered information on the morphological structures, semantic features, syntactic functions, and grammaticalization of demonstratives. I used two criteria for selecting the languages of my sample: (i) genetic diversity and (ii) geographical distance.[2] For the genetic classification, I consulted two sources: Ruhlen (1991) and the Ethnologue (Grimes 1997). With two exceptions, my sample includes at least one language of every major language family that Ruhlen suggests. The two exceptions are Miao-Yao and Chukchi-Kamchatkan. Both families include fewer than half a dozen languages in Ruhlen's classification. My sample also includes several language isolates (Burushaski, Basque, Korean, Ainu) and an English-based creole (Tok Pisin). Large and diverse phyla are better represented than small and homogeneous phyla. For instance, Niger-Congo, which comprises several hundred languages, is represented by five languages in my sample, while Khoisan, which subsumes 30 languages, is only represented by one.

In order to ensure geographical diversity I used the geographical divisions suggested by Dryer (e.g. 1992a). He distinguishes six major geographical areas: North America, South America, South East Asia and Oceanic, Africa, Eurasia, and Australia and New Guinea (Dryer 1989c distinguishes only five areas). My sample includes at least eight languages of each of the six geographical areas that Dryer suggests. Below, I have given a list of all 85 languages that are included in my sample. The sources that I have used for each language are listed in Appendix A.

North America

1. Halkomelem	Salishan
2. Kiowa	Kiowa-Tanoan
3. Lealao Chinantec	Oto-Manguean
4. Mam	Mayan
5. Mojave	Hokan
6. Oneida	Iroquoian
7. Passamaquoddy-Maliseet	Algonquian
8. Picurís	Kiowa-Tanoan
9. Quileute	Chimakuan
10. Slave	Athapaskan-Eyak
11. Tümpisa Shoshone	Uto-Aztecan
12. Tuscarora	Iroquoian
13. Tzutujil	Mayan
14. Ute	Uto-Aztecan
15. West Greenlandic	Eskimo-Aleut

South America

16. Apalai	Carib
17. Barasano	Tucanoan
18. Canela-Krahô	Ge-Kaingang
19. Epena Pedee	Choco
20. Hixkaryana	Carib
21. Urubu-Kaapor	Tupi-Guarani
22. Wari'	Chapakuran
23. Yagua	Peba-Yaguan

South East Asia and Oceanic

24. Acehnese	Western Malayo-Polynesian
25. Ao	Tibeto-Burman
26. Byansi	Tibeto-Burman
27. Khasi	Mon-Khmer
28. Kusaiean	Central-Eastern Malayo-Polynesian
29. Lahu	Tibeto-Burman
30. Manam	Central-Eastern Malayo-Polynesian
31. Mandarin Chinese	Sinitic
32. Mulao	Daic
33. Nùng	Daic
34. Pangasinan	Western Malayo-Polynesian
35. Ponapean	Central-Eastern Malayo-Polynesian
36. Santali	Munda
37. Vietnamese	Mon-Khmer
38. West Futuna-Aniwa	Central-Eastern Malayo-Polynesian

Africa

39. Duwai	Chadic
40. Ewondo	Niger-Congo
41. Gulf Arabic	Semitic
42. Izi	Niger-Congo
43. Karanga	Niger-Congo
44. Koyra Chiini	Songhay (wider affiliation unknown)
45. Kunuz-Nubian	Eastern Sudanic
46. Lango	Nilotic
47. Logbara	Central Sudanic
48. Margi	Chadic
49. Modern Hebrew	Semitic
50. Nama	Khoisan
51. Nandi	Nilotic
52. Ngiti	Central Sudanic
53. Supyire	Niger-Congo
54. Swazi	Niger-Congo
55. Turkana	Nilotic
56. Western Bade	Chadic

Eurasia

57. Ainu	Isolate
58. Basque	Isolate
59. Burushaski	Isolate
60. Czech	Slavic
61. Finnish	Finno-Ugric
62. French	Romance
63. Georgian	Kartvelian
64. German	Germanic
65. Japanese	Japanese
66. Kannada	Dravidian
67. Korean	Isolate
68. Lezgian	North Caucasian
69. Punjabi	Indo-Aryan
70. Swedish	Germanic
71. Turkish	Turkic

Australia and New Guinea

72. Alamblak	Sepik
73. Ambulas	Sepik
74. Dyirbal	Pama-Nyungan
75. Guugu Yimidhirr	Pama-Nyungan
76. Hua	East New Guinea Highlands
77. Ngiyambaa	Pama-Nyungan
78. Nunggubuyu	Gunwingguan
79. Tauya	Madang-Adelbert Range
80. Tok Pisin	Creole
81. Urim	Torricelli
82. Usan	Madang-Adelbert Range
83. Wardaman	Gunwingguan
84. Yankunytjatjara	Pama-Nyungan
85. Yimas	Nor-Pondo

CHAPTER 2

Morphology

This chapter is concerned with the morphological structures of demonstratives. Some languages have only a few demonstrative particles; they are uninflected and do not combine with any other morpheme. Other languages employ demonstratives that are marked for gender, number and/or case and may combine with derivational affixes or other free forms. Languages of this sort can have several hundred demonstrative forms. For instance, Denny (1982: 372) reports that the demonstrative system in Inuktitut comprises 686 different forms, formed from twelve demonstrative roots and a wide variety of inflectional and derivational morphemes. Another language with an extremely complex demonstrative system is Santali, a Munda language spoken in northeastern India. According to Bodding's description (1929: 118–147), there are well over 200 distinct forms in the demonstrative system in Santali.

In this chapter, I first describe the demonstratives of four individual languages, and then I examine the morphological structures of demonstratives more systematically from a typological perspective.

2.1 Demonstratives in Guugu Yimidhirr, Ambulas, Ewondo, and Korean

The following four sections describe the demonstratives in Guugu Yimidhirr, Ambulas, Ewondo, and Korean, respectively. The purpose of these descriptions is to illustrate the extent of formal variation among demonstratives in different languages. We will see that the demonstratives of some languages are morphologically invariable, while the demonstratives of other languages are formed from a demonstrative root and a wide variety of other morphemes.

2.1.1 *Guugu Yimidhirr*

Guugu Yimidhirr is a Pama-Nyungan language spoken in northeastern Australia.

The language has two demonstrative roots, *yii* 'proximal' and *nhaa* 'distal', which are inflected for case:

Table 2. *Demonstratives in Guugu Yimidhirr (Haviland 1979: 73)*

	PROXIMAL	DISTAL
ABS	*yii, yiyi*	*nhaa, nhaayun*
ERG/INSTR	*yiimuun*	*nhaamuun*
LOC/ALL	*yiway, yuway, yiimu*	*nhaway, nhaamu*
ABL/CAUSAL	*yiimunganh*	*nhaamunganh, nhaawanun* (ABL only)
PURP		*nhaamuu*
COM	*yimudhirr, yimidhirr*	*nhamudhirr, nhamidhirr*

The demonstratives in Table 2 refer to "things", "places" and "times" (Haviland 1979: 72). They may function as independent pronouns (1a), noun modifiers (1b), locational deictics (1c), or identificational demonstratives in nonverbal clauses (1d). That is, Guugu Yimidhirr does not distinguish between demonstrative pronouns, determiners, adverbs, and identifiers; rather, it uses the same demonstrative forms in various syntactic contexts:

(1)   Guugu Yimidhirr (Haviland 1979: 73, 165, 92, 54)

    a. *ngayu   nhinaan **yiimuun**   gunda-l*
       1SG.NOM 2SG.ACC PROX.INSTR hit-NONPAST
       'I'll hit you with this (thing I have here).'

    b. ***nhayun** nambal bada gada-y   iii*
       DIST.ABS rock.ABS down come-PAST ...
       'That rock dropped...'

    c. *ngayu **yiway**   nhin.ga-l*
       1SG   PROX.LOC sit-NONPAST
       'I'll stay here.'

    d. ***yii***   *yugu   yalmba-aga*
       PROX.ABS tree.ABS sandhill-ABES
       'This is a tree of the sandhill.'

The demonstratives in absolutive case have plural forms: *yinharrin* 'these/this kind' and *nhanharrin* 'those/that kind'. They seem to be the only demonstratives in plural. An example is given in (2).

(2)   Guugu Yimidhirr (Haviland 1979: 74)
        yinharrin bama   binaal-mul
        these.ABS people.ABS know-PRIVATE
        'These (sort of) peope don't know (about it).'

The absolutive form *nhaayun* 'proximal' is often glossed as 'it' and might be considered a third person pronoun:

(3)   Guugu Yimidhirr (Haviland 1979: 73)
        *buligi   gada-y,   nyulu   **nhaayun** gunda-y*
        bullock.ABS come-PAST 3SG.NOM DIST.ABS kill-PAST
        'The bullock came and he killed it.'

The purposive form *nhaamuu* refers to propositions and is usually translated by 'therefore':

(4)   Guugu Yimidhirr (Haviland 1979: 74)
        nyulu   wawu-murrgarra bama-agal yirrga-nda
        3SG.NOM breath-unable   man-ADES speak-CONTRF
        *guugu   wangaarr-ga-m-i **nhaamuu** nyulu*
        speech.white man-GEN-mu-DAT DIST.PURP 3SG.NOM
        guugu   yi-mi-dhirr   maa-ni
        speech.ABS PROX-mu-COM take-PAST
        'He was unable to talk to Aboriginals in the white man's language, and therefore he learned Guugu Yimidhirr.'

There are two other deictic expressions in Guugu Yimidhirr that one might classify as demonstratives: *yarra* 'yonder' and *yarrba* 'there, that way, that's the way'. Unlike the demonstratives in Table 2, these two forms are uninflected. Haviland (1979: 72) points out that they normally accompany gestures, but their status and function remain somewhat unclear.

2.1.2   Ambulas

Ambulas, a Sepik language spoken in New Guinea, has three demonstrative roots: *kén* 'proximal', *an* 'medial' and *wan* 'distal'. In contrast to Guugu Yimidhirr, where the same demonstrative forms occur in a variety of syntactic contexts, Ambulas has several categories of demonstratives serving specific syntactic functions.

To begin with, the demonstrative roots, *kén* and *wan*, are used as demonstrative identifiers in nonverbal clauses.

16 DEMONSTRATIVES

(5)   Ambulas (Wilson 1980: 454)
   kén bakna walkamu taalé
   this just little   place
   'This is just a little place.'

Demonstrative pronouns are formed by combining *kén* and *wan* with the third person pronouns *dé* 'he', *lé* 'she', *bét* 'they (dual)', and *de* 'they (plural)', yielding the forms in Table 3.

Table 3. *Demonstrative pronouns in Ambulas (1) (Wilson 1980: 56)*

	PROXIMAL	DISTAL
SG.M	*dé-kén*	*dé-wan*
SG.F	*lé-kén*	*lé-wan*
DU	*bét-kén*	*bét-wan*
PL	*de-kén*	*de-wan*

Ambulas has a second series of demonstrative pronouns, which is used only with inanimate referents. The forms are given in Table 4; they are unmarked for gender and number. Note that the inanimate demonstratives express a three way contrast while the (animate) demonstratives in Table 3 have only two deictic roots: proximal and distal. The medial demonstrative *an* does not combine with third person pronouns.

Table 4. *Demonstrative pronouns in Ambulas (2) (Wilson 1980: 56)*

PROXIMAL	*kénikénan, kénikinan*
MEDIAL	*anikénan, anikinan*
DISTAL	*wanikénan, wanikinan, waninan*

Ambulas also has two series of demonstrative determiners, shown in Table 5. Both series distinguish three degrees of distance. The demonstratives of the first series are also used as "an introducer and closure marker of a discourse" and as temporal adverbs meaning 'now' and 'then' (Wilson 1980: 56). Demonstrative determiners always precede the noun and other noun modifiers, as shown in (6a–b).

Table 5. *Demonstrative determiners in Ambulas (Wilson 1980: 57)*

	SERIES 1	SERIES 2
PROXIMAL	*kéni*	*kénina*
MEDIAL	*ani*	*aniké, aniki*
DISTAL	*wani*	*waniké, waniki, wanina*

(6)   Ambulas (Wilson 1980: 433, 86)
        a.   ***kéni*** *kudi*
             this talk
             'This talk'
        b.   ***kénina*** *bét-ku   jébaa*
             this   3DU-POSS work
             'This work of theirs'

Table 6 shows the demonstrative adverbs. Wilson (1980: 58) argues that they might have developed from two morphemes: the demonstratives *kén* and *wan* and a locational adverb or adposition. However, from a synchronic perspective these forms are monomorphemic.

Finally, there is a series of manner demonstratives, shown in Table 7.

Table 6. *Demonstrative adverbs in Ambulas (Wilson 1980: 57)*

PROXIMAL	*kéba*
DISTAL	*waba*
TO.PROXIMAL	*kénét*
TO.DISTAL	*wanét*

Table 7. *Manner demonstratives in Ambulas (Wilson 1980: 57)*

LIKE THIS (forward referring)	*kéga*
LIKE THIS (forward referring)	*aga*
LIKE THAT (backward referring)	*waga*

Manner demonstratives are commonly used to refer to a chunk of the surrounding discourse (cf. 4.2). They are discourse deictics that indicate an overt link between two propositions. The distal form *waga* refers back to an element of the preceding discourse, while the proximal and medial forms anticipate upcoming information. Example (7) shows the distal demonstrative *waga* referring back to the preceding clause.

(7) Ambulas (Wilson 1980: 464–5)
     gayéba   kutdu   méné gayéba   kutkéyo   ména
     in.village he.catch.and you   in.village must.catch your
     *naawi wale waaru waatbete   **waga** de   yo*
     peer with argue be.angry.and thus they do
     'If he catches a pig in the village, you must catch one in the village.
     When you quarrel with your peer, that is what they do.'

2.1.3   Ewondo

Ewondo is a Northwest Bantu language spoken in southern Cameroon. It distinguishes three distance categories — proximal, medial, and distal — and six noun classes:

Table 8. *Demonstrative pronouns/determiners in Ewondo (Redden 1980: 67–70)*

| | NEAR S | | NEAR H | | AWAY FROM S+H | |
	SG	PL	SG	PL	SG	PL
NC1	ɲɔ́	bá	ɲɔ́lō	bálā	ɲɔ́lí	bálí
NC2	ɲū	mī̄	ɲūlú	mīlí	ɲūlí	mīlíí
NC3	dī̄	mā	dīlí	mālá	dílí	mālí
NC4	dzī̄	bī̄	dzīlí	bīlí	dzílí	bīlíí
NC5	ɲī̄	mā	ɲīlí	mālá	ɲílí	mālí
NC6	ɲū	dī̄	ɲūlú	dīlí	ɲūlí	dīlíí

The demonstratives in Table 8 can be used as independent pronouns or as noun modifiers. That is, Ewondo does not distinguish between demonstrative pronouns and determiners.[3]

Both pronominal and adnominal demonstratives always cooccur with the definite article *é*. If a demonstrative is used adnominally, the article and the demonstrative frame the noun as in the following example:

(8) Ewondo (Redden 1980: 67)
     é   mod ɲɔ́
     ART man DEM
     'this man'

Occasionally the definite article is repeated before the demonstrative as in (9):

(9)   Ewondo (Redden 1980: 67)
       é   mod é   ɲɔ́
       ART man ART DEM
       'this man'

The second article in this example can be omitted, but the initial *é* is obligatory if the demonstrative after the noun functions as a noun modifier. If the noun is not preceded by *é* the demonstrative does not form an NP with the cooccurring noun; instead, it functions as an identificational demonstrative in a nonverbal clause. Compare the following two examples:

(10)   Ewondo (Redden 1980: 67, 67)
       a.   *é   kádá ɲɔ́*
             ART crab DEM
             'this crab'
       b.   *kádá ɲɔ́*
             crab DEM
             'This is a crab.'

Due to the definite article that precedes the noun in (10a), *ɲɔ́* is interpreted as a demonstrative noun modifier; that is, *ɲɔ́* is an adnominal demonstrative in this case. Since the noun in (10b) does not occur with the definite article *é*, the following demonstrative is interpreted as an identificational demonstrative rather than a noun modifier.

Like adnominal demonstratives, pronominal demonstratives are generally accompanied by the definite article *é:*

(11)   Ewondo (Redden 1980: 178–9)
       ɲgɔ́ wa-yi   é   ŋɔ́lə te w-ee-yaŋga   kóám
       if   you-want ART DEM   you-FUT-wait a.long.time
       'If you want that one you'll wait quite a while.'

Identificational demonstratives are formally indistinguishable from pronominal (and adnominal) demonstratives, but adverbial demonstratives have a different phonological form. There are two sets of adverbial demonstratives in Ewondo, shown in Table 9.

While adnominal and pronominal demonstratives comprise three deictic forms, adverbial demonstratives express a four way deictic contrast. They indicate a location (i) near the speaker, (ii) near the hearer, (iii) away from speaker and hearer, and (iv) far away from speaker and hearer. The last category is probably also used for locations out of sight. The demonstratives of set 1 are used to indicate an "exact location", while the demonstratives of the second set indicate

Table 9. *Demonstrative adverbs in Ewondo (Redden 1980: 145)*

	SET 1 (precise)	SET 2 (vague)
NEAR S	vá	mú
NEAR H	válā	múlū
AWAY FROM S+H	válí	wóé
FAR AWAY FROM S+H	álí	múlí

that the location is somewhere "around" or "in the vicinity of" the speaker, hearer or some other reference point (cf. Redden 1980: 145–6). The adverbial demonstratives of both sets may coalesce with the preposition *à* 'in/on/at/to', yielding the following forms:

Table 10. *Complex demonstrative adverbs in Ewondo (Redden 1980: 147)*

	SET 1 (precise)	SET 2 (vague)
NEAR S	ává	ámú
NEAR H	áválā	ámúlú
AWAY FROM S+H	áválí	áwóé
FAR AWAY FROM S+H	álí	ámúlí

2.1.4   Korean

Korean has three demonstrative particles: *i*, referring to an object or person near the speaker, *ku*, indicating a referent near the hearer, and *ce*, referring to an object or location that is away from both speaker and hearer. The Korean demonstratives are determiners; they cannot be used as independent pronouns. The semantic equivalent of a pronominal demonstrative in English is a noun phrase consisting of *i*, *ku* or *ce* and a "defective noun", which indicates the type of referent (Sohn 1994: 294). The examples in (12a-c) show *i*, *ku* and *ce* followed by the defective nouns *kes* 'thing/fact', *i* 'person' and *il* 'thing/fact'.[4]

    (12)   Korean (Sohn 1994: 294–6)
        a. **i**   *kes*
           this thing/fact
           'this (one/thing/fact)'

b. *ku i*
   that person
   'that (one/person)/he/she/it'
c. *ce il*
   that.away thing/fact
   'that (one/thing/fact)'

The demonstratives in (12a–c) are determiners; they have the same syntactic function as demonstratives that precede a regular noun, as in the following examples:

(13) Korean (Sohn 1994: 114, 114, 114)
   a. *i cip*
      this house
      'this house'
   b. *ku cha*
      that car
      'that car (near you)'
   c. *ce san*
      that mountain
      'that mountain over there'

I, ku and *ce* are morphologically invariable. Number and case is indicated through affixes on the (defective) noun:

(14) Korean (Sohn 1994: 297)
   i kes-tul-i
   this THING-PL-NOM
   'these (things/facts)'

Korean has three demonstrative adverbs that correspond to *i, ku* and *ce:*

Table 11. *Demonstrative adverbs in Korean (Sohn 1994: 296)*

NEAR S	*yeki*
NEAR H	*keki*
AWAY FROM S+H	*ceki*

Synchronically *yeki, keki* and *ceki* are monomorphemic, but historically they are composed of the base form *eki* meaning 'place' and the demonstrative determiners *i, ku* and *ce* (cf. Sohn 1994: 296). In place of the demonstrative adverbs, the demonstratives *i, ku* and *ce* may be used with the defective noun *kos* 'place' in order to indicate a location:

(15)   Korean (Sohn 1994: 295)
        ku *kos-ey kathi   kaca*
        that place-to together go
        'Let's go there together.'

Finally, there are three diminutive demonstratives in Korean: *yo* 'near speaker',
ko 'near hearer', and *co* 'away from speaker and hearer' (Sohn 1994: 114). Like
i, ku and *ce,* the diminutive demonstratives are determiners; they cannot occur
without a subsequent noun.

2.2 The morphology of demonstratives

The four previous sections exemplified the extent of formal variation among demonstratives of different languages. We saw that the demonstratives of some
languages are morphologically invariable (e.g. Korean), while the demonstratives
of other languages inflect for gender, number and/or case (e.g. Guugu Yimidhirr,
Ewondo). We also saw that some languages distinguish demonstrative pronouns,
determiners, adverbs, and identifiers (e.g. Ambulas), while other languages have
only a single series of demonstratives that they employ in various syntactic
contexts (e.g. Guugu Yimidhirr). And finally we saw that the semantic features
of demonstratives vary across languages: some languages have only two deictic
terms (e.g. Guugu Yimidhirr), others have three (e.g. Korean), and yet others
have four (e.g. demonstrative adverbs in Ewondo). In what follows I examine the
form, meaning and syntax of demonstratives more systematically. In the remainder of the current section, I investigate their morphological structures. I describe
in turn the properties of demonstrative clitics (2.2.1), the inflectional features of
demonstratives in different syntactic contexts (2.2.2), and the formation of demonstrative stems (2.2.3). The semantic and syntactic features will be examined
in Chapter 3 and 4, respectively.

2.2.1   *Demonstrative clitics*

Most demonstratives are phonologically unbound. There is, however, a substantial
number of languages in my sample in which some demonstratives may cliticize
to an element in their environment: Acehnese, Ponapean, Lango, Margi, Nandi,
and several others. All of the demonstrative clitics that are included in my sample
are enclitics (i.e. clitics that follow their host); demonstrative proclitics do not
occur, but they seem to occur in other languages. An example from Yagaria is
shown in (16b):

(16)   Yagaria (Renck 1975: 64, 66)
        a. *ma'i nina*
            this water
            'this water'
        b. *m=ígopa*
            this=ground
            'this ground'

Example (16a) shows an unbound demonstrative, which is commonly replaced by a proclitic, as in (16b), if the referent is not emphasized (clitic boundaries are indicated by the equal sign =).

All demonstrative clitics that are included in my sample are used adnominally; pronominal, adverbial and identificational demonstratives are always unbound. There are, however, languages in which the latter are clitics. Consider, for instance, the following examples from Kilba (Chadic), in which both adnominal and identificational demonstratives are attached to a preceding noun:

(17)   Kilba (Schuh 1983b: 315, 318)
        a. *kí=nà*
            house=this
            'this house'
        b. *kàtàŋ=ná*
            sheep=this
            'This/it is a sheep.'

The demonstrative clitics in (17a-b) have the same segmental shape, but they are tonally distinguished. The demonstrative in (17a) is a determiner marked by falling tone, while the demonstrative identifier in (17b) carries a rising tone.

Like adnominal and identificational demonstratives, pronominal demonstratives may cliticize to an element in their environment. The following example from Kawaiisu (Numic) shows a pronominal demonstrative that is attached to the first word of the clause. The pronominal enclitics are usually translated by third person pronouns, but since they are marked for distance *(=ina* 'proximal' vs. *=ana* 'distal') one might consider them demonstratives (cf. Zigmond et al. 1991: 47–48).

(18)   Kawaiisu (Zigmond 1991: 172)
        mee-gi-pigadi=ina   *ʔuna wiigara*
        say-BEN-PERF=DEM.PROX.SG.ANIM that red.racer
        'Red Racer said to her.'

Unlike adnominal, pronominal and identificational demonstratives, adverbial demonstratives are always unbound. I am at least not aware of any language in which adverbial demonstratives are clitics.[5]

While demonstratives may cliticize to an element in their environment, they are probably never bound to a specific word. Some of the sources that I consulted refer to bound demonstratives as suffixes (e.g. Creider and Tapsubei Creider 1989: 40; Noonan 1992: 86), but they seem to use the term suffix in a broad sense subsuming all bound forms including enclitics. Among other things, suffixes and enclitics differ in their syntactic behavior: while suffixes are associated with a specific word, enclitics are attached to a phrase (cf. Zwicky 1977; Klavans 1985; Anderson 1992: 198–223).[6] Although the distinction between suffixes and enclitics is theoretically well defined, it is empirically often difficult to decide whether an (adnominal) demonstrative is bound to a word or a phrase. The distinction is especially problematic if adjectives and other noun modifiers precede the noun. In such a case, it is usually impossible to determine whether a bound demonstrative is a suffix of the noun or an enclitic of the noun phrase. If, on the other hand, the modifiers follow the noun, it is immediately obvious whether a bound demonstrative is used as an enclitic or suffix. Consider, for instance, the following examples from Lango.

(19)   Lango (Noonan 1992: 155, 155, 156)
   a.   *gwók=kî*
        dog=this
        'this dog'
   b.   *gwôkk à   dwóŋ=ŋî*
        dog   ATT big.SG=this
        'this big dog'
   c.   *gwóggî à   dɔŋɔ̀   àryɔ́=nî*
        dogs ATT big.PL two-this
        'these two big dogs'

The demonstratives in (19a–c) attach to the last free form of the noun phrase: in (19a) the demonstrative follows a noun, in (19b) it follows an adjective, and in (19c) a numeral. Noonan (1992: 86) refers to the adnominal demonstratives in Lango as suffixes, but these examples show that they are enclitics of the noun phrase rather than suffixes of the noun (as Noonan points out in a footnote). I suspect that all demonstratives being referred to as suffixes in my sources are in fact enclitics. Suffixes tend to be obligatory in the contexts in which they occur, while enclitics are often interchangeable with unbound (stressed) forms. Since demonstratives are commonly used to emphasize a referent, I hypothesize that bound demonstratives can always be replaced by an unbound stressed form. If this is correct, it would suggest that all bound demonstratives are clitics and that demonstrative affixes do not exist.

2.2.2   The inflection of demonstratives

Most languages included in my sample have at least some demonstratives that are inflected for gender, number and/or case. The inflectional features of demonstratives vary with their syntactic function. Pronominal demonstratives are more likely to inflect than adnominal and identificational demonstratives, which, in turn, are more often inflected than adverbial demonstratives. Table 12 shows the number and percentage of pronominal demonstratives that are inflected for number, gender and case in my sample; a detailed overview of the inflectional features of pronominal demonstratives is given in Appendix B.

Table 12. *The inflectional features of pronominal demonstratives (cf. Appendix B)*

	Inflected	Uninflected	Number	Gender	Case	Total
Number	68	17	64	38	25	85
Percentage	80%	20%	75%	45%	30%	100%

There are 68 languages in my sample in which pronominal demonstratives are marked for gender, number, and/or case, and 17 languages in which pronominal demonstratives are uninflected. In some of the latter, (pronominal) demonstratives are always accompanied by a nominal such as a defective noun (e.g. Korean; cf. 2.1.4), a third person pronoun (e.g. Kusaiean; cf. 4.1.3), or a classifier (e.g. Nùng; cf. 4.1.3). Such demonstratives are strictly speaking not pronominal. They are demonstrative determiners that are embedded in a noun phrase. Demonstratives of this sort will be discussed in Section 4.1.3.

Apart from such 'pronominal NPs', there are only ten languages in my sample in which pronominal demonstratives are uninflected, namely Acehnese, Izi, Koyra Chiini, Mulao, Oneida, Tuscarora, Tok Pisin, Urim, Urubu-Kaapor, and Usan. In all of these languages, nouns are in general uninflected (or, at least, they are not regularly inflected as in English). The demonstratives of these languages behave therefore just like other nominals and can be considered pro-nouns even though they lack the trappings of a typical pronoun.

The most common inflectional feature of pronominal demonstratives is number followed by gender and case. There are sixty-four languages in my sample in which pronominal demonstratives are inflected for number, thirty-eight languages in which they are inflected for gender, and twenty-five languages in which they are case-marked. The case endings of pronominal demonstratives are usually the same as, or very similar to, the case endings of nouns, while the gender and number features are either expressed by special endings or, more frequently, by stem alternations (see below).

Like pronominal demonstratives, the majority of adnominal demonstratives is uninflected. However, there is a significant number of languages in my sample in which adnominal demonstratives are morphologically invariable while pronominal demonstratives are inflected for gender, number, and/or case. In fact, if a language employs adnominal demonstratives that are marked for gender, number and/or case, one can predict that the pronominal demonstratives are marked for the same feature(s). Table 13 lists some of the languages in my sample in which adnominal demonstratives are uninflected while pronominal demonstratives are marked for gender, number and/or case (note that some of the case endings might be enclitics of the noun phrase rather than suffixes of the noun).

Table 13. *Inflected DEM PROs vs. uninflected DEM DETs*

	Pronominal			Adnominal
Ambulas	*number*	*gender*		Ø
Byansi	*number*		*case*	Ø
Duwai	*number*			Ø
Epena Pedee	*number*	*gender*	*case*	Ø
Hua			*case*	Ø
Kannada	*number*	*gender*	*case*	Ø
Lezgian	*number*		*case*	Ø
Nama	*number*	*gender*		Ø
Tauya			*case*	Ø
Turkish	*number*		*case*	Ø
Total:	8	4	7	10

In all of the languages shown in Table 13, adnominal demonstratives cooccur with an inflected noun. The grammatical features of the noun phrase are thus sufficiently marked by the inflectional endings of the noun. This is illustrated by the following example from Lezgian.

(20)   Lezgian (Haspelmath 1993: 259)
        a   *insan-ar*
        that human-PL
        'these people'

Like adnominal demonstratives, identificational demonstratives are often morphologically invariable in languages in which pronominal demonstratives are marked for gender, number and/or case. Table 14 shows that there are (at least) nine languages in my sample in which pronominal demonstratives have certain inflectional features while identificational demonstratives are morphologically unmarked. Languages in which pronominal demonstratives are uninflected while identificational demonstratives are marked for gender, number and/or case do not occur in my sample.

Table 14. *Inflected DEM PROs vs. uninflected DEM IDENTs*

	Pronominal			Identificational	
Ambulas	number	gender		Ø	(*kén* PROX)
Czech	number	gender	case	Ø	(*to*)
Duwai	number			Ø	(*nə́mù*)
French	number	gender		Ø	(*ce*)
German	number	gender	case	Ø	(*das*)
Margi	number			Ø	(*ŋú*)
Pangasinan	number			Ø	(*nía* PROX)
Swedish	number	gender		Ø	(*det*)
T. Shoshone	number		case	Ø	(*isün* PROX)
Total:	9	5	3	9	

Demonstrative adverbs are almost always uninflected. In Section 2.1.1, we saw that the semantic equivalents of 'here' and 'there' in Guugu Yimidhirr are demonstratives with certain (locational) case endings, but since they belong to the same paradigm as demonstratives that are used as independent pronouns and noun modifiers, they cannot be classified as adverbs. Guugu Yimidhirr does not have a particular class of demonstrative adverbs.

There are, however, a few languages in my sample in which demonstrative adverbs are case-marked and categorially distinguished from demonstrative pronouns. One of them is Hua, in which both demonstrative pronouns and adverbs are inflected for case. Demonstrative adverbs consist of two morphemes in Hua, a demonstrative root and one of four locative case markers, while demonstrative pronouns are formed from three elements: a demonstrative root, a (non-locative) case marker, and the suffix *-bo'*, which Haiman (1980:259) analyzes as a nominalizer (see next section). Compare the following two forms:

(21)   Hua (Haiman 1980:259, 259)
        a.   *ma-bo'-mamu'*
              PROX-NLZ-ERG
              'this (one)'
        b.   *ma-roga*
              PROX-LOC
              'here/hither'

The demonstrative pronoun in (21a) consists of three morphemes: the demonstrative root *ma*, the nominalizer *-bo'*, and the case marker *-mamu'*. (21b) shows a demonstrative adverb formed from two morphemes: a demonstrative root and a locative case marker. Unlike the demonstrative pronoun in (21a), the demonstrative adverb does not include the nominalizer *-bo'*, and therefore it cannot be classified as a demonstrative pronoun in locative case. Both pronominal and adverbial demonstratives are case-marked in Hua, but they are categorially distinguished due to the absence and presence of *-bo'*.

2.2.3   Demonstrative stems

Having described the inflectional endings of demonstratives, I now examine the formation of demonstrative stems. A demonstrative stem is a demonstrative without its inflectional endings. It consists of a demonstrative root (i.e. a deictic element) and possibly some other morpheme: a derivational affix or another free form. In the following I concentrate on the stem formation of demonstrative pronouns and adverbs; demonstrative determiners and identifiers will not be considered because they have either the same stems as pronominal demonstratives or they consist only of a demonstrative root.

In the literature, it has often been argued that demonstrative pronouns and determiners are derived from demonstrative adverbs (cf. Anderson and Keenan 1985:279; Greenberg 1985:277; Himmelmann 1996:246), but Brown (1985) and Woodworth (1991) present evidence that challenges this view. Their studies show that demonstrative adverbs are often morphologically more complex than demonstrative pronouns and determiners, which seems to suggest that they are derived from demonstrative pronouns or noun modifiers that combined with some other morpheme. My data include examples that would support either one of these hypotheses. I assume therefore that there is no unidirectional pathway leading from demonstrative adverbs to demonstrative pronouns/determiners or vice versa. Both developments seem to occur. Furthermore, it is conceivable that in some languages demonstrative pronouns, determiners, and adverbs developed independently of one another from a deictic particle with no specific syntactic function (see below).

The stems of demonstrative pronouns are often formed from a demonstrative root and a nominalizing affix, a third person pronoun, or a classifier. In the previous section we saw that the stems of demonstrative pronouns in Hua are formed from a demonstrative root and the suffix *-bo'*. Haiman (1980: 259) characterizes *-bo'* as a "nominalizing suffix", used to derive pro-nominals from a demonstrative root. Similar stem formations occur in several other languages in my sample. Lezgian, for instance, has two demonstrative roots, *i* 'proximal' and *a* 'distal', which may function as noun modifiers (e.g. *a insan-ar* that human-PL 'those people'; Haspelmath 1993: 259). The demonstrative pronouns are formed by combining *i* and *a* with the suffix *-da* 'ergative/oblique' *(-di* 'absolutive'), which is otherwise used to derive nouns from adjectives. Haspelmath (1993: 110) characterizes the demonstrative pronouns in Lezgian as "substantivised forms":

(22)   Lezgian (Haspelmath 1993: 110, 111)
        a.   *-da* deriving a noun from an adjective
              q̃acu   >   *q̃acu-da*
              'green'   '(the) green one'
        b.   *-da* deriving a DEM pronoun from a DEM root
              i   >   *i-da*
              'this'   'this one'

In other languages, demonstrative pronouns are composed of a demonstrative root and a third person pronoun. Consider, for instance, the demonstrative in (23) from Margi, which consists of the third person pronoun *nàjà*, the plural marker *-'yàr,* and the demonstrative root *-tà.*

(23)   Margi (Hoffmann 1963: 86)
        nádà   nàjà-'yàr-tà
        give.me 3-PL-that
        'Give me those!'

Apart from Margi, there are six other languages in my sample in which demonstrative pronouns are formed by combining a demonstrative root with a third person pronoun: Acehnese, Ambulas, Ao, Barasano, Kokborok, and Khasi. In some of these languages, the combination of a demonstrative root and a third person pronoun is optional (e.g. Acehnese), but in others it is obligatory (e.g. Ao). Table 15 shows the demonstrative pronouns in Ao. They are formed from two demonstrative roots, *ya* 'proximal' and *ci* 'distal', and one of five third person pronouns: *pá* 'he', *lá* 'she', *ipá* 'it', *paḷʰnok* 'they (human)', and *item* 'they (non-human)':

Table 15. *Demonstrative pronouns in Ao (Gowda 1975: 34)*

	PROXIMAL	DISTAL
SG.M.HUMAN	*pá-ya*	*pá-ci*
SG.F.HUMAN	*lá-ya*	*lá-ci*
SG.NONHUMAN	*ipá-ya*	*ipá-ci*
PL.HUMAN	*paḷʰnok-ya*	*paḷʰnok-ci*
PL.NONHUMAN	*item-ya*	*item-ci*

The demonstratives in Table 15 can be viewed as '(grammatical) compounds' formed from two independent words. Since they are only slightly different from demonstratives with inflectional endings, I suspect that third person pronouns are a common historical source for gender and number markers on demonstratives. The grammaticalization path that I suggest is schematized in (24a–b).

> (24) a.   3.PRO DEM   >   3.PRO-DEM   >   AFFIX-DEM
>   b.   DEM 3.PRO   >   DEM-3.PRO   >   DEM-AFFIX

At the initial stage of the grammaticalization process, demonstratives and third person pronouns are two independent forms that commonly cooccur. Such pronominal NPs occur, for instance, in Kusaiean (cf. 4.1.3). At the next stage, demonstratives and third person pronouns coalesce and form a complex word consisting of two elements that are still used as independent words in other contexts. This stage is exemplified by the demonstratives in Ao in Table 15. At the final stage, demonstratives and third person pronouns must cooccur and can no longer be used in isolation. At this point, the third person pronouns have basically assumed the function of gender/number markers.[7]

Finally, pronominal demonstratives are quite frequently formed from a demonstrative root and a classifier, which may evolve into a noun class marker. Examples from Mandarin Chinese, Yagua and Barasano are shown in (25) to (27), respectively.

(25)   Mandarin Chinese (Li and Thompson 1981: 533)
        nèi-ge
        that-CLASS
        'that (one)'

(26)   Yagua (Payne and Payne 1990: 374)
        jiy-nù
        this-CLASS:ANIM:SG
        'this (one)'

(27)   Barasano (Jones and Jones 1991: 57)
        ti-a-re
        that-CLASS-OBJ
        'that (one)'

The stems of demonstrative adverbs are usually distinguished from the stems of
demonstrative pronouns, determiners and identifiers. They are often formed from
a demonstrative root and a locative or directional affix, as in the following
example from Kiowa:

(28)   Kiowa (Watkins 1984: 189)
        é̠:-dé   Ø-dɔ́:-+ą́:   gɔ̀   ó-y
        here-toward 3SG-move-come and over.there-widely.bounded
        Ø-pʰɔ̀:
        3SG-stop
        'He was coming here and stopped over there.'

Example (28) includes two demonstrative adverbs: one is marked by the locative
suffix -y 'location.widely.bounded' and the other by the directional marker -dé
'toward speaker'. The corresponding demonstrative pronouns/determiners are built
on the same demonstrative roots (é̠:-'proximal' and ó- 'distal'), but they combine
with other suffixes.

Similar demonstrative adverbs occur in many other languages in my sample.
Demonstrative adverbs in Yimas, for instance, are formed from three deictic
roots, k 'proximal', m 'medial', and n 'distal', and a locative affix. As shown in
Table 16, the proximal and distal roots combine with the prefix ta-, while the
medial form occurs with the suffix -nti.

Other languages form demonstrative adverbs from a demonstrative root and
a noun meaning 'place'. For instance, in Section 2.1.4 we saw that the demonstrative adverbs in Korean developed from a demonstrative particle and the defective
noun eki 'place' (cf. 29).

Table 16. *Demonstrative adverbs in Yimas (Foley 1991: 114)*

PROXIMAL	*ta-k*
MEDIAL	*m-nti*
DISTAL	*ta-n*

(29) Korean (Sohn 1994: 296)

yeki	<	*i*	*eki*
'here (NEAR S)'		'this	place'
keki	<	*ku*	*eki*
'there (NEAR H)'		'that	place'
ceki	<	*ce*	*eki*
'there (AWAY FROM S+H)'		'that	place'

Similar demonstrative adverbs seem to occur in Kokborok (cf. Gowda 1975: 33).

2.3 Summary

In this chapter, I first described the demonstrative systems of four individual languages and then I examined the morphological features of demonstratives more systematically. The major findings of my investigation can be summarized as follows:

1. Though the demonstratives of most languages are independent words, there are some languages in which certain demonstratives may cliticize to an element in their environment.
2. The occurrence of demonstrative clitics is largely restricted to adnominal demonstratives; pronominal, adverbial and identificational demonstratives are almost always free forms.
3. Though (adnominal) demonstratives may cliticize to an adjacent element, they are probably never bound to a specific word; that is, there are probably no demonstrative affixes.
4. The inflectional features of demonstratives vary with their syntactic function: pronominal demonstratives are more likely to inflect than adnominal and identificational demonstratives, which, in turn, are more often inflected than adverbial demonstratives. The latter are usually uninflected unless they occur with a set of locational case markers.

5. The most frequent inflectional feature is number, followed by gender and case.

6. In languages in which nouns are inflected for gender, number and/or case, pronominal demonstratives are always marked for the same features whereas adnominal and identificational demonstratives are often uninflected. In fact, if adnominal and/or identificational demonstratives are inflected, one can predict that the pronominal demonstratives of the same language occur (at least) with the same inflectional features.

7. Though the stems of most demonstratives are monomorphemic, there are demonstratives whose stems are composed of multiple morphemes. The stems of demonstrative pronouns may consist of a deictic root and a nominalizer, a third person pronoun or a noun classifier, and the stems of demonstrative adverbs may be formed from a deictic root and a locative/directional affix or a locational noun. Demonstrative determiners and identifiers have either the same stems as demonstrative pronouns or their stems consist solely of a deictic root.

CHAPTER 3

Semantics

The previous chapter examined the morphological properties of demonstratives. This chapter investigates their meaning. The meaning of demonstratives comprises two kinds of features: (i) deictic features, which indicate the location of the referent relative to the deictic center, and (ii) qualitative features, which characterize the referent (cf. Lyons 1977: 648; cf. also Fillmore 1982; Rauh 1983; Hanks 1989, 1990). The deictic features indicate whether the referent is near or removed from the deictic center, whether it is at a higher or lower elevation, uphill or downhill, or whether it is moving toward or away from the deictic center. These features are primarily encoded by demonstrative roots. The qualitative features provide classificatory information about the referent. They indicate, for instance, whether the referent is animate or inanimate, female or male, or human or non-human. These features are usually expressed by morphemes that attach to a demonstrative root, but in some languages the root itself is classifying. The following two sections investigate the deictic and qualitative features of demonstratives, respectively. The final section provides an overview of all features — semantic, pragmatic and syntactic — that are commonly encoded by demonstratives.

3.1 The semantic features of demonstratives

3.1.1 Deictic features

Demonstratives are deictics. Deictic expressions are linguistic elements whose interpretation makes crucial reference to some aspect of the speech situation. As Levinson (1983: 54) puts it, "deixis concerns the ways in which languages encode or grammaticalize features of the context of utterance or speech event, and thus also concerns ways in which the interpretation of utterances depends on the analysis of that context". Deictic expressions are traditionally divided into three semantic categories: person, place and time (cf. Bühler 1934: 102). Person deixis comprises the personal pronouns *I* and *you*, which denote the speech participants; place deictic expressions refer to objects, locations or persons (apart from the speech participants); and time deictic expressions indicate a temporal reference point relative to the time of the speech event. Demonstratives are place (or spatial) deictics. They indicate the relative distance of an object, location or person vis-à-vis the deictic center (also called the *origo*), which is usually associated with the location of the speaker.

In addition to person, place and time deixis, Levinson (1983: 61–96) discusses two other deictic categories: "social deixis", which concerns the social status of the speech participants (for which some languages employ honorifics), and "discourse deixis", which applies to deictic elements that refer to aspects of the surrounding discourse (cf. Fillmore 1997: 103–125). In Chapter 5, I show that demonstratives are often used as discourse deictics, which can be seen as an extension of their primary use as spatial deictics.

All languages have at least two demonstratives locating the referent at two different points on a distance scale: a proximal demonstrative referring to an entity near the deictic center, and a distal demonstrative indicating a referent that is located at some distance to the deictic center. English, for instance, has such a two-term deictic system, consisting of the proximal demonstratives *here* and *this* and their distal counterparts *there* and *that*. There are many other languages in my sample that have a two-term deictic system. Consider, for instance, the demonstratives in Table 17 from Vietnamese. Like English, Vietnamese has two demonstrative pronouns/determiners and two demonstrative adverbs. Note that the proximal and distal forms of the demonstrative pronouns/determiners are only distinguished by tone; they have the same segmental features.

Table 17. *Demonstratives in Vietnamese (Thompson 1965: 142)*

	DEM PROS/DETS	DEM ADVS
PROXIMAL	này	đây
DISTAL	nọ	đãy

Both English and Vietnamese indicate the contrast between proximal and distal referents through different demonstrative roots. Alamblak expresses the same contrast through bound morphemes that attach to a demonstrative root unmarked for distance.

As shown in Table 18, the deictic suffixes *-ar* 'proximal' and *-ur* 'distal' are not obligatory to form pronominal/adnominal demonstratives in Alamblak. Bruce

Table 18. *Demonstrative pronouns/determiners in Alamblak (Bruce 1984: 81)*

	NEUTRAL	PROXIMAL	DISTAL
SG.M	*ind-r*	*ind-ar-r*	*ind-ur-r*
SG.F	*ind-t*	*ind-ar-t*	*ind-ur-t*
DU	*ind-f*	*ind-ar-f*	*ind-ur-f*
PL	*ind-m*	*ind-ar-m*	*ind-ur-m*

(1984: 81–82) does not explain when and why a demonstrative root is used without a distance marker, but there are many examples in his grammar in which *ind* does not occur with *-ar* or *-ur*. In such a case, *ind* is often translated by a definite article, but it is always glossed as 'DEM'. It seems that *ind* serves a pragmatic function that is somewhere in between a definite article and a demonstrative.

Like Alamblak, French uses two bound morphemes, *ci* 'proximal' and *là* 'distal', to indicate the relative distance of the referent to the deictic center. The demonstrative roots themselves are distance-neutral. Table 19 shows that *ci* and *là* are attached either to a demonstrative pronoun or to a noun that is preceded by a demonstrative determiner.

Table 19. *Demonstrative pronouns/determines in French*

	DEM PROS		DEM DETs	
	PROXIMAL	DISTAL	PROXIMAL	DISTAL
SG.M	*celui-ci*	*celui-là*	*ce livre-ci*	*ce livre-là*
SG.F	*celle-ci*	*celle-là*	*cette maison-ci*	*cette maison-là*
PL.M	*ceux-ci*	*ceux-là*	*ces livres-ci*	*ces livres-là*
PL.F	*celles-ci*	*celles-là*	*ces maisons-ci*	*ces maisons-là*

The distance markers *ci* and *là* are usually obligatory to form a demonstrative pronoun; they can only be omitted if *celui, celle, ceux,* or *celles* are modified by a relative clause or a prepositional phrase (cf. Calvez 1994: 62). The demonstrative determiners *ce, cette* and *ces*, on the other hand, are frequently used without *ci* or *là*. Harris (1978, 1980) argues that *ce, cette* and *ces* can be viewed as definite articles rather than demonstratives when they occur without a distance marker. This raises the interesting question whether distance is a necessary feature of the category demonstrative. Are demonstratives generally marked for distance or are there reasons to consider an item a demonstrative even if it does not indicate the relative distance of its referent to the deictic center? Anderson and Keenan (1985: 280) argue that a deictic expression unmarked for distance "would be little different from a definite article" or third person pronoun (cf. Frei 1944: 119). In their view, demonstratives are generally distance-marked.

Himmelmann (1997: 53–62) takes a different view. He argues that demonstratives do not always encode a deictic contrast. His hypothesis is primarily based on data from colloquial German. There are two expressions in colloquial German that one might consider demonstratives: *dies* and stressed *das*. *Dies* is almost always used adnominally, but *das* can be both an independent pronoun and a modifier of a cooccurring noun. *Dies* and *das* do not contrast deictically: both forms may occur with proximal and distal meaning. In order to indicate that *dies* or *das* are used contrastively, they are commonly accompanied by a demonstrative adverb (e.g. *das da* 'this/that there', *das Haus da* 'this/that house there'). Himmelmann argues that at least one of these forms, *dies,* functions as a demonstrative.[8] He shows that *dies* serves the same pragmatic functions as demonstratives that are deictically contrastive. Like *this* and *that* in English, *dies* focuses the hearer's attention on entities in the speech situation, often in combination with a pointing gesture. Since definite articles and third person pronouns do not function to orient the hearer in the surrounding situation, *dies* must be a demonstrative despite the fact that it does not encode a deictic contrast. Similar demonstratives seem to occur in other languages. Supyire, for instance, has only one series of demonstratives which, according to Carlson (1994: 160), is "used with both proximal and distal meaning". I assume therefore, with Himmelmann, that demonstratives are not generally distance-marked. Some languages have demonstratives that do not indicate a deictic contrast. The occurrence of distance-neutral demonstratives is, however, crosslinguistically infrequent. Apart from German and Supyire there are only five other languages in my sample in which some demonstratives are distance-neutral: Alamblak, French, Czech, Koyra Chiini, and Tok Pisin. Moreover, even though pronominal and adnominal demonstratives are not always deictically contrastive, adverbial demonstratives are generally distance-marked (cf. Himmelmann 1997: 49). All eighty-five languages included in my sample have at least two adverbial demonstratives that indicate a deictic contrast. The occurrence of distance-neutral demonstratives is thus restricted to certain syntactic contexts. All languages employ at least some demonstratives that are distance-marked, and, as the examples from Alamblak, French, and German have shown, distance-marked demonstratives are often used to reinforce demonstratives that are distance-neutral (also in Koyra Chiini; cf. Heath 1999: 61). Distance is thus after all a feature that occurs in the demonstrative system of all languages even though individual elements of the system may lack a distance feature. Turning to languages with three deictic terms, one has to distinguish between systems in which the middle term refers to a location in medial distance relative to the deictic center, and systems in which the middle term denotes a referent close to the hearer. Anderson and Keenan (1985: 282–286) refer to these two systems as *distance-oriented* and *person-oriented* systems, respectively (cf. Fillmore 1982: 49–50). Spanish, for instance, has a distance-oriented system, consisting of the demonstratives *este* 'proximal', *ese* 'medial' and *aquel* 'distal' (Anderson and Keenan 1985: 283–5), while Japanese has a person-oriented system, in which the middle terms (based on the deictic root *so-*) refer to a location near the hearer: *sore* 'that (near hearer), *soko* 'there (near hearer)' etc. (cf. Kuno 1973; Imai 1996). Two other examples from Yimas and Pangasinan are shown in Table 20 and 21, respectively.

Table 20. *Demonstrative pronouns/determiners in Yimas (Foley 1991: 112)*

	SG	DU	PL
PROXIMAL	*p-k*	*pla-k*	*pia-k*
MEDIAL	*m-n*	*mpl*	*m-ra*
DISTAL	*p-n*	*pla-n*	*pia-n*

Table 21. *Demonstrative pronouns in Pangasinan (Benton 1971: 88)*

	SG	PL
NEAR S	*(i)yá*	*(i)rá-ya*
NEAR H	*(i)tán*	*(i)rá-tan*
AWAY FROM S+H	*(i)mán*	*(i)rá-man*

The demonstratives in Yimas are built on three demonstrative roots: *k* 'proximal' and *n* 'distal', which take number prefixes, and *m* 'medial', which takes number suffixes. They form a distance-oriented system, while the demonstratives in Pangasinan are person-oriented: the middle term *tan* refers to a location near the hearer. Anderson and Keenan (1985) point out that in both distance-oriented and person-oriented systems the middle term is often the preferred form for anaphoric reference.

Not every deictic system that includes three deictic terms is either a distance or a person-oriented system. Nama, for instance, has three deictic terms which, according to Anderson and Keenan (1985: 285–286), are basically used as a variant of a two-term system. Nama uses the demonstrative *nee* to indicate a referent near the deictic center, and it uses ‖ *nāá* (‖ is a click) in order to refer to objects or persons that are not included in the domain that is conceptualized as the deictic center. However, the latter term is only used in "neutral deictic settings" and it does not occur in contrast to *nee*. That is, *nee* and ‖ *nāá* are never used within the same construction to indicate that one of two referents is closer to the deictic center than the other. In order to express a deictic contrast between two referents, Nama employs a third demonstrative, *náú* 'distal', which is used only in contrast either to *nee* or ‖ *nāá*; it never occurs in sentences without one of the other two forms. Examples are given in (1a–b).

(1)　　Nama (Anderson and Keenan 1985: 286, 286)
　　　a.　*nee kxòep tsīí* *náú* *kxòep*
　　　　　this man　and that man
　　　　　'this man and that one'
　　　b.　‖ *nāá kxòep tsīí* *náú*　　　*kxòep*
　　　　　that　man　and that (other) man
　　　　　'that man and that other one'

Returning to the contrast between distance and person-oriented systems, it is interesting to note that distance-oriented systems tend to have fewer deictic terms than person-oriented systems. A distance-oriented system is usually confined to three deictic terms. Anderson and Keenan (1985: 286–295) report languages having four, five or even more demonstratives distinguished by pure distance, but such systems do not occur in my data. Based on the languages in my sample, I would support Fillmore (1982: 48–9), who maintains that "that there are never really more than three [distance categories]" and that all larger systems either involve the hearer as a point of reference or other deictic dimensions such as visibility or elevation.

Unlike distance-oriented systems, person-oriented systems may involve four deictic terms. In Section 2.1.3 we saw, for instance, that Ewondo has four adverbial demonstratives: *vá* 'near speaker', *válā* 'near hearer', *válí* 'away from speaker and hearer', and *álí* 'far away from speaker and hearer'. The corresponding pronominal and adnominal demonstratives have only three deictic terms in Ewondo, but as shown in Table 22, Quileute uses four distance categories throughout the entire deictic system.

Note that the location of the hearer is only relevant to the first and second terms within this system. The third and fourth distance categories relate the

Table 22. *Demonstratives in Quileute (Andrade 1933: 246, 252)*

| | DEM PROS/DETS | | DEM ADVS |
	NON-FEM	FEM	
NEAR S	*yü´x:o*	*yü´k:o*	*xo"a*
NEAR H	*yi´tca*	*yi´tca*	*so"o*
NEAR S+H	*sa"a*	*ksa'*	*sa"a*
AWAY FROM S+H	*ha*	*ha*	*á:tca'a*

referent to a domain that includes both speaker and hearer. In other words, the deictic center is conceptualized in two different ways in this system: it is conceptualized as the sole domain of the speaker (excluding the hearer) for the first and second deictic terms (i.e. NEAR S and NEAR H); and it is conceptualized as the common domain of speaker and hearer for the two other terms (i.e. NEAR S+H and AWAY FROM S+H). None of the demonstratives in this system involves more than three reference points: (i) the referent, (ii) the deictic center, and, depending on the term, (iii) another reference object. A person-oriented system including four deictic terms is thus basically a variant of a three-term deictic system with an additional category for referents near the hearer.[9]

In addition to distance, demonstratives may indicate whether the referent is visible or out of sight, at a higher or lower elevation, uphill or downhill, upriver or downriver, or moving toward or away from the deictic center. Fillmore (1982: 51) considers these features non-deictic, but based on the information that I have gathered from my sources I would contend that they have a deictic character. Like the features 'proximal' and 'distal', these features are deictic because they indicate the location of the referent relative to the deictic center: the referent is 'out of sight' or 'downriver' from the perspective of the speaker (or some other reference point to which the deictic center has been shifted). It is conceivable that some of the morphemes that encode these feature can also be used non-deictically (e.g. *uphill from the village),* but in all of the sources that I consulted their meaning is described in such a way that it involves the speaker as the unmarked point of reference. This suggests that these features are deictic and that the non-deictic use of these morphemes (if it exists) is due to pragmatic extensions. In the remainder of this section, I discuss examples of demonstratives that encode features of such semantic categories as visibility or elevation that receive a deictic interpretation.

Visibility is a common deictic category in Native American languages. In my sample, there are seven American Indian languages that have particular demonstrative forms for invisible referents: West Greenlandic, Halkomelem, Quileute, Passamaquoddy-Maliseet, Tümpisa Shoshone, Ute, and Epena Pedee. Table 23 shows the demonstrative pronouns/determiners in Ute (only the subject forms are shown). Two of the three demonstratives in this table are distinguished by pure distance while the third term is used for referents out of sight.

Table 23. *Demonstratives in Ute (Givón 1980: 55)*

	PROXIMAL	DISTAL	INVISIBLE
INANIMATE	'íca	máru̧	'úru̧
SG.ANIMATE	'ína	máa	'ú
PL.ANIMATE	'ímu̧	mámu̧	'úmu̧

Most languages in which visibility is a feature of the deictic system have a single deictic term to indicate a referent out of sight, but Quileute has three: one for referents nearby (which may be partly visible), one for referents whose location is known, and one for referents whose location is unknown (cf. Andrade 1933: 252). Table 24 shows the three forms of the invisible demonstrative adverbs in this language.

Table 24. *Invisible demonstrative adverbs in Quileute (Andrade 1933: 252)*

NEAR (maybe partly visible)	χa'x:e
KNOWN PLACE	tci''tc'
UNKNOWN PLACE	xu'xwa'

Another deictic dimension that is relatively frequent in my sample is elevation. Nine languages have demonstratives that indicate whether the referent is at a higher or lower elevation relative to the deictic center. These demonstratives occur in languages spoken in New Guinea (Usan, Hua, Tauya) in the Himalayan area (Lahu, Khasi, Byansi), in Australia (Dyirbal, Ngiyambaa), and in the Caucasus (Lezgian). Table 25 shows the deictic system in Khasi, which is based on six demonstrative roots: three of them locate the referent on a distance scale, two others indicate a referent at a higher or lower elevation, and one refers to objects or locations out of sight. The demonstrative roots are either combined with personal pronouns or with adpositions.

A similar system is employed in Lahu, which has five demonstrative adverbs: three of them are distinguished by (pure) distance and the other two

Table 25. *Demonstratives in Khasi (Nagaraja 1985: 11–12; Rabel 1961: 67)*

	DEM PROS			DEM ADVS
	M.SG (*u* 'he')	F.SG (*ka* 'she')	PL (*ki* 'they')	(*ša* 'to')
PROXIMAL	*u-ne*	*ka-ne*	*ki-ne*	*ša-ne*
MEDIAL (NEAR H)	*u-to*	*ka-to*	*ki-to*	*ša-to*
DISTAL	*u-tay*	*ka-tay*	*ki-tay*	*ša-tay*
UP	*u-tey*	*ka-tey*	*ki-tey*	*ša-tey*
DOWN	*u-thie*	*ka-thie*	*ki-thie*	*ša-thie*
INVISIBLE	*u-ta*	*ka-ta*	*ki-ta*	*ša-ta*

indicate whether the referent is above or below the deictic center. The demonstratives in Lahu are monomorphemic, they are uninflected and do not combine with any other morpheme.

Table 26. *Demonstrative adverbs in Lahu (Matisoff 1973: 110–1)*

PROXIMAL	*chò*
MEDIAL	*ô*
DISTAL	*cô*
UP	*nô*
DOWN	*mô*

While Khasi and Lahu employ particular demonstrative roots in order to refer to entities at different elevations, Tauya expresses the same deictic contrast through prefixes that are attached to a demonstrative root: *pise-* refers to a location above the deictic center, and *tofe-* indicates a referent at a lower elevation.

Table 27. *Elevation in Tauya (MacDonald 1990: 102)*

	ABOVE	BELOW
PROXIMAL	*pise-me*	*tofe-me*
DISTAL	*pise-ʔe*	*tofe-ʔe*

Like Tauya, Dyirbal indicates the horizontal location of a referent through bound morphemes: *-gali* 'down' and *-gala* 'up' (cf. Dixon 1972: 48). In addition,

Dyirbal has also a series of bound forms that indicate whether the referent is
uphill or downhill from the perspective of the speaker:

Table 28. *Downhill and uphill in Dyirbal (Dixon 1972: 48)*

SHORT DISTANCE DOWNHILL	-*bayḍi*
MEDIUM DISTANCE DOWNHILL	-*bayḍa*
LONG DISTANCE DOWNHILL	-*bayḍu*
SHORT DISTANCE UPHILL	-*dayi*
MEDIUM DISTANCE UPHILL	-*daya*
LONG DISTANCE UPHILL	-*dayu*

Dixon treats the forms in Table 28 as single morphemes, but Anderson and
Keenan (1985: 292) break them down into two elements: -*bayḍ* and -*day*, which
encode the geographical features 'downhill' and 'uphill', and the word final
vowels, -*i*, -*a* and -*u*, which indicate the distance features: 'short', 'medium' and
'long' (i.e. 'proximal', 'medial' and 'distal'). The forms in Table 28 are part of
a more complex system in which the feature 'hill' contrasts with the feature
'river', encoded by the following forms:

Table 29. *Downriver and upriver in Dyirbal (Dixon 1972: 48)*

MEDIUM DISTANCE DOWNRIVER	-*balbala*
LONG DISTANCE DOWNRIVER	-*balbulu*
MEDIUM DISTANCE UPRIVER	-*dawala*
LONG DISTANCE UPRIVER	-*dawulu*
ACROSS THE RIVER	-*guya*

According to Dixon (1972: 48), "'river' is the marked feature in the system 'river
versus hill'". Like the 'hill' suffixes, the 'river' suffixes consist of two morphemes, -*balb* 'downriver' and -*daw* 'upriver', and the distance markers, -*ala*
'medial' and -*ulu* 'distal'.[10]
    Geographical features such as uphill and downhill or upriver and downriver
are crosslinguistically uncommon. Apart from Dyirbal, there are only two other
languages in my sample in which they occur: Hua and West Greenlandic. Like
Dyirbal, Hua has demonstratives which indicate whether the referent is uphill or
downhill. They distinguish two degrees of distance: *buga* refers to a location a
short distance uphill; *biga* indicates a location a long distance uphill; *muna* refers

to a location a short distance downhill; and *mina* indicates a referent a long distance downhill.

Table 30. *Uphill and downhill in Hua (Haiman 1980: 258)*

	UPHILL	DOWNHILL
SHORT DISTANCE	*buga*	*muna*
LONG DISTANCE	*biga*	*mina*

West Greenlandic has two demonstratives that refer to objects or locations along the coastline: *anna* indicates a referent to the north along the coastline from the perspective of the speaker, and *qanna* refers southwards relative to the location of the speaker. The deictic system of West Greenlandic is especially complex. Apart from *anna* and *qanna*, it includes three demonstrative roots that are marked for pure distance: *ma(t)-* 'proximal', *u(a)-* 'medial', and *ik-* 'distal'; four demonstrative roots that indicate distance and elevation: *kat-/kan-* 'down a medial distance', *sam-* 'down a long distance', *pik-* 'up a medial distance', and *pav-* 'up a long distance'; and two demonstrative roots that refer to an object or location that is either "outside beyond a wall" or "on the other side (interior or exterior) of some intervening surface, usually a wall or door": *qam-* 'interior/exterior' and *kig-* 'exterior' (Fortescue 1984: 260). In addition, there is an archaic form used for referents out of sight: *im-* 'invisible'. Table 31 shows the twelve demonstrative roots employed in West Greenlandic combined with an absolutive case marker.

All demonstratives that we have seen thus far in this section indicate a stationary referent. In some languages, demonstratives are also used to indicate that the referent is moving in a certain direction relative to the deictic center. Movement (or direction) is often expressed by bound morphemes that attach to a demonstrative stem. For instance, Nunggubuyu has three "kinetic suffixes" (Heath 1980: 152) that indicate whether the referent is moving (i) toward the speaker, (ii) away from the speaker, or (iii) across the speaker's line of vision. The examples in (2a–b) illustrate the use of the directional markers. They are suffixed to demonstrative identifiers in these examples, but they also occur with demonstrative pronouns/determiners and adverbs (Heath 1984: 281–291).

Table 31. *Demonstrative roots in West Greenlandic (Fortescue 1984: 259–262)*

		DEM.ABS	ROOT
DISTANCE	PROXIMAL	*manna*	*ma(t)-*
	MEDIAL	*una*	*u(a)-*
	DISTAL	*innga*	*ik-*
ELEVATION	DOWN.MEDIAL	*kanna*	*kat-/kan-*
	DOWN.DISTAL	*sanna*	*sam-*
	UP.MEDIAL	*pinnga*	*pik-*
	UP.DISTAL	*panna*	*pav-*
IN/EXTERIOR	IN/OUT	*qanna*	*qam-*
	OUTSIDE	*kinnga*	*kig-*
COASTLINE	IN.THE.NORTH	*anna*	*av-*
	IN.THE.SOUTH	*qanna*	*qav-*
VISIBILITY	INVISIBLE	*inna*	*im-*

(2)   Nunggubuyu (Heath 1980: 152, 152, 152)
      a.   *yuwa:-gi:-'la*
         DISTAL-NC-TOWARD.S
         'There he/she comes.'
      b.   *yuwa:-gi:-'li*
         DISTAL-NC-AWAY.FROM.S
         'There he/she goes away.'
      c.   *yuwa:-gi-yaj*
         DISTAL-NC-ACROSS
         'There he/she goes across.'

Similar demonstratives occur in several other languages in my sample. Kiowa, for instance, has three directional markers that have the same meaning as the kinetic affixes in Nunggubuyu: *-dé* indicates a referent moving toward the deictic center; *-p* marks referents that are moving away from the deictic center; and *-pé* attaches to demonstratives that refer to entities moving across the visual field of the speaker.

(3)   Kiowa (Watkins 1984: 189, 189, 190)
      a.   *ɔ́:-**dé***   *Ø-dɔ́-+ą́:*
         there-toward 3SG-move-come
         'He was coming here (toward me from far away).'
      b.   *ɔ́-**p***   *Carnegie-kù Ø-dɔ́:-+hɔ́:*
         there-away Carnegie-to 3SG-move-go
         'He went off there toward Carnegie.'

c. *ɔ́:-pé* *Ø-q́:*
there-along 3SG-come.PAST
'She came along there.'

Finally, Inuktitut has a deictic prefix which indicates that the deictic center has been shifted from the speaker to another person in the speech situation. Demonstratives that are marked by this prefix refer to a location relative to the person to which the deictic center has been shifted. Compare the following two examples:

(4) Inuktitut (Denny 1982: 362, 362)
a. *pik-unga*
up.there-to
'up there from my perspective' (speaker's perspective)
b. *ta-ik-unga*
SHIFT-up.there-to
'up there from your/his/her/their perspective(s)'

The demonstrative in (4a) consists of a deictic root and a locative marker; it refers to a location that is 'up there' from the perspective of the speaker. The demonstrative in (4b) occurs with the same locative marker, but in addition it is marked by the "field shifting prefix" *ta-* (Denny 1982: 362). *Ta-* indicates that the deictic center has been transferred from the speaker to another person so that the referent of the demonstrative is 'up there' from the perspective of the person to which the deictic center has been shifted.

3.1.2 Qualitative features

In addition to deictic information, demonstratives usually provide some qualitative information about the referent. They may indicate, for instance, whether the referent is animate or inanimate or whether it is a single entity or a set. I have divided the qualitative features into six categories: (i) ontology, (ii) animacy, (iii) humanness, (iv) sex, (v) number, and (vi) boundedness. I will discuss these categories in turn.

The category of ontology subsumes two semantic features which indicate whether a demonstrative refers to a location or to an object or person. In most languages, demonstrative adverbs can only refer to a location while demonstrative pronouns are used to indicate a person or object. In other words, the semantic distinction between locational and non-locational referents corresponds rather closely with the categorial distinction between demonstrative adverbs and pronouns.[11]

The categories animacy, humanness and sex overlap to some extent: a demonstrative that indicates a human referent presupposes, for instance, that the referent is also animate. However, since animacy, humanness and sex are not synonymous, they must be kept separate.

Animacy distinctions are encoded by the demonstratives in several American Indian languages in my sample (e.g. Apalai, Barasano, Hixkaryana, Passamaquoddy-Maliseet, Ute). Table 32 shows the animate and inanimate demonstratives in Apalai.

Table 32. *(In)animate demonstratives in Apalai (Koehn and Koehn 1986: 95)*

	ANIMATE		INANIMATE	
	NON-COLL	COLL	NON-COLL	COLL
PROXIMAL	*mose*	*moxiamo*	*seny*	*senohne*
MEDIAL	*mokyro*	*mokaro*	*moro*	*morohne*
DISTAL	*moky*	*mokamo*	*mony*	*monohne*

One of the few languages in which demonstratives are marked for humanness in my sample is Burushaski, an isolate language spoken in Pakistan. Burushaski indicates humanness and animacy through distinct demonstrative roots. In addition, it expresses sex as a secondary feature through certain case suffixes. Table 33 shows the nominative/accusative, genitive and dative forms of the proximal demonstrative pronouns. The nominative/accusative forms are unmarked for sex, but the genitive and dative forms indicate the sex features of the referent indirectly through their case endings.

Table 33. *Demonstrative pronouns in Burushaski (Lorimer 1935: 141)*

	HUMAN ANIMATE MASC	HUMAN ANIMATE FEM	NON-HUMAN ANIMATE (+few others)	NON-HUMAN INANIMATE
NOM/ACC	*kiːnɛ/kiːn*	*kiːnɛ/kiːn*	*gʊsɛ*	*gʊtɛ*
GEN	*kiːnɛ*	*kiːnɛmo*	*gʊsɛ*	*gʊtɛ*
DAT	*kiːnɛr/kiːnər*	*kiːnɛmʊr*	*gʊsɛr*	*gʊtɛr*

In addition to animacy, humanness and sex, demonstratives may be marked for number. Number is the most frequent non-deictic category of the demonstratives in my sample (cf. 2.2.2). Most languages distinguish between singular and plural forms only, but some languages have also a dual (cf. Ambulas 2.1.2). Table 34 shows that the demonstratives in Wardaman have as many as four number features: (i) singular, (ii) dual, (iii) plural, and (iv) collective:

Table 34. *Demonstrative pronouns/determiners in Wardaman (Merlan 1994: 139)*

	PROXIMAL	MEDIAL	DISTAL
ABS.SG	*dana*	*nana*	*darni*
ABS.DU	*dan-guya*	*nan-guya*	*dang-guya*
ABS.PL	*dan-mulu*	*nan-mulu*	*dang-mulu*
ABS.COLL	*dan-ganung*	*nan-ganung*	*dang-ganung*

The last semantic category to be discussed in this section is boundedness (for a general discussion of the category 'boundedness' see Talmy 1988: 178–80). Boundedness is a central category of the deictic system in Inuktitut. Inuktitut has two series of demonstratives: one indicates a restricted referent and the other is specifically used to indicate an unbound or extended referent. The two series are shown in Table 35.

Table 35. *Demonstrative roots in Inuktitut (Denny 1982: 372)*

	RESTRICTED	EXTENDED
PROXIMAL	*uv-*	*maj-*
DISTAL	*ik-*	*av-*
UP.THERE	*pik-*	*pag-*
DOWN.THERE	*kan-*	*ug-*
IN.THERE	*qav-*	*qav-*
OUT.THERE	*kig-*	*qag-*

The bound forms, which Denny (1982: 360) calls "restricted", refer to an object or location "whose entire extent is comprehensible to the eye in a single glance", while the unbound forms, which Denny calls "extended", refer to objects and locations "whose entire extent is not comprehensible in a single glance" (Denny 1982: 360). The choice between these forms is not determined by the objective size of the referent; crucial is how the speaker conceptualizes the entity to which s/he refers.

3.1.3   Summary: the semantic features of demonstratives

The two previous sections described the semantic features of demonstratives, which were divided into two categories: (i) deictic features, which indicate the location of the referent relative to the deictic center, and (ii) qualitative features, which provide some classificatory information about the referent. The major results of these two sections are summarized in 1 to 6:

1. All languages have at least two demonstratives that are deictically contrastive: a proximal demonstrative referring to an entity near the deictic center and a distal demonstrative indicating a referent that is located in some distance to the speaker.

2. In some languages, pronominal, adnominal and/or identificational demonstratives are distance-neutral, but adverbial demonstratives are always deictically contrastive.

3. Deictic systems that involve more than two deictic terms can be divided into distance-oriented systems, in which the deictic center is the only point of reference for the location of the referent, and person-oriented systems, in which, in addition to the deictic center, the location of the hearer serves as another reference point.

4. Distance-oriented systems have usually not more than three deictic terms while person-oriented systems may have up to four.

5. In addition to distance, demonstratives often encode a number of 'special' deictic features: they may indicate, for instance, whether the referent is visible or out of sight, at a higher or lower elevation, uphill or downhill, upriver or downriver, or moving toward or away from the deictic center.

6. Apart from deictic information, demonstratives usually provide some qualitative information about the referent: they may indicate whether the referent is a location, object or person, whether it is animate or inanimate, human or non-human, female or male, a single entity or set, or conceptualized as a restricted or extended entity.

3.2   The features of demonstratives: a systematic overview

In addition to semantic information, demonstratives often provide some information concerning aspects of their pragmatic use and syntactic function. There are, for instance, languages in which exophoric, anaphoric, discourse deictic, and recognitional demonstratives have different forms, and there are also languages in which pronominal, adnominal, adverbial, and identificational demonstratives are formally distinguished. Thus, there are three kinds of features that demonstratives encode: (i) semantic features, which indicate the kind of referent and its location; (ii) pragmatic features, which indicate how demonstratives are used; and (iii) syntactic features, which indicate their syntactic functions. Table 36 provides an overview of all features — semantic, pragmatic and syntactic — that are encoded by demonstratives in my sample.

Table 36. *An overview of the features encoded by demonstratives*

Semantics

(i) Deixis

Distance	Visibility	Elevation	Geography	Movement
neutral	visible	up	uphill	toward S
proximal	invisible	down	downhill	away from S
medial			upriver	across the visual
etc.			downriver	field of S

(ii) Quality

Ontology	Animacy	Humanness	Sex	Number	Boundedness
location	animate	human	female	singular	bound
object/person	inanimate	nonhuman	male	plural	unbound
				etc.	

Syntax

Category	Case	Agreement			
pronoun	nom	*(i) Gender*	*(ii) Number*	*(iii) Case*	
determiner	acc	masc	singular	nom	
adverb	etc.	fem	plural	acc	
identifier		etc.	etc.	etc.	

Pragmatics

Use	Reference			
exophoric	*(i) Emphasis*	*(ii) Contrast*	*(iii) Precision*	
anaphoric	emphatic	contrastive	precise	
discourse deictic	non-emphatic	non-contrastive	vague	
recognitional				

The features in Table 36 are organized into three main categories: semantics, syntax and pragmatics (given in bold italics). The three main categories are divided into several subcategories (in italics), which subsume the features that are directly encoded by demonstratives (in roman type). The features listed under each subcategory are in contrastive distribution, but they may cooccur with features of other subcategories. For instance, a demonstrative cannot have two case features, but it may have a case feature, a category feature, up to three agreement features, and so on. Let me emphasize that these features are meant to characterize the information that is directly encoded in the morphological form of a demonstrative. A demonstrative may be used, for example, as an anaphoric pronoun referring to a human being, but if this is not reflected in its *form* it will not have the features 'anaphoric', 'pronoun' and 'human'. Each feature is either expressed by a demonstrative root or by one of the morphemes with which it combines. In addition, there are a few forms in which a feature is associated with the combination of a demonstrative root and a particular affix. For instance, some languages have demonstratives that are interpreted as pronouns when they are case-marked due to the fact that case markers only occur with pronominal demonstratives in these languages (cf. 2.2.2 and 4.1). In such a case, the feature 'pronoun' is associated with the entire form rather than with one of its components.

The semantic features are divided into two categories: *Deixis* and *Quality*. The category *Deixis* has five subcategories: (i) *Distance*, (ii) *Visibility*, (iii) *Elevation*, (iv) *Geography*, and (v) *Movement* (or *Direction*). The category *Quality* is divided into six subcategories: (i) *Ontology*, (ii) *Animacy*, (iii) *Humanness*, (iv) *Sex*, (v) *Number*, and (vi) *Boundedness*. The features of these categories were discussed at length in the previous two sections.

The syntactic features are divided into three categories: (i) *Category*, (ii) *Case*, and (iii) *Agreement*. *Category* subsumes four features which indicate the categorial status of a demonstrative: (i) 'pronoun', (ii) 'determiner', (iii) 'adverb', and (iv) 'identifier'. The categorial status of demonstratives will be examined in the following chapter. The agreement features are subsumed by three subcategories: (i) *Gender*, (ii), *Number* and (iii) *Case*. *Case* is listed twice because case is not only an agreement feature; its primary function is to indicate grammatical relations.

The pragmatic features are divided into two categories: *Use* and *Reference*. The category *Use* has four features: (i) 'exophoric', (ii) 'anaphoric', (iii) 'discourse deictic', and (iv) 'recognitional'. Chapter 5 will show that many languages employ distinct demonstrative forms for these four uses. The category *Reference* is further divided into (i) *Emphasis*, (ii) *Contrast*, and (iii) *Precision*. The features of these categories indicate the kind of reference that is expressed by a demonstrative. More specifically, they indicate whether a demonstrative is (i) emphatic or non-emphatic, (ii) contrastive or non-contrastive, and (iii) whether it is used with vague or precise reference. Since these features are not discussed anywhere else in this study, I use the remainder of this section to illustrate their form and function.

Emphasis is usually expressed by emphatic suffixes that attach to a demonstrative root, as in the following example from Ngiti.

(5)   Ngiti (Kutsch 1994: 374)
       wɔ̀-rí   nɔ́nyù tsìtsì
       DEM-EMPH eat.PF banana(s)
       'That one has eaten bananas.'

Similar emphatic affixes augment demonstratives in Basque (Saltarelli 1988: 215–6), Dyirbal (Dixon 1972: 48), Logbara (Crazzolara 1960: 55), Ewondo (Redden 1980: 70), and Ponapean (Rehg 1981: 143–154).[12] Table 37 shows the emphatic and non-emphatic demonstrative determiners in Ponapean (allomorphs are omitted). The emphatic forms consist of the non-emphatic singular forms and a numeral classifier. The classifier shown in this table is *men,* which indicates an animate referent. Inanimate demonstrative pronouns involve a different classifier. The emphatic plural forms are formed by combining the non-emphatic demonstratives with the morpheme *pwu-,* which does not occur in any other context.

Table 37. *Emphatic demonstrative determiners in Ponapean (Rehg 1981: 144, 149)*

	NON-EMPHATIC		EMPHATIC	
	SG	PL	SG	PL
NEAR S	*-e(t)*	*-ka(t)*	*mene(t)*	*pwuka(t)*
NEAR H	*-en*	*-kan*	*menen*	*pwukan*
AWAY FROM S+H	*-o*	*-kau*	*meno*	*pwukau*

Like *Emphasis, Contrast* is usually expressed through a particular affix. Woleaian, for instance, has a suffix that indicates a contrastive referent "as when pointing out one member of a group" (Anderson and Keenan 1985: 289):

(6)   Woleaian (Anderson and Keenan 1985: 289)
       mwu(u)-l
       that.NEAR.H-CONTRAST
       'that one near you'

Like Woleaian, Manam marks contrastiveness by a particular suffix. Demonstratives being marked by this suffix indicate that the speaker selects the referent "out of a set" (Lichtenberk 1983:334).

(7)   Manam (Lichtenberk 1983:334)
       tomóata ŋáe-ni-Ø   *y-ún-a*
       man   this-SELECT-3SG 3SG-hit-1SG.OBJ
       'This man (out of several) hit me.'

Finally, there are demonstratives that indicate either vague or precise reference. Ewondo, for instance, has two series of adverbial demonstratives that convey this kind of information: *vá* 'near speaker', *válá* 'near hearer', *válí* 'away from speaker and hearer, and *álí* 'far away from speaker and hearer' are used with precise reference, while *mú* 'around the location of the speaker', *múlū* 'around the location of the hearer', *wóé* 'away from the location of speaker and hearer' and *múlí* 'far away from the location of speaker and hearer' indicate a location somewhere around (or in the vicinity of) a certain point of reference (cf. 2.3). Similarly, in Daga, a language spoken in New Guinea, demonstratives occur with the suffix *-na* if the location of the referent is vague, and they are unmarked if they refer to a precise location (cf. Anderson and Keenan 1985:291).[13]

Concluding this chapter, I describe some demonstratives using the features in Table 36. The number of features that are encoded by a demonstrative varies with the size of the demonstrative system: demonstratives of complex systems provide more information than demonstratives of small systems. Acehnese, for instance, has only three invariable demonstratives which carry one semantic feature (cf. 8), while the demonstratives in Tümpisa Shoshone, which has more than a hundred different forms, indicate seven features (cf. 9).

(8)   Acehnese   *nyoe*
       Syntax   –
       Semantics   proximal
       Pragmatics   –

(9)   Tümp. Shoshone   *s-u-tungku* 'ANA-INVIS-NOM.DU'
       Syntax   pronoun/determiner
                         dual
                         nom
       Semantics   invisible
                         object/person
                         dual
       Pragmatics   anaphoric

(10)   English   *there*
        Syntax   adverbial
        Semantics   distal
                         location
        Pragmatics   exophoric/anaphoric

(11)   Ngiyambaa   *ŋa-ni-la:* 'DIST-LOC-GIVEN'
        Syntax   pronoun/determiner/(adverb/identifier)
                         locative
                         singular
        Semantics   distal
                         location
        Pragmatics   anaphoric

(12)   Korean   *i*
        Syntax   determiner
        Semantics   proximal
        Pragmatics   exophoric/anaphoric

(13)   German   *dessen*
        Syntax   pronoun/determiner
                         singular
                         masculin/neuter
                         genitive
        Semantics   neutral
                         object/person
                         singular
                         (male)
        Pragmatics   exophoric/anaphoric

CHAPTER 4

Syntax

Having described the morphological and semantic properties of demonstratives, I now examine their syntactic features. As pointed out in the introduction, I distinguish between the use of a demonstrative in a specific syntactic context and its categorial status. Demonstratives occur in four different syntactic contexts: (i) they are used as independent pronouns in argument position of verbs and adpositions, (ii) they may cooccur with a noun in a noun phrase, (iii) they may function as verb modifiers, and (iv) they occur in copular and nonverbal clauses. I refer to demonstratives being used in one of these four contexts as (i) *pronominal*, (ii) *adnominal*, (iii) *adverbial*, and (iv) *identificational* demonstratives, respectively. Some languages have only one series of demonstratives that they use in all four contexts, but most languages employ distinct demonstrative forms in some or all of these positions. If adnominal, pronominal, adverbial, and identificational demonstratives are formally distinguished, I assume that they belong to different grammatical categories, which I refer to as (i) demonstrative *pronouns*, (ii) demonstrative *determiners*, (iii) demonstrative *adverbs*, and (iv) demonstrative *identifiers,* respectively.

The term demonstrative pronoun is probably the most transparent term of these four notions. Demonstrative pronouns are pro-nominals; they are used in lieu of a noun (phrase) and have the usual morphological features of nominals (i.e. gender, number and case), if the nominals of a particular language are marked for these features (cf. 2.2.2).

The term demonstrative determiner applies to adnominal demonstratives that are formally distinguished from demonstratives in other syntactic contexts. Traditional grammar assumes that demonstrative determiners are noun modifiers (e.g. Bloomfield 1933), but Hudson (1984), Abney (1987) and others have argued that the determiner is head of NP (or DP). Below I argue against the "Determiner-as-head hypothesis". More specifically, I show that some of the head features are shared by a demonstrative determiner and a cooccurring noun.

The term demonstrative adverb is adopted from Fillmore (1982: 47), who uses this notion for locational deictics such as English *here* and *there* (and also for manner demonstratives, cf. 4.2). The category adverb applies to a variety of items that are semantically quite diverse and morphologically often not consistently marked as a particular word class (cf. Schachter 1985: 20). Syntactically, adverbs are used as modifiers of verbs, adjectives and other adverbs. Since locational deictics are primarily used to indicate the location of the event or situation denoted by a cooccurring verb they may be classified as adverbs.

The term demonstrative identifier is used for demonstratives in copular and nonverbal clauses that are formally distinguished from demonstratives in other sentence types. The term has the connotation of a semantic or pragmatic notion, but I use it as a label for a grammatical category on a par with demonstrative pronouns, determiners and adverbs. In two previous studies (Diessel 1997a, forthcoming) I referred to demonstrative identifiers as "predicative demonstratives". I adopted this notion from studies by Denny (1982: 365) and Heath (1984: 269–336), where it is used to refer to a particular class of demonstratives in Inuktitut and Nunggubuyu. Other notions that I have found in the literature that seem to correspond to the notion of demonstrative identifier are "demonstrative predicator" (Schuh 1977), "predicative pronoun" (Marconnès 1931: 110), "copulative demonstrative" (Ziervogel 1952: 47–8), "existential demonstrative" (Benton 1971: 90), "pointing demonstrative" (Rehg 1981: 143), and "deictic identifier pronoun" (Carlson 1994: 160). Since demonstrative identifiers often occur in nonverbal clauses, they are sometimes considered to be functionally equivalent to a demonstrative plus copula, which many languages require in this construction (Hengeveld 1992). In fact, demonstrative identifiers are often glossed as 'this/that.is' or 'here/there.is' (e.g. Carlson 1994: 241; Dayley 1989: 145). This explains why some studies use the attribute 'predicative' in order to characterize demonstrative identifiers. The occurrence of demonstrative identifiers is, however, not restricted to nonverbal clauses. Demonstratives in copular sentences are also often distinguished from (pronominal) demonstratives in other sentence types. Since the demonstratives in copular clauses are certainly not predicative, I decided to replace the notion predicative demonstrative by demonstrative identifier.

In the following three sections, I discuss the evidence for the distinction between demonstrative pronouns, determiners, adverbs, and identifiers, and I take a closer look at languages in which these categories are not distinguished. I begin by examining the distinction between demonstrative pronouns and determiners, then I discuss demonstrative adverbs, and finally I consider the evidence for my hypothesis that many languages have a class of demonstrative identifiers.

4.1 Demonstrative pronouns and demonstrative determiners

The majority of languages uses the same demonstrative forms as independent pronouns and as modifiers of a cooccurring noun. In my sample, there are only twenty-four languages in which pronominal and adnominal demonstratives are formally distinguished. In some of these languages they have different stems, as in the following examples from Mulao and Japanese:

Table 38. *Demonstratives in Mulao (Wang and Guoqiao 1993: 52)*

	DEM PROS	DEM DETS
PROXIMAL	ni^5	$na{:}i^6$
DISTAL	hui^5	ka^6

Table 39. *Demonstratives in Japanese (Kuno 1973: 27)*

	DEM PROS	DEM DETS
NEAR S	*kore*	*kono*
NEAR H	*sore*	*sono*
AWAY FROM S+H	*are*	*ano*

Mulao uses the demonstratives ni^5 and hui^5 as independent pronouns and $na{:}i^6$ and ka^6 as modifiers of a cooccurring noun (the superscript numbers indicate tone). The Japanese demonstratives consist of a distance and a category marker: *ko-*, *so-* and *a-* indicate the relative distance between the referent and the deictic center, and *-re* and *-no* indicate whether the demonstrative functions as a pronoun or determiner.

In other languages, pronominal and adnominal demonstratives have the same stems but differ in their inflection (cf. 2.2.2). Two examples from Turkish and Lezgian are shown in Table 40 and 41 respectively.

Turkish has three demonstrative roots: *bu* 'proximal', *şu* 'medial', and *o* 'distal' (Lewis 1967 glosses *şu* 'the following'). The demonstrative determiners are uninflected, but the demonstrative pronouns occur with number and case suffixes, which are joined to the demonstrative root by an alveolar nasal. Like Turkish, Lezgian has three demonstrative roots, *i* 'proximal', *a* 'distal' and *at'a* 'yonder'. They are marked for gender and number when they are used as

Table 40. *Demonstratives in Turkish (Kornfilt 1997: 106, 311)*

		DEM PROS				DEM DETS		
		PROX	MED	DIST		PROX	MED	DIST
SG	ABS	*bu*	*şu*	*o*	SG/PL	*bu*	*şu*	*o*
	ACC	*bun-u*	*şun-u*	*on-u*				
	GEN	*bun-un*	*şun-un*	*on-un*				
	DAT	*bun-a*	*şun-a*	*on-a*				
	LOC	*bun-da*	*şun-da*	*on-da*				
PL	ABS	*bun-lar*	*şun-lar*	*on-lar*				

Table 41. *Demonstratives in Lezgian (Haspelmath 1993: 111)*

		DEM PROS				DEM DETS		
		PROX	DIST	YONDER		PROX	DIST	YONDER
SG	ABS	*i-m*	*a-m*	*at'a-m*	SG/PL	*i*	*a*	*at'a*
	ERG	*i-da*	*a-da*	*at'a-da*				
	GEN	*i-da-n*	*a-da-n*	*at'a-da-n*				
PL	ABS	*i-bur*	*a-bur*	*at'a-bur*				

independent pronouns, but they are uninflected when they cooccur with an (inflected) noun (cf. 2.2.2).

If pronominal and adnominal demonstratives have different stems as in Mulao and Japanese or if they differ in their inflectional behavior as in Turkish and Lezgian, I assume that they belong to different grammatical categories, which I refer to as demonstrative pronouns and demonstrative determiners, respectively.

4.1.1   Adnominal demonstrative pronouns

Unlike Mulao, Japanese, Turkish, and Lezgian, most languages use the same demonstrative forms in the position of independent pronouns and adjacent to a cooccuring noun. In my sample, there are sixty-one languages in which adnominal and pronominal demonstratives have the same stems and the same inflectional features. In most of these languages there is no evidence that pronominal and adnominal demonstratives belong to different categories. Both demonstratives are often independent pronouns, which are either used as arguments of verbs and adpositions or adjoined to a coreferential noun in apposition (cf. Hale 1983; Heath 1986; Baker 1996: chap4). Tuscarora, for instance, has two demonstratives, *hè:ní:kɔ̀:* 'this/these' and *kyè:níkɔ̀:* 'that/those', which are either used as independent pronouns or with a cooccurring noun (Mithun 1987). When *hè:ní:kɔ̀:* and *kyè:níkɔ̀:* are used adnominally they are only loosely combined with the juxtaposed noun: (i) both noun and demonstrative can represent the entire NP without the other element, (ii) their position with respect to each other is flexible (cf. 1a–b), and (iii) they are often separated by an intonational break (cf. 1c):

(1)   Tuscarora (Mithun 1987: 184, 184, 186)
   a.   ***hè:ní:kɔ̀:*** *áha:θ*
         that   horse
         'that horse'
   b.   *uʔné:wa:k **hè:ní:kɔ̀:***
         ghost   that
         'that ghost'
   c.   *waʔtkahá:hi:θ **hè:ní:kɔ̀:**, ... ruyaʔkwáhehr*
         it.met.it   that   he.body.carries
         'It met that dinosaur.'

Based on these examples, Mithun (1987) argues that adnominal demonstratives in Tuscarora are free nominals that cooccur with a coreferential noun in apposition. There are several other languages in my sample in which adnominal demonstratives behave in the same way as in Tuscarora and have been analyzed as independent pronouns that are juxtaposed to a coreferential noun (e.g. Dyirbal, Nunggubuyu, Wardaman, Oneida, West Greenlandic, Karanga). In some of these languages, adnominal demonstratives may even be separated from the noun by an intervening constituent. Such discontinuous noun phrases are quite common in Australian languages (cf. Dixon 1972; Hale 1983; Heath 1986). An example from Wardaman is shown in (2).

(2)   Wardaman (Merlan 1994: 143)
       dang-nyi *wunggun-bu-ndi   yibiyan-yi*
       yonder-ERG 3SG:3NON.SG-hit-PAST man-ERG
       'That man hit them.'

In Tuscarora and Wardaman, adnominal demonstratives are not categorially distinguished from demonstrative pronouns. These languages do not have a particular class of demonstrative determiners. Adnominal demonstratives are demonstrative pronouns that are adjoined to a neighboring noun in some kind of appositional structure.[14]

4.1.2 *Adnominal demonstratives in English*

At this point one might ask whether adnominal and pronominal demonstratives generally belong to the same category if they are phonologically and morphologically indistinguishable. Consider, for instance, the adnominal demonstratives in English. They have the same form as pronominal demonstratives, but are they independent pronouns that are joined to an appositive noun, or do they function as determiners? The categorial status of demonstratives in English is controversial.

To begin with, Van Valin and LaPolla (1997: 62) argue that "demonstratives are pronominal in nature". In their view, *this* and *that* are pronouns no matter where they occur. If they are used adnominally they occupy a particular slot in the noun phrase. Van Valin and LaPolla use tree diagrams with two "projections" in order to describe the syntactic and semantic relationships between the elements of a noun phrase: a "constituent projection", which represents the major constituents of the noun phrase, and an "operator projection", which represents the operators of the noun and the entire NP. Both the constituent and operator projection have several layers: nucleus, core, periphery, and the whole noun phrase. For Van Valin and LaPolla's treatment of adnominal demonstratives, it is essential to distinguish between elements that occur inside of the core layer and elements outside of the core. To be precise, there is only one slot outside of the core, called the "NP-initial position", which is the place where possessor NPs usually occur. Articles, adjectives and numerals are treated as operators of the core; they are only represented in the operator projection:

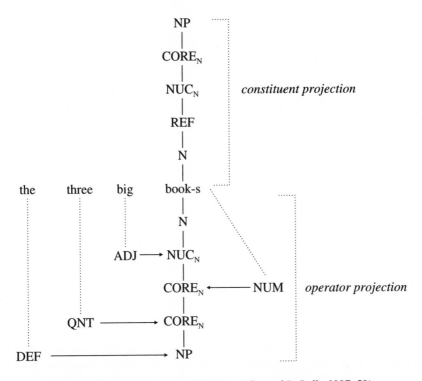

Figure 2. *Layered structure of NP (Van Valin and LaPolla 1997: 59)*

Adnominal demonstratives are also treated as operators by Van Valin and LaPolla. But unlike articles, demonstratives are not 'pure' operators in their view. They are also represented in the constituent projection where they occupy the NP-initial position (NPIP) outside of the core.

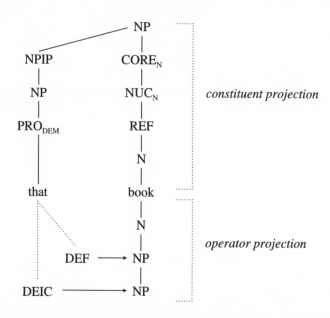

Figure 3. *Layered structure of NP with adnominal DEM (Van Valin and LaPolla 1997: 62)*

In this analysis, adnominal demonstratives are pronouns that occur in a specific syntactic slot in which independent nominals (i.e. pronouns or nouns) function as operators of a juxtaposed noun (phrase). Van Valin and LaPolla (1997: 62) point out that in their analysis *the house* has a different syntactic structure from *this house* because articles and adnominal demonstratives are treated as members of two distinct categories, which are associated with different slots in the noun phrase: articles are pure operators inside of the core, while (adnominal) demonstratives are treated as independent pronouns that may "occur as NP modifiers" outside of the core (Van Valin and LaPolla 1997: 62). In defense of their analysis, Van Valin and LaPolla argue that although this "might seem odd from an English perspective" there is good crosslinguistic evidence that articles and adnominal demonstratives are categorially distinguished. They point out that in some languages articles and adnominal demonstratives may cooccur, and they cite Dryer's work on word order correlations (Dryer 1989a, 1992a), which shows that articles and demonstratives follow different word order patterns across languages: while the order of article and noun correlates with the order of verb and object, the order of demonstrative and noun is in principle independent of the basic word order pattern that characterizes a particular language (cf. Dryer 1989a: 89, 1992a: 103–4). Crosslinguistically, demonstratives tend to precede the noun regardless of the order of verb and object (cf. Dryer 1989a: 95, 1992a: 96). This might indicate, as Dryer points out, that articles and demonstratives do not always belong to the same category.

Though articles and demonstratives are not always members of the same category, there is good evidence that English *the* and *this/that* have the same categorial status. English is one of the few languages in my sample in which adnominal demonstratives are in paradigmatic relationship with articles, possessives and other noun operators (e.g. *every*), which share a number of syntactic features. This is a clear indication that adnominal *this* and *that* belong to a category of determiners subsuming (adnominal) demonstratives, articles, possessives and several other items such as *every*. Van Valin and LaPolla's argument is based on the assumption that adnominal demonstratives have the same categorial status across all languages, but that is not the case. As shown above, there are languages in which adnominal demonstratives are independent pronouns that are adjoined to a coreferential noun in apposition, and there are other languages in which adnominal demonstratives are determiners, which require a cooccurring noun.

To summarize the discussion thus far, I consider adnominal demonstratives determiners if they are formally distinguished from demonstratives in other contexts. They might differ from demonstrative pronouns, adverbs and identifiers in three ways. First, they might have a particular phonological form, as in Mulao and Japanese (cf. 4.1). Second, they might differ in their inflectional behavior, as in Turkish and Lezgian (cf. 4.1). And third, they might have specific syntactic properties, as in English, where adnominal demonstratives belong to the same paradigm as articles and possessives. Adnominal *this* and *that* cannot be treated as pro-nominals, unless one wants to claim that all determiners are independent pronouns in English.

Assuming that the adnominal demonstratives in English are determiners, one could argue, as an alternative to Van Valin and LaPolla's analysis, that pronominal *this* and *that* are determiners that accompany an empty head instead of a cooccurring noun. This view is captured in the tree diagram in Figure 4, which I adopted from Abney (1987: 279–280). Abney discusses this structure as an alternative to the analysis that he eventually suggests (see below).

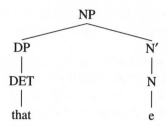

Figure 4. *Demonstrative determiner with empty head noun (Abney 1987: 280)*

Figure 4 provides an analysis that solves the problem in theory: if pronominal demonstratives in English generally cooccur with an empty head, they are indeed determiners. But as far as I can see, there is no empirical evidence for this claim. Pronominal *this* and *that* do not constitute empty-headed NPs. There is no structural and no psycholinguistic evidence that would support such a claim. The assumption that adnominal demonstratives accompany an empty head is motivated by theory internal considerations, which are irrelevant to the current investigation.

After considering the structure in Figure 4, Abney (1987) presents an alternative analysis. He maintains that pronouns and determiners are in principle not distinguished. That is, Abney claims that pronouns such as *I, he* and *someone* belong to the same category as determiners such as *a, the* and *every* (cf. Postal 1969; Vennemann and Harlow 1977; Hudson 1984: 90–2). Abney refers to the members of this category as determiners, but they should be called 'pro-terminers' to be neutral.

In order to understand Abney's hypothesis, one has to consider the context in which it is proposed. Abney is not interested in the categorial status of *this* and *that*; he is primarily concerned with the structure of the noun phrase in English and constituency in universal grammar. His ultimate goal is to show that NP has basically the same constituent structure as IP. Abney assumes, for conceptual reasons, that the constituent structure of all phrases is essentially the same and should be reduced to a single X-bar schema. IP is a maximal projection of a functional category, namely of INFL. Abney suggests that determiners are the equivalent of INFL in NP. That is, he claims that determiners project a phrase in which the determiner functions as head and the noun as a complement of the former.

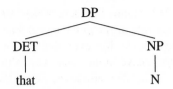

Figure 5. *Determiner phrase (Abney 1987: 279)*

In order to account for the different behavior of traditional pronouns and traditional determiners, Abney distinguishes between different subtypes of determiners. More specifically, he claims that the category determiner is sub-categorized in the same way as the category verb. Like verbs, determiners can be transitive or intransitive. Traditional determiners such as the definite article *the* are transitive; they take a noun as their complement. Traditional pronouns, on the other hand, are intransitive determiners that do not take a complement. In this approach, demonstratives are treated as determiners with variable valency: they may be used intransitively without a nominal complement, or they are used transitively in a determiner phrase. Demonstratives correspond to verbs such as *eat* or *burn,* which can also be both transitive and intransitive.[15]

Abney's analysis is largely motivated by conceptual and theory internal considerations, as he himself points out (Abney 1987: 351). He abandons the distinction between determiners and pronouns primarily because this strengthens the "Det-as-head analysis", which, in turn, allows him to maintain that the structure of NP/DP is basically the same as the structure of IP.[16] If determiners belong to the same category as pronouns it appears to be more plausible to analyze determiners as the head of NP/DP because pronouns are commonly treated as the head of NP. There is, however, only little empirical support for this claim. The only piece of evidence that might suggest that pronouns and deter-miners are not distinguished comes from items such as *this* and *that* that can be both independent pronouns and determiners. But since most pronouns cannot function as determiners and most determiners cannot be used as independent pronouns this argument alone is not convincing. Abney seeks to support his analysis by two other empirical observations. First, he argues that in certain contexts personal pronouns such as *I* and *you* are also used as determiners, as in *I Claudius* and *you idiot(s)* (Abney 1987: 282). This argument is, however, based on false assumptions. The personal pronouns that are used in these examples are not restrictive. They do not determine the referential scope of the associated nominal; rather, they are used as independent pronouns that cooccur with an appositive noun.[17]

Second, Abney (1987: 283) claims that determiners are also similar to pronouns in that they are the basic site of the grammatical features that characterize a noun phrase. Chapter 2 has shown, however, that pronominal and adnominal demonstratives do not always behave in the same way in this respect. There are many languages in which adnominal demonstratives are not the site of grammatical features even though pronominal demonstratives inflect. Abney's hypothesis that determiners and pronouns form a single category is thus empirically unmotivated and therefore I suggest that pronominal and adnominal *this* and *that* are to be categorially distinguished.

To summarize, we have considered three analyses of *this* and *that* providing three different answers to the question: what is the categorial status of adnominal demonstratives in English? Van Valin and LaPolla argue that both adnominal and pronominal *this* and *that* are independent pronouns. Alternatively, it has been argued that they function as determiners, which cooccur either with a noun or an empty head. Finally, Abney suggests that one should abandon the distinction between pronouns and determiners altogether. All three analyses treat pronominal and adnominal demonstratives as members of the same category, but ultimately they are not convincing. I follow therefore the traditional view, which holds that pronominal and adnominal *this* and *that* belong to different categories despite the fact that they are phonologically and morphologically not distinguished (cf. Bloomfield 1933). Adnominal *this* and *that* occur in a specific syntactic slot where they cannot be analyzed as pronouns, and there is no evidence that pronominal *this* and *that* would function as determiners. The English demonstratives have the syntactic properties of two distinct word classes, and it seems that one can only account for this if one assumes that adnominal and pronominal demonstratives are categorially distinguished. Like many other languages, English has both demonstrative pronouns and demonstrative determiners.

It is, of course, no accident that pronominal and adnominal *this* and *that* share the same phonological and morphological features. Historically, the determiners can be traced back to independent pronouns. Old English did not have demonstrative determiners. Unlike adnominal demonstratives in Modern English, adnominal demonstratives in Old English were not obligatory to form a noun phrase and could cooccur with other elements that determine a noun semantically such as possessives (cf. Traugott 1992: 173):

(3)   Old English (Traugott 1992: 173)
        þa   com   þær   gan   in to me heofoncund Wisdom, &
        then came there going in to me heavenly   Wisdom and
        þæt min murnede mod mid his wordum gegrette
        that my sad   spirit with his words   greeted
        'Then heavenly Wisdom came to me there and greeted my sad spirit
        with his words.'

In example (3), the demonstrative *þæt* cooccurs with a possessive pronoun. In
such a case, the demonstrative usually precedes the possessor as in (3), but
Traugott (1992: 173) points out that there are also examples in Old English in
which the demonstrative follows the possessor. Both the fact that demonstratives
could cooccur with a possessive (pro)noun and that their position vis-à-vis the
possessor was not entirely fixed shows that the noun phrase in Old English was
not as tightly constrained as the noun phrase in Modern English. Traugott
(1992: 173) argues that there are examples in the Old English data in which
adnominal demonstratives can only be analyzed as independent pronouns.
Consider, for instance, the demonstrative in (4):

(4)   Old English (Traugott 1992: 173)
        se   heora cyning ongan ða   singan
        that their king   began then to.sing
        'He (that one), their king, then began to sing.'

Old English is a so-called 'verb-second language' in which the finite verb occurs
after the first constituent of a clause, which is typically an adverb (cf. Traugott
1992: 275). Sentence (4) includes the temporal adverb *ða* 'then', which was
strongly preferred in sentence initial position. Traugott (1992: 173) argues that *ða*
does not occur before the verb in this example because the demonstrative *se* "is
probably a pronoun in a topicalized construction", which motivates the unusual
occurrence of the subject NP before the verb, where it is joined to the coreferential demonstrative in some kind of appositional structure. If it is correct that the
adnominal demonstratives of Old English were independent pronouns, as the
analysis of (4) suggests, one has to assume that the demonstrative determiners of
Modern English developed from a pronominal source.

 Himmelmann (1997) argues that the evolution of determiners from independent pronouns is due to a common historical process whereby pragmatic discourse
structures develop into tightly organized phrase structure configurations (cf. Givón
1979; Hopper 1987; Lehmann 1995a). In his view, syntactic structure is the result
of a grammaticalization process by which elements in apposition (or juxtaposition)

are reanalyzed as hierarchically organized phrases (cf. Givón 1979: chap5). Himmelmann points out that this process has an effect on the categorial status of the elements that are involved in an emergent phrase structure configuration. An appositional noun phrase, for instance, consists of two nominals, one of which might be a pronoun. When such a structure is reanalyzed as a hierarchically organized NP the categorial statuses of the items involved in this structure change and new grammatical categories emerge. In the case of the English noun phrase, pronominal elements such as demonstratives and possessives were reanalyzed as determiners. They are distinguished from independent pronouns in that they fill a specific slot in the NP, which can only be occupied by an element that belongs to a particular class of linguistic items. The categorial change that led from pronouns to determiners is not yet reflected in the morphology of *this* and *that,* but as the grammaticalization process continues pronouns and determiners might eventually assume different forms.

The grammaticalization process that gave rise to the structure of the noun phrase in Modern English did not only affect the demonstratives and other adnominal elements, it also changed the status of the cooccurring noun. In Old English, nouns were free nominals which could form a noun phrase without a cooccurring article, demonstrative or possessive. In Modern English, the occurrence of bare nouns is restricted to certain types of nouns (e.g. proper names, mass nouns) and certain uses (e.g. indefinite plural). In all other contexts, a noun requires a cooccurring determiner as much as a determiner requires a cooccurring noun. The noun phrase of Modern English is a *grammatical construction* in which neither the noun nor the determiner can be the sole representation of the whole phrase.[18] Himmelmann (1997: 144–157) argues that the head and dependent properties of the English NP is split between its components. Following Zwicky (1985, 1993), he assumes that the distinction between heads and dependents is based on a set of semantic, syntactic and morphological features, as shown in Table 42.

In the unmarked case, the head and dependent features are divided among the constituents of the phrase, but both Zwicky and Himmelmann argue that in some constructions the head and dependent features are split among their components. The noun phrase of Modern English provides an excellent example. Semantically, the noun is the head of the construction, and since many determiners do not inflect (e.g. *a, the, every*) one might argue that the noun is also the morphosyntactic locus. However, the syntactic head features are represented by both the noun and the determiner: (i) both constituents are usually required, (ii) both the demonstrative and the noun have word rank (i.e. there can only be one element of each in a noun phrase), and (iii) together they determine the categorial

Table 42. *Head and dependent features (Zwicky 1993: 298)*

	Head	Dependent
Semantics	characterizing	contributory
Syntax	required	accessory
	word rank	phrase rank
	category determinant	non-determinant
	external representative	externally transparent
Morphology	morphosyntactic locus	morphosyntactically irrelevant

status of the phrase and its external syntax (Lyons 1977: 392). The adnominal demonstratives in English have therefore both head and dependent features. They must be distinguished from pure modifiers such as adjectives, which have only dependent features. Unlike demonstratives, adjectives (i) are not obligatory, (ii) they do not have word rank (i.e. they can be iterated and modified by an adverb), and (iii) they are irrelevant to the external syntactic behavior of a noun phrase. In order to indicate that determiners are distinguished from ordinary noun modifiers, they are sometimes given a special status. In the generative literature, demonstratives are often classified as *specifiers* (Chomsky 1981), which are distinguished from modifiers such adjectives due to the fact that they have both head and dependent features (cf. Zwicky 1993; Pollard and Sag 1994; Borsley 1996).

4.1.3   *Pronominal demonstrative determiners*

In the previous two sections, we have seen that some languages distinguish between demonstrative pronouns and determiners while other languages have only demonstrative pronouns. In this section, I show that there are also languages that have only demonstrative determiners and lack a class of demonstrative pronouns. We have already seen an example of such a language in Chapter 2, where I have argued that Korean uses a demonstrative determiner and a defective noun in lieu of a demonstrative pronoun. Korean does not have demonstratives that are used as independent pronouns; (pronominal) demonstratives are always accompanied by a nominal constituent, as in the following example:

(5)   Korean (Sohn 1994:   295)
        [ce   il-ul]   nwu-ka   mak-keyss-ni
        that thing-ACC who-NOM block-will-Q
        'Who would be able to block that?'

There are several other languages in my sample in which demonstratives are
generally embedded in a noun phrase. In some of these languages demonstratives
are accompanied by a classifier, as in the following example from Nùng:

(6)   Nùng (Saul and Freiberger Wilson 1980: 61)
        [tú   té] non   cá mu'n
        CLASS that sleep all night
        'That one slept all night.'

In other languages, demonstratives cooccur with a third person pronoun, as in (7)
from Kusaiean:

(7)   Kusaiean (Lee 1975: 101)
        el   uh
        3SG this
        'this (one)'

In Chapter 2, we saw that some languages form demonstrative pronouns from a
demonstrative root and a classifier (e.g. Barasano) or a third person pronoun (e.g.
Ao). The examples from Nùng and Kusaiean suggest that these demonstratives
are historically derived from a noun phrase in which the two elements were
independent.

Although some languages do not have independent demonstrative pronouns,
there are two contexts in which demonstratives usually do not cooccur with a
nominal constituent: (i) in copular and nonverbal clauses, and (ii) in contexts
where a demonstrative refers to an adjacent proposition. Consider the following
two examples:

(8)   Kusaiean (Lee 1975: 109)
        Sohn pa   nge
        John (COP) this
        'This is John.'

(9)   Nùng (Saul and Freiberger Wilson 1980: 21)
        dạ lão   tê   vạ tê
        grandmother that say that
        'That grandmother said that.'

SYNTAX 73

Example (8) shows a demonstrative in a copular clause; and example (9) shows a demonstrative that refers to an adjacent proposition or speech act. Although demonstratives are usually accompanied by a third person pronoun or a classifier in Kusaiean and Nùng, the demonstratives in (8) and (9) are used without a cooccurring nominal. The missing nominal reflects the fact that the demonstratives in these examples do not have the status of a common pronoun. The demonstrative in (8) is an identificational demonstrative, which many languages distinguish from demonstrative pronouns (cf. 4.3), and the demonstrative in (9) is a discourse deictic demonstrative referring to a chunk of the surrounding discourse. Discourse deictic demonstratives can be seen as pro-forms of the proposition(s) to which they refer, but unlike ordinary pronouns they do not substitute for a common noun or noun phrase denoting a person or object (cf. 5.3). In other words, discourse deictic demonstratives are not prototypical pronouns. If one takes the notion of pronoun in its narrow sense as a pro-nominal that replaces a common noun (i.e. a noun denoting an object or person) in an ordinary main clause (i.e. a clause with a common main verb rather than a copula), the demonstratives in (8) and (9) do not qualify as pronouns. I maintain therefore my hypothesis that Kusaiean and Nùng do not have a class of demonstrative pronouns.

4.1.4 Pronominal and adnominal demonstratives: an overview

Table 43 summarizes what I have said in this section about the categorial status of adnominal and pronominal demonstratives. It distinguishes three types of languages: (i) languages in which adnominal and pronominal demonstratives

Table 43. *Demonstrative pronouns and demonstrative determiners*

	DEM PROS	DEM DETS
Mulao	x	x
Japanese	x	x
Turkish	x	x
Lezgian	x	x
English	x	x
Tuscarora	x	
Wardaman	x	
Korean		x
Kusaiean		x
Nùng		x

belong to different categories; (ii) languages that have only demonstrative pronouns; and (iii) languages that have only demonstrative determiners.

4.2 Demonstrative adverbs

Having examined the categorial status of pronominal and adnominal demonstratives, I turn now to demonstrative adverbs. The term demonstrative adverb applies to locational deictics such as *here* and *there* in English. Locational deictics are adverbial in that they are primarily used to indicate the location of the event or situation that is expressed by a cooccurring verb; that is, locational deictics function as some sort of verb modifiers. In many languages, locational deictics can also be used adnominally as in English *this guy here* or German *das Haus da* 'this/that house there'. In this use, they usually cooccur with a demonstrative determiner that they intensify. That is, if a demonstrative adverb is used adnominally it usually does not function as an operator of the noun; rather, it is used to reinforce a cooccurring demonstrative determiner. In some languages, this use has been grammaticalized and has given rise to new demonstrative forms that consist of an old demonstrative determiner and a locational adverb. Afrikaans, for instance, has two demonstratives, *hierdie* 'this' and *daardie* 'that', which are historically derived from the Dutch demonstrative/article *die* and the demonstrative adverbs *hier* 'here' and *daar* 'there' (cf. Raidt 1993). When these forms first appeared they were only used adnominally, but now they are also increasingly used as independent pronouns. Similar demonstratives occur in Swedish (e.g. *det här hus-et* 'the/this here house-the') and French (e.g. *cette maison-là* 'this/that house-there').[19]

Apart from locational deictics, manner demonstratives are usually classified as demonstrative adverbs (cf. Fillmore 1982: 48).[20] Manner demonstratives have been largely ignored in the literature on deixis. Most of the sources that I consulted list only their forms and gloss them as 'in this/that way' or 'like this/that', but they do not explain their meaning or function. Manner demonstratives seem to involve some sort of comparison and they are often used as discourse deictics (cf. 5.3). Some examples are given in Table 44. Since the use and function of manner demonstratives is not sufficiently explained in most of my sources, the following discussion concentrates on locational deictics.

Most languages distinguish locational deictics from pronominal and adnominal demonstratives, but there are a few languages in my sample in which they have the same form. In Chapter 2 we saw, for instance, that Guugu Yimidhirr

Table 44. *Manner demonstratives*

Japanese	*koo* 'in this way', *soo* 'in that way', *aa* 'in that way'
Ainu	*taa* 'in this way', *too* 'in that way'
Ambulas	*kéga* 'like this', *aga* 'like that', *waga* 'like that'
Finnish	*näin* 'in this way', *noin* 'in that way', *niin* 'so' etc.
T. Shoshone	*inni* 'this way'/'like that', *enni* 'this way'/'like that' etc.
Pangasinan	*onyá* 'like this', *ontán* 'like that (near H)', *onmán* 'like that'

uses demonstratives with certain (locative) case endings as locational deictics. They belong to the same morphological paradigm as demonstratives that correspond to *this* and *that* in English. There is no evidence for the existence of an independent class of demonstrative adverbs in Guugu Yimidhirr.

My sample includes only a few other languages in which adverbial demonstratives are members of the same category as pronominal and adnominal demonstratives. Ponapean is one of them. Unlike Guugu Yimidhirr, Ponapean distinguishes demonstrative pronouns from demonstrative determiners, but adverbial demonstratives have the same form as the singular demonstrative pronouns. That is, adverbial and pronominal demonstratives belong to the same category in Ponapean:

Table 45. *Demonstratives in Ponapean (Rehg 1981: 143–154)*

	DEM DETS		DEM PROS		DEM ADVS
	SG	PL	SG	PL	
NEAR S	*-e(t)*	*-ka(t)*	*me(t)*	*metakan*	*me(t)*
NEAR H	*-en*	*-kan*	*men*	*menakan*	*men*
AWAY FROM S+H	*-o*	*-kau*	*mwo*	*mwohkan*	*mwo*

Finnish is particularly interesting in this regard. In Finnish, demonstratives can be arranged on a cline of adverbiality ranging from forms that are clearly pronominal to forms that are primarily adverbial (cf. Laury 1997: 128–146). Finnish has three demonstrative roots: *tämä, tuo* and *se*. *Tämä* refers to entities near the deictic center, *tuo* indicates a referent at some distance to the deictic center, and *se* is mostly used anaphorically and is perhaps best analyzed as a definite article in contemporary Finnish (cf. Laury 1995, 1997: 147–264). The three demonstratives are always case-marked. Finnish has a complex case system including six locational case forms, which are divided into two groups: three

76   DEMONSTRATIVES

"internal case forms" — inessive, elative and illative — and "three external case forms" — adessive, ablative and allative. The internal and external case forms of *tämä, tuo* and *se* are shown in Table 46.

Table 46. *Locational case forms of the Finnish demonstratives (Laury 1997: 129)*

(a) Internal case forms = Internal demonstratives

| | INESSIVE | | ELATIVE | | ILLATIVE | |
	SG	PL	SG	PL	SG	PL
PROXIMAL	*tässä*	*näissä*	*tästä*	*näistä*	*tähän*	*näihin*
DISTAL	*tuossa*	*noissa*	*tuosta*	*noista*	*tuohon*	*noihin*
ANAPHORIC	*siinä*	*niissä*	*siitä*	*niistä*	*siihen*	*niihin*

(b) External case forms = External demonstratives

| | ADESSIVE | | ABLATIVE | | ALLATIVE | |
	SG	PL	SG	PL	SG	PL
PROXIMAL	*tällä*	*näillä*	*tältä*	*näiltä*	*tälle*	*näille*
DISTAL	*tuolla*	*noilla*	*tuolta*	*noilta*	*tuolle*	*noille*
ANAPHORIC	*sillä*	*niillä*	*siltä*	*niiltä*	*sille*	*niille*

The external demonstratives are primarily used to indicate a possessor, recipient or instrument; they are only occasionally used to indicate a location. The internal demonstratives, on the other hand, are primarily used with reference to places.

In addition to the forms shown in Table 46, Finnish has a set of "locational demonstratives", which occur in three different case forms: adessive, ablative and lative. The locational demonstratives are morphologically similar to the singular forms of the external demonstratives, but they do not have plural forms.

Table 47. *Locational demonstratives in Finnish (Laury 1997: 129)*

	ADESSIVE	ABLATIVE	LATIVE
PROXIMAL	*täälla*	*täältä*	*tänne*
DISTAL	*tuolla*	*tuolta*	*tuonne*
ANAPHORIC	*siellä*	*sieltä*	*sinne*

The adessive and ablative forms of *tämä* and *se* have a long or diph-thongized vowel in the first syllable, which distinguishes these forms from the corresponding external forms. The adessive and ablative forms of *tuo* are indistinguishable from the external demonstratives in written Finnish, but Laury points out that they are differently pronounced. Finally, the lative forms of all three locational demonstratives — *tänne, tuonne*, and *sinne* — are clearly distinguished from the corresponding allative forms, *tälle, tuolle*, and *sille*.

The external demonstratives are usually considered demonstrative pronouns by Finnish linguists, but the status of the internal and locational demonstratives is controversial. Traditionally, they have been considered adverbs (cf. Laury 1997: 134), but Laury points out that there is no morphological evidence in support of this view. Although the internal demonstratives are commonly used to refer to a location they behave morphologically like ordinary demonstrative pronouns rather than adverbs. Moreover, Laury shows that even the locational demonstratives are not prototypical adverbs. Unlike demonstrative adverbs such as English *here* and *there*, the locational demonstratives in Finnish are case-marked and they are frequently used adnominally. These are typical properties of demonstrative determiners (or pronouns). However, when the locational demonstratives are used adnominally they do not always agree with the cooccurring noun as a demonstrative determiner (or pronoun). The following example shows a locative demonstrative in lative case preceding a noun with an illative case marker.

(10)   Finnish (Laury 1997: 135)
        katotaas **sinne**   *?kurkkuu*
        look.PASS DEM.LOC.LAT throat.ILL
        'Let's look at that throat.'

The lack of agreement between a locational demonstrative and a cooccurring noun suggests that the case endings of the locational demonstratives do not have a syntactic function: they do not indicate grammatical relations, rather they are used to specify the location of the referent. In other words, the case markers have primarily a semantic function (similar to a locational adposition). The locational demonstratives can therefore be seen as demonstrative adverbs despite the fact that they are case-marked.

The internal demonstratives are integrated into the morphological paradigm of demonstrative pronouns, but like locational demonstratives they do not generally agree with a noun when they are used adnominally. The following example shows an internal demonstrative in inessive case followed by a noun with an adessive case marker.

(11)   Finnish (Laury 1997: 136–7)
   ja **siin** *?puuhellalla,... kerran ni,... mää*
   and DEM.INE wood.stove.ADE once so 1SG
   illalla   ?paistoin
   evening.ADE fry.PAST.1SG
   'And on the wood stove, one time, I was frying.'

According to Laury, the internal demonstratives have features of both demonstrative pronouns and demonstrative adverbs. Morphologically, they behave like ordinary demonstrative pronouns, but syntactically they are often used like demonstrative adverbs, and semantically they are equivalent to locational deictics (i.e. adverbial demonstratives). Laury (1997: 138) argues that the Finnish demonstratives can be arranged on a cline of adverbiality ranging from forms that are primarily used as pronouns to forms that behave more like typical adverbs:

Table 48. *Locational demonstratives in Finnish arranged on a cline of adverbiality (cf. Laury 1997: 138)*

<< LESS ADVERBIAL << EXTERNAL DEMS	INTERNAL DEMS	>> MORE ADVERBIAL >> LOCATIONAL DEMS
• they are case- and number-marked like DEM PROS	• they are case- and number-marked like DEM PROS	• they are case-marked like DEM PROS, but they are unmarked for number
• they do not always agree with a cooccurring noun	• they do not always agree with a cooccurring noun	• they behave syntactically like DEM ADVs, but they may cooccur with a noun
• they are primarily used to indicate a possessor, recipient, or instrument	• they are semantically equivalent to locational deictics	• they are semantically equivalent to locational deictics

Up to this point, I have argued that demonstratives can be divided into four syntactic categories, but the Finnish demonstratives show that the boundaries between these categories are not always clear-cut.

4.3 Demonstrative identifiers

While demonstrative pronouns, determiners, and adverbs are well established categories of linguistic analysis, the last category to be discussed in this chapter is widely unknown. Demonstrative identifiers have been described under various names in reference grammars, but they have never been recognized in the typological and theoretical literature on demonstratives (but see Himmelmann 1997: 126).

Demonstrative identifiers occur in copular and nonverbal clauses. Like other demonstratives, they are used to focus the hearer's attention on entities in the surrounding situation or in the universe of discourse. Most studies consider the demonstratives in copular and nonverbal clauses demonstrative pronouns, but as pointed out in the introduction, the demonstratives being used in these constructions are often formally distinguished from pronominal demonstratives in other contexts: they may have a different phonological form or may differ in their inflection. If the demonstratives in copular and nonverbal clauses are phonologically or morphologically distinguished from pronominal demonstratives in other clause types, I assume that they form a class of demonstrative identifiers independent of demonstrative pronouns. If, on the other hand, the demonstratives in copular and nonverbal clauses are formally indistinguishable from demonstrative pronouns, I assume that they belong to the same grammatical category. English, for instance, does not distinguish between demonstrative pronouns and demonstrative identifiers. The demonstratives in copular clauses have the same phonological and morphological features as pronominal demonstratives in other contexts and hence they are considered demonstrative pronouns.[21]

Demonstrative identifiers are similar to deictic presentatives such as French *voilà,* Latin *ecce,* and Russian *vot.* Fillmore (1982: 47) calls such presentatives "sentential demonstratives". Both demonstrative identifiers and sentential demonstratives are commonly used to introduce new discourse topics, but they have different syntactic properties. Demonstrative identifiers are embedded in a specific grammatical construction, a copular or nonverbal clause, while sentential demonstratives are syntactically more independent. Although they might occur in sentences that are functionally equivalent to copular and nonverbal clauses (e.g. *Voilà un taxi.* 'Here is a taxi.'), they are more commonly used as one word utterances, which may be loosely adjoined to a neighboring constituent. I assume therefore that demonstrative identifiers are distinguished from sentential demonstratives, but the distinction is not clear-cut (see the discussion of Nunggubuyu below).

In Chapter 6 I will show that demonstrative identifiers are a common historical source for nonverbal copulas. The distinction between demonstrative identifiers and copulas is not always immediately obvious: a demonstrative identifier is easily confused with a copula that appears in a sentence with no overt subject. Consider, for instance, the following example from Ambulas.

(12)   Ambulas (Wilson 1980: 454)
        kén bakna walkamu taalé
        this just   little   place
        'This is just a little place.'

Example (12) shows a nonverbal clause consisting of the demonstrative identifier *kén* and a predicate nominal (DEM Ø NP). Without further evidence, example (12) could be taken as a copular clause with no overt subject, in which *kén* would function as a copula (Ø COP NP). However, since *kén* refers to a location and is deictically contrastive (*kén* 'proximal' vs. *wan* 'distal'), it would be mistaken to analyze it as a copula. If *kén* were a copula it would be non-referential and non-contrastive. Thus, although (12) is syntactically ambiguous, *kén* can only be interpreted as a demonstrative because of its meaning. There is, in other words, a clear semantic contrast between a nonverbal copula and an identificational demonstrative in a nonverbal clause.

The following two sections present evidence for my hypothesis that many languages have a distinct class of demonstrative identifiers. In Section 4.3.1, I consider demonstrative identifiers whose stems are phonologically distinguished from the stems of demonstrative pronouns, and in Section 4.3.2, I examine demonstrative identifiers that differ from demonstrative pronouns in their inflection.

4.3.1   Phonological evidence

The strongest evidence for my hypothesis that many languages have a particular class of demonstrative identifiers comes from languages in which the stems of identificational demonstratives are phonologically distinguished from the stems of demonstrative pronouns. In this section, I discuss examples from Supyire, Karanga, Ponapean, Western Bade, and Kilba. My sample includes further examples from Izi, Swazi, Margi, and Pangasinan, which will not be considered (the Pangasinan demonstratives are discussed in Section 4.4).

Table 49 shows the demonstrative pronouns and demonstrative identifiers in Supyire. The demonstrative pronouns have an initial nasal consonant, which does not occur with the demonstrative identifiers. Both demonstrative pronouns and demonstrative identifiers are inflected for gender (noun class) and number. Note that Supyire does not distinguish between proximal and distal forms (cf. 3.1.1). Carlson (1994: 240) points out that the demonstrative identifiers might have developed from a pronominal demonstrative and a copula. Their use is restricted to affirmative nonverbal clauses. In negative contexts, Supyire uses a particular negative identifier; and in copular clauses demonstrative identifiers are replaced

Table 49. *Demonstrative pronouns — identifiers in Supyire (Carlson* 1994: 159–61)

	DEM PROS (DETS)		DEM IDENTS	
	SG	PL	SG	PL
NC1	ŋgé	m̀píí	we	pii
NC2	ŋké	ɲ̀jé	ke	ye
NC3	ǹdé	ɲ̀cíí	le	cii
NC4		ǹté		te
NC5		m̀pé		pe

by demonstrative pronouns. Example (13a) shows a demonstrative pronoun, and example (13b) shows one of the demonstrative identifiers.

(13)   Supyire (Carlson 1994: 190, 241)
   a.   *mu   à   pyi   a   ŋgé   cè   la*
        you PERF PAST PERF DEM.G1SG know Q
        'Did you know this/that one?'
   b.   *ku   kè*
        it.G2SG here.is.G2SG
        'Here/there it is.'

Supyire has also a set of "simple identifier pronouns", which occur in the same syntactic context as the demonstrative identifiers in Table 49. The identifier pronouns are, however, non-deictic; they are usually glossed as 'it.is' (cf. Carlson 1994: 160).

Table 50 shows the demonstrative pronouns and demonstrative identifiers of three gender classes in Karanga, which are inflected for number and noun class; proximal and distal demonstratives are formally distinguished. The demonstrative pronouns begin with a vowel, while the demonstrative identifiers occur with an initial *h-*. Both the demonstrative pronouns and identifiers have allomorphs that are omitted in Table 50. Marconnès (1931: 110) argues that the demonstrative identifiers, which he calls "predicative pronouns", form "a complete predicate, i.e. include the verb 'to be' or some other verb, and correspond to English 'here is', 'here are', 'there is', 'there are', 'there goes' etc." Examples of demonstrative pronouns and demonstrative identifiers are given in (14a–b) respectively.

Table 50. *Demonstrative pronouns — identifiers in Karanga (Marconnès 1931: 101–10)*

		DEM PROS (DETS)		DEM IDENTS	
		SG	PL	SG	PL
PROX	NC1	*iyi*	*idzi*	*heyi*	*hedzi*
	NC2	*uyu*	*ava*	*hoyu*	*hava*
	NC3	*ichi*	*izvi*	*hechi*	*hezvi*
	etc.				
DIST	NC1	*iyo*	*idzo*	*heyo*	*hedzo*
	NC2	*uyo*	*avo*	*hoyo*	*havo*
	NC3	*icho*	*izvo*	*hecho*	*hezvo*
	etc.				

(14)   Karanga (Marconnès 1931: 102, 111)
a.   *ndi no da **uyu***
         I   like   this
         'I like this one.'
b.   ***hero***   *sadza*
         there.is porridge
         'There is the porridge.'

Western Bade has three demonstrative roots: one referring to an object or location
near the speaker, one referring to an object or location away from the speaker,
and another one which Schuh (1977: 19–20) glosses as "particular". The distal demonstrative pronouns have the same form as the distal demonstrative identifiers,
but the proximal and particular forms are different: the demonstrative pronouns
end in a rounded mid back vowel, which is replaced by a long low vowel in the
corresponding forms of the demonstrative identifiers. Moreover, the proximal and
particular forms of the demonstrative identifiers occur optionally with the suffix
-ni which, according to Schuh, does not change their meaning. Both demonstrative pronouns and demonstrative identifiers are inflected for gender and number.[22]
The demonstrative identifiers, which Schuh calls "deictic predicators", occur only
in nonverbal clauses:

(15)   Western Bade (Schuh 1977: 20)
         m̀sàa   *wúnáajàaŋíi*
         this/here your.dog
         'Here's your dog.'

Table 51. *Demonstrative pronouns — identifiers in Western Bade (Schuh 1977: 19–20)*

	DEM PROS (DETS)			DEM IDENTS		
	SG.M	SG.F	PL	SG.M	SG.F	PL
PROXIMAL	m̀só	m̀có	m̀dó	m̀sàa(ní)	m̀càa(ní)	m̀dàa(ní)
DISTAL	m̀síi	m̀cíi	m̀díi	m̀sîi	m̀cîi	m̀dîi
PARTICULAR	m̀sə́nò	m̀cə́nò	m̀də́nò	m̀sə́náa(ní)	m̀cə́náa(ní)	m̀də́náa(ní)

Table 52 shows the demonstrative pronouns and demonstrative identifiers in Ponapean. The demonstrative pronouns begin with a bilabial nasal and the demonstrative identifiers have an initial high front vowel.

Table 52. *Demonstrative pronouns — identifiers in Ponapean (Rehg 1981: 150–53)*

	DEM PROS		DEM IDENTS	
	SG	PL	SG	PL
NEAR S	me(t)	metakan	ie(t)	ietakan
NEAR H	men	menakan	ien	ienakan
AWAY FROM S+H	mwo	mwohkan	io	iohkan

Example (16a–b) illustrate the use of these forms: (16a) shows a demonstrative pronoun functioning as the subject of the verb *mengila* 'wither', and example (16b) shows a demonstrative identifier in a nonverbal clause.

(16)   Ponapean (Rehg 1981: 143, 150)
   a.   **met** *pahn mengila*
        this will   wither
        'This will wither.'
   b.   **iet**   *noumw naipen*
        this/here your   knife
        'Here is your knife.'

Finally, in Kilba demonstrative identifiers are monosyllabic enclitics while demonstrative pronouns are free forms consisting of two or more syllables. It is unclear whether the demonstratives in Kilba are marked for number. Schuh (1983b) does not discuss their inflectional features; he only provides the forms in Table 53.

Table 53. *Demonstrative pronouns — identifiers in Kilba (Schuh 1983b: 315–317)*

	DEM PROS (DETS)	DEM IDENTS
PROXIMAL	(nə́)nə́nnà	=ná
DISTAL	(nà)ndándà	=ndá
REMOVED	(ŋgə̀)ŋgə́ŋgà	=ŋgá

(17)   Kilba (Schuh 1983b: 318)
        kə̀nə̀ŋ=**ná**
        sheep=DEM
        'It's a sheep.'

Schuh (1983b: 317) classifies the enclitics =*ná*, =*ndá* and =*ŋgá* as demonstratives, but he commonly translates them by a third person pronoun or an expletive. The demonstrative enclitics are usually unstressed like third person pronouns, but since they indicate a deictic contrast I consider them demonstratives. Note that all demonstrative identifiers cited in this section are marked for distance. Demonstrative identifiers are genuine deictic expressions; they are not expletives such as English *it* in *It is Friday*. In fact, in some languages demonstrative identifiers are primarily used exophorically. This is reflected in the terminology that some of my sources use for demonstrative identifiers: Rehg (1981: 15) calls them "pointing demonstratives" and Carlson (1994: 160) uses the notion "deictic identifier pronoun".

4.3.2   Morphological evidence

The previous section has shown that demonstratives in copular and nonverbal clauses are often phonologically distinguished from pronominal demonstratives in other sentence types. This section shows that they may also differ in their inflection. As pointed out in Chapter 2, in the majority of languages pronominal demonstratives have the same grammatical features as other nominals: if nouns are inflected for gender, number and/or case, pronominal demonstratives usually have the same inflectional features. Unlike pronominal demonstratives, identificational demonstratives do not always occur with the same inflectional endings as other nominals. There is a substantial number of languages in my sample in which pronominal demonstratives are inflected for gender, number and/or case while identificational demonstratives are morphologically invariable. If pronominal and identificational demonstratives differ in their inflection, I assume that they belong to distinct categories. That is, if identificational demonstratives are not inflected in a language in which pronominal demonstratives are marked for gender, number and/or case, I assume that they belong to a particular class of demonstrative identifiers. This section discusses examples from Duwai, Nunggubuyu, Tümpisa Shoshone, Inuktitut, French, and German. Other examples from Ambulas (cf. 2.1.2), Pangasinan (cf. 4.4), and Modern Hebrew (cf. 6.6.1) are discussed elsewhere in this study.

Duwai has two demonstrative identifiers, *nə́mù* 'proximal' and *náamù* 'distal', which are uninflected. They are distinguished from the demonstrative pronouns shown on the left hand side of Table 54. The pronouns have a different stem form and are differentiated for number.[23]

Table 54. *Demonstrative pronouns — identifiers in Duwai (Schuh 1977: 25–26)*

	DEM PROS (DETS)		DEM IDENTS
	SG	PL	
PROXIMAL	*ŋgàannó*	*ǹdìiwnó*	*nə́mù*
DISTAL	*ŋgàanàwó*	*ǹdìiwnàwó*	*náamù*

In Nunggubuyu, demonstrative pronouns occur with two noun class markers, a prefix and a suffix, while demonstrative identifiers take only the suffix. The noun class affixes are also used to indicate number distinctions. Both demonstratives occur optionally with a case marker. Table 55 shows only the masculine singular forms; the demonstratives of other noun classes have the same structure.

Table 55. *Demonstrative pronouns — identifiers in Nunggubuyu (Heath 1984: 272–4)*

	DEM PROS (DETS)	DEM IDENTS
PROXIMAL	*naː-'-gi*	*yaː-gi*
MEDIAL	*naː-da-gi*	*da-gi*
DISTAL	*nuː-'waː-gi*	*yuwaː-gi*
ANAPHORIC	*nuː-'baː-gi*	*ba-gi*

In Nunggubuyu, demonstrative identifiers are often used without a cooccurring nominal so that one might argue that they are better analyzed as sentential demonstratives (see above). However, since Nunggubuyu is a non-configurational language, in which all constituents are syntactically more independent than in languages with rigid phrase structure configurations (cf. Heath 1984, 1986), I assume that the ability to use demonstrative identifiers without a cooccurring noun is not a property of the demonstratives but rather a consequence of general typological characteristics. Example (18) shows a demonstrative identifier that is accompanied by a coreferential noun.

(18)   Nunggubuyu (Heath 1984: 278)
         ya:-gi   na-walyi-n^{y}un^g
         this-M.SG M.SG-male-HUMAN.SG
         'Here is the man.'

In Tümpisa Shoshone, demonstrative pronouns are inflected for number and case and may take the prefix *s-*, which Dayley (1989: 136) calls an "obviative marker". The demonstrative identifiers are unmarked for number, they take the suffix *-sü(n)* instead of a regular case ending, and they never occur in the obviative form. Table 56 shows only the proximal and medial forms; there are parallel forms built on three other demonstrative roots.

Table 56. *Demonstrative pronouns — identifiers in T. Shoshone (Dayley 1989: 137–43)*

		DEM PROS (DETS)		DEM IDENTS
		SUBJ	OBJ	
PROXIMAL	SG	*(s)-i-tü*	*(s)-i-kka*	*i-sü(n)*
	DU	*(s)-i-tungku*	*(s)-i-tuhi*	
	PL	*(s)-i-tümmü*	*(s)-i-tümmi*	
MEDIAL	SG	*(s)-e-tü*	*(s)-e-kka*	*e-sü(n)*
	DU	*(s)-e-tungku*	*(s)-e-tuhi*	
	PL	*(s)-e-tümmü*	*(s)-e-tümmi*	

The use of demonstrative pronouns and identifiers is exemplified in (19a–b) respectively.

(19)   Tümpisa Shoshone (Dayley 1989: 141, 145)
    a.   *u punikka setü*
         it see   that
         'This one saw it.'
    b.   *esü   nahim pungku*
         this.is our.DU pet
         'This is our pet.'

Inuktitut has demonstrative identifiers that behave syntactically like demonstrative identifiers in Nunggubuyu: since they are frequently used as one word utterances they could be classified as sentential demonstratives rather than demonstrative identifiers. However, since Inuktitut is a non-configurational language like Nunggubuyu, I assume that the specific properties of the identificational demonstratives are due to the particular structure of this language.

Table 57 shows the demonstrative identifiers in Inuktitut in comparison to the demonstrative pronouns. The demonstrative pronouns consist of three morphemes: a deictic root, a case suffix, and the nominalizer -*sum*-. The demonstrative identifiers, on the other hand, are formed by a morphological process which doubles the final consonant and adds a low back vowel:

Table 57. *Demonstrative pronouns — identifiers in Inuktitut (Denny 1982: 364–5)*

	DEM PROS (DETS)	DEM IDENTS
PROXIMAL	*uv-sum-ing* 'PROX-the.one-ACC'	*uvva* 'here'
DISTAL	*ik-sum-ing* 'DIST-the.one-ACC'	*ikka* 'there'
UP.DISTAL	*pik-sum-ing* 'UP.DIST-the.one-ACC'	*pikka* 'up there'
DOWN.DISTAL	*kan-sum-ing* 'DOWN.DIST-the.one-ACC'	*kanna* 'down there'

The following sentences illustrate the use of demonstrative pronouns and demonstrative identifiers respectively:

(20)   Inuktitut (Denny 1982: 365)
    a. ***pik-sum-inga***   *takujuq*
        UP.DIST-the.one-ACC he.sees
        'He sees the (one) up there.'
    b. *Piita* **uvva**
        Peter DEM.PROX
        'Here is Peter.'

French has a demonstrative particle, *ce* 'this/that/there/it', which is used only in copular clauses.[24] *Ce* does not generally function as a demonstrative. In fact, in most instances *ce* is non-deictic and functions either as a third person pronoun or as an expletive (cf. Reed 1994). However, in those cases in which *ce* has a deictic interpretation, it can be analyzed as a demonstrative identifier. The demonstrative pronouns, *celui* and *celle*, are morphologically and phonologically distinguished from *ce*. They are marked for gender and number, and they are usually reinforced by the deictic particles *ci* and *là* (cf. 3.1.1). *Ce* does not inflect for gender and number and is replaced by *celui, celle, ceci,* or *cela* if the speaker seeks to indicate the relative distance between the referent and the deictic center. In other words, French has a demonstrative identifier, but its use is not obligatory in copular clauses.

Table 58. *Demonstrative pronouns — identifiers in French (Calvez 1993: 33, 62)*

	DEM PROS				DEM IDENTS
	SG.M	SG.F	PL.M	PL.F	
PROXIMAL	celui-(ci)	celle-(ci)	ceux-(ci)	celles-(ci)	ce
DISTAL	celui-(là)	celle-(là)	ceux-(là)	celles-(là)	ce

Finally, in German, where pronominal demonstratives are inflected for gender, number, and case, identificational demonstratives are uninflected. Consider the examples in (21a–b).

(21) German

    a. **Das**   *ist meine Schwester.*
       DEM.NOM/ACC.SG.N is my   sister.SG.F
       'This is my sister.'

    b. **Das**   *sind meine Freunde.*
       dem.nom/ACC.SG.N are my   friend.PL
       'These are my friends.'

Example (21a–b) show two copular clauses including the demonstrative *das*. The demonstrative has the same form as the nominative/accusative, singular, neuter form of the demonstrative pronouns, but unlike pronominal demonstratives it is uninflected. Note that the coreferential predicate nominal in (21a) has feminine gender and that the predicate nominal in (21b) occurs in plural. Since the demonstratives in these examples are uninflected and do not agree with the coreferential noun, they must be distinguished from demonstrative pronouns. They are demonstrative identifiers, which occur only in copular clauses.

4.4 Summary

In this chapter, I have examined the syntactic properties of demonstratives. I have argued that one has to distinguish between the use of a demonstrative in a specific syntactic context and its categorial status. Demonstratives occur in four different syntactic contexts: (i) they are used as independent pronouns in argument positions of verbs and adpositions; (ii) they occur together with a noun in a noun phrase; (iii) they may function as locational adverbs modifying a cooccurring verb; and (iv) they are used in copular and nonverbal clauses. I have shown that the demonstratives being used in these four contexts are often formally distinguished from one another. They might have different stem forms, they might differ in their inflection, or they might have different syntactic properties. If they are distinguished by any of these criteria, they belong to different grammatical categories, for which I suggested the terms (i) demonstrative pronoun, (ii) demonstrative determiner, (iii) demonstrative adverb, and (iv) demonstrative identifier. I have shown that languages differ as to how they exploit these categories. Many languages distinguish between demonstrative pronouns and demonstrative determiners, but some languages have only one of these two categories. Languages that do not have demonstrative determiners use instead demonstrative pronouns with a coreferential noun in apposition, while languages that do not have demonstrative pronouns use demonstrative determiners together with a classifier or a third person pronoun in lieu of a demonstrative pronoun. Unlike pronominal and adnominal demonstratives, adverbial demonstratives usually have a special form. There are only a few languages in my sample that do not have a distinct class of demonstrative adverbs. Demonstrative identifiers occur in copular and nonverbal clauses. They may differ from demonstrative pronouns in two ways: they may have a particular phonological form or they may have other inflectional features. The category demonstrative identifier is crosslinguistically not as common as the category demonstrative adverb, but the distinction between demonstrative pronouns and demonstrative identifiers is at least as frequent as the distinction between demonstrative pronouns and determiners.

I will conclude this chapter with a short discussion of the demonstratives from two languages that exemplify the extent of variation in this domain: one in which pronominal, adnominal, adverbial, and identificational demonstratives are formally distinguished, and one in which they belong to the same category. Acehnese represents the latter. The Acehnese demonstratives are shown in Table 59.

Acehnese has three demonstrative particles that indicate three degrees of

Table 59. *Demonstratives in Acehnese (Durie 1985: 130)*

	FREE FORMS	BOUND ALLOMORPHS
PROXIMAL	*nyoe*	=*noe*
MEDIAL	*nyan*	=*nan*
DISTAL	*jêh*	=*dêh*

distance: *nyoe* 'proximal', *nyan* 'medial' and *jêh* 'distal'. The three demonstratives have three bound allomorphs: =*noe* 'proximal', =*nan* 'medial' and =*dêh* 'distal'. All six demonstratives may occur in every possible syntactic context (cf. the discussion of demonstratives in Guugu Yimidhirr in 2.1.1). That is, they may be used adnominally as in (22a), they may function as independent pronouns or as locational adverbs (cf. 22b-c), and they are also used as identificational markers in nonverbal clauses (cf. 22d).

(22)   Acehnese (Durie 1985: 191, 268, 256, 132)

    a.   *ureueng=**nyan***
       person=that
       'that person.'

    b.   *neu=peusom **nyan** bek ji=teu-peu   lê=gop*
       2=hide   that NEG 3=know-what by=other.person
       'Hide that so that no one else will know.'

    c.   ***nyan** ji=pura-pura   teungeut jih*
       there 3=pretend-pretend sleep   he
       'There he goes pretending to be asleep.'

    d.   ***nyan** aneuk=lông*
       that child=1SG
       'That is my child.'

All four examples include the medial demonstrative *nyan*. In (22a), *nyan* is used adnominally. Adnominal demonstratives usually cliticize to a preceding noun, but they are not generally bound.[25] In (22b), *nyan* is used as an independent pronoun functioning as the object of the verb *peusom* 'to hide'. The demonstrative in (22c) is ambiguous: it is either used to indicate a location or it functions as a presentational marker. Durie (1985: 132) points out that the Acehnese demonstratives may serve as locational adverbs (which he calls "locative pronouns"), but apart from (22c) I did not find any example in Durie's grammar in which *nyan* might be interpreted as an adverbial demonstrative. There are, however, several examples in which some of the other demonstratives are used adverbially (often after a preposition). In the final example, *nyan* serves as an identificational marker in a nonverbal clause. The sentences in (22a-d) show that adnominal, pronominal, adverbial, and identificational demonstratives are formally indistinguishable in Acehnese. They belong to the same grammatical category, which may occur in four different syntactic contexts.

The demonstratives in Pangasinan represent the other end of the spectrum. Pangasinan uses particular demonstrative forms in each of the four contexts in which demonstratives occur. The Pangasinan demonstratives are shown in Table 60.

Table 60. *Demonstratives in Pangasinan (Benton 1971: 51–52, 88–91)*

	DEM DETS	DEM PROS	DEM ADVS	DEM IDENTS
PROXIMAL	*sá-ta-y* (SG/PL)	(*i*)*yá* (SG)	*diá*	*nía*
	sa-rá-ta-y (PL)	(*i*)*rá-ya* (PL)		
NEAR H	–	(*i*)*tán* (SG)	*ditán*	*nítan*
	–	(*i*)*rá-tan* (PL)		
DISTAL	*sá-ma-y* (SG/PL)	(*i*)*mán* (SG)	*dimán*	*níman*
	sa-rá-ma-y (PL)	(*i*)*rá-man* (PL)		

The Pangasinan demonstratives are divided into four grammatical categories: determiners, pronouns, adverbs, and identifiers.[26] The demonstrative determiners are formed from the article *sa*, the deictic roots *ta* 'proximal' and *ma* 'distal', and the suffix *-y*, which Benton calls a topic marker, but which is probably a linker (Nikolaus Himmelmann p.c.). In the plural, demonstrative determiners are marked by *-ra-*, which precedes the deictic root and the linker. Benton (1971:51–2) classifies these forms as articles, but since they indicate a deictic contrast I consider them demonstratives. The demonstrative pronouns consist of the demonstrative roots *ya* 'proximal', *tan* 'nearer hearer' and *man* 'distal', which optionally occur with an initial high front vowel; the plural forms are also marked by *-ra-*. The demonstrative adverbs occur with an initial stop and do not have plural forms, while the demonstrative identifiers take an initial nasal and are also unmarked for number. The sentences in (23a-d) exemplify the use of these forms.

(23)   Pangasinan (Benton 1971:53, 89, 90, 91)
        a. *sá-ma-y*   *apók*
            ART-DEM-LK grandchild.my
            'My grandchild' (i.e 'that grandchild of mine')
        b. *sikató so*   *analíw* **imán**
            he   TOPIC bought that
            'He (is the one who) bought that.'
        c. *sikató-y inmogíp* **ditán**
            he-LK   slept   here/there
            'He (was the one who) slept here/there.'
        d. **nía**   *so*   *kánen mo*
            here.is TOPIC food   your
            'Here's your food.'

The demonstrative in (23a) is a demonstrative determiner; the demonstrative in
(23b) is a pronoun; the one in (23c) is a demonstrative adverb; and the final
example shows a demonstrative identifier.

Acehnese and Pangasinan represent the two ends of a spectrum ranging from
languages in which all demonstratives belong to the same category to languages
in which demonstratives are divided into four distinct classes. Most languages fall
somewhere in between these two extremes. English, for instance, distinguishes
three demonstrative categories: demonstrative adverbs, demonstrative determiners,
and demonstrative pronouns. It does not have a separate class of demonstrative
identifiers; the demonstratives being used in copular constructions are ordinary
demonstrative pronouns. Korean has two demonstrative categories: demonstrative
determiners and demonstrative adverbs. It does not have demonstrative pronouns
and demonstrative identifiers. The functional equivalent of the latter two are noun
phrases that consist of a demonstrative determiner and a defective noun (cf.
2.1.4). To cite one other example, Nunggubuyu has demonstrative pronouns, demonstrative adverbs and demonstrative identifiers. Adnominal demonstratives are
demonstrative pronouns that cooccur with an appositive noun (Heath 1986). The
three demonstrative categories are formally distinguished through noun class
markers: the demonstrative pronouns take two noun class markers, a prefix and
a suffix, the demonstrative identifiers do not take noun class prefixes, and the demonstrative adverbs do not occur with noun class suffixes (Heath 1984:274–318).

CHAPTER 5

Pragmatic use

Demonstratives serve important pragmatic functions in the communicative interaction between the interlocutors. They are primarily used to orient the hearer in the speech situation, focusing his or her attention on objects, locations, or persons, but they also serve a variety of other pragmatic functions. Following Halliday and Hasan (1976: 57–76), I use the notion *exophoric* for demonstratives that are used with reference to entities in the speech situation, and I use the term *endophoric* for all other uses. The endophoric use is further subdivided into the *anaphoric, discourse deictic* and *recognitional* uses. Anaphoric and discourse deictic demonstratives refer to elements of the ongoing discourse (cf. Fillmore 1997; Lyons 1977; Levinson 1983; Himmelmann 1996, 1997). Anaphoric demonstratives are coreferential with a prior NP; they keep track of discourse participants. Discourse deictic demonstratives refer to propositions; they link the clause in which they are embedded to the proposition to which they refer. Recognitional demonstratives do not refer to elements of the surrounding discourse; rather, they are used to indicate that the hearer is able to identify the referent based on specific shared knowledge. The recognitional use is restricted to adnominal demonstratives, while the demonstratives of all other uses may occur in any possible syntactic context. That is, recognitional demonstratives are always used with a cooccurring noun, while exophoric, anaphoric and discourse deictic demonstratives may also be used pronominally, adverbially and in copular and nonverbal clauses.

This chapter examines the various pragmatic uses of demonstratives from a crosslinguistic perspective. It follows rather closely the work by Himmelmann (1996, 1997), which I have cited above. My analysis is consistent with Himmelmann's investigation except for one claim that he makes regarding the status of the exophoric use. Himmelmann argues, in disagreement with much previous work, that all four uses have equal status. Challenging this hypothesis, I maintain that the exophoric use is indeed the basic use from which all other uses derive. I support my hypothesis with evidence from language acquisition, markedness theory, and grammaticalization. My analysis proceeds as follows: Sections 5.1 to

5.4 examine the exophoric, anaphoric, discourse deictic, and recognitional uses respectively, and Section 5.5 argues that the exophoric use is basic.

5.1 The exophoric use

Exophoric demonstratives focus the hearer's attention on entities in the situation surrounding the interlocutors. They have three distinctive features: first, they involve the speaker (or some other person) as the deictic center; second, they indicate a deictic contrast on a distance scale (unless they belong to the small minority of demonstratives that are distance-neutral; cf. 3.1.1); and third, they are often accompanied by a pointing gesture. None of these features is shared by the three endophoric uses.

Fillmore (1997: 63) distinguishes between two uses that are exophoric from my perspective: the *gestural* and the *symbolic* use (cf. Levinson 1983: 65–66). The gestural use requires monitoring the speech event in order to identify the referent, whereas the symbolic use involves activating knowledge about the communicative situation and the referent. The two uses are exemplified by the following examples, which Levinson (1983) provides in order to illustrate the difference.

(1)   English (Levinson 1983: 66, 66)
        a.   *This finger hurts.*
        b.   *This city stinks.*

The demonstratives in both sentences involve the speaker (or some other person) as the deictic center. They are anchored in the speech situation, which indicates that they are exophoric. However, only the demonstrative in (1a) can be accompanied by a pointing gesture. This example illustrates the gestural use. The demonstrative in (1b), which does not involve a pointing gesture, draws on knowledge about the larger situational context, which involves more than what is immediately visible in the surrounding situation. This example illustrates the symbolic use.

The symbolic use shows that the exophoric use is not limited to concrete referents that are present in the surrounding situation. Exophoric demonstratives are sometimes described as 'pointers' which simply locate an object in the physical world, but this view is too simplistic (for a critique of this view see Hanks 1990, De Mulder 1996, and Himmelmann 1996). Exophoric demonstratives may also refer to entities that are not immediately visible in the speech situation, as in (1b) (where the city as a whole is not visible) and in the following example.[27]

(2)   English (Levinson 1983: 66)
        Hello, is Peter there? (on the telephone)

Moreover, exophoric demonstratives are also commonly used with reference to entities that do not have a physical existence, as in (3):

(3)   English
        This *is a nice feeling.*

Even more abstract than the demonstratives in (2) and (3) is the use that Bühler calls "Deixis am Phantasma" (Bühler 1934: 121–140). This use involves shifting the deictic center from the speaker in the current speech situation to a person in a different situation that is evoked by the ongoing discourse. This phenomenon, which Lyons (1977: 579) calls "deictic projection" (cf. Jakobson 1957; Ehlich 1979; Sitta 1991), is characteristic of narratives and descriptions. Himmelmann (1996) cites the following example from the Pear Stories, in which the proximal demonstrative *this* refers to a location that only exists in the imagination of the interlocutors.

(4)   English (Himmelmann 1996: 222)
        And he's... you see a scene where he's... coming on his bicycle ***this***
        way.

In (4), the deictic center has been shifted from the speaker to an imaginary observer in the story world. The demonstrative is deictically anchored in the situation evoked by the ongoing discourse (cf. Linde and Labov 1975; Ullmer-Ehrich 1979).

McNeill, Cassell and Levy (1993) show that demonstratives 'am Phantasma' can also be accompanied by a pointing gesture, just like demonstratives that are anchored in the immediate speech situation. The referents are physically absent, but they do exist in the universe of discourse, and speakers point to them as if they were there. The use of deictic gestures provides strong evidence for my hypothesis that the use of demonstratives 'am Phantasma' is a subtype of the exophoric usage.

5.2 The anaphoric use

Anaphoric demonstratives are coreferential with a noun or noun phrase in the previous discourse. They refer to the same referent as their antecedent (cf. Lyons 1977: 660). Unlike exophoric demonstratives, which are primarily used to orient the hearer in the outside world, anaphoric demonstratives serve a language-internal function: they are used to track participants of the preceding discourse.[28]

Anaphoric demonstratives interact with other tracking devices such as personal pronouns, definite articles, zero anaphors, and pronominal affixes on the verb. There are a number of studies that examine the specific properties of anaphoric demonstratives in comparison to other tracking means (cf. Linde 1979; Ehlich 1979, 1982; Givón 1983; Sidner 1983; Ariel 1988; Gundel et al. 1993; Lichtenberk 1988, 1996; Himmelmann 1996; Comrie forthcoming). These studies show that anaphoric demonstratives are often used to indicate a referent that is somewhat unexpected and not currently in the focus of attention. Comrie (forthcoming) observes, for instance, that anaphoric demonstratives in Dutch, German and Russian exclude the topic of the preceding discourse as a possible antecedent. Continuing topics are tracked by third person pronouns or definite noun phrases in these languages, while anaphoric demonstratives are coreferential with non-topical antecedents, which are usually less expected. Consider the following example from German.

(5)   German
       Der Anwalt$_i$ sprach mit   einem Klienten$_j$. Da   er$_i$/der$_j$
       the lawyer talked with a   client   since he/this.one
       nicht viel   Zeit hatte, vereinbarten sie   ein weiteres
       not   much time had   agreed.on   they a   further
       Gespräch   nächste Woche.
       conversation next   week
       'The lawyer talked to a client. Since he didn't have much time, they agreed to have another meeting next week.'

The referent of the third person pronoun *er* is the subject NP *der Anwalt* 'the lawyer' of the preceding sentence. The pronoun continues the topic of the previous discourse. By contrast, the demonstrative *der* can only be coreferential with the non-topical NP at the end of the first sentence, *einen Klienten* 'a client'. Anaphoric demonstratives in German do not track continuing topics; rather, they indicate a *topic shift*. Very often, they occur after the first mention of a thematically prominent referent that persists in the subsequent discourse (cf. Himmelmann 1997: 229).

Similar conditions license the use of anaphoric demonstratives in many other languages. For instance, Lichtenberk (1996) points out that in To'aba'ita demonstratives are especially frequent after a new referent has been mentioned for the first time. The following example is characteristic in this respect.

(6)   To'aba'ita (Lichtenberk 1996: 387–8)
Si   u'unu 'eri 'e   lae suli-a   te'e wane bia
CLASS story that it:FACT go about-them one man and
kwai-na   bia 'a-daro'a   te'e wela, wela wane.
spouse-his and BEN-their.DU one child child man
Wela 'eri kali wela fa'ekwa ni   bana. 'e a'i
child that little child small   PART only it NEG
si   tala   'a-na   kai   lae 'a-si
NEG be.possible BEN-his he:NONFACT go to-CLASS
kula n-e   nii   daa.
place REL-it:FACT be.located far
'This story is about a man, his wife, and their child, a boy. The child
was very little. He wasn't able to go faraway places.'

Example (6) shows the first paragraph of a narrative about a man, his wife, and
their child. The three major participants are mentioned for the first time in the
initial sentence. The subsequent discourse concentrates on *wela* 'the child', which
is the main topic of the sentences that follow. When the child is mentioned for
the second time (at the beginning of the second sentence), it is marked by the
anaphoric demonstrative *'eri* 'that'. Similar to the demonstrative in (5), the demonstrative in (6) functions to establish a new discourse topic. Note that *wela* is
tracked by a third person pronoun once it is in the focus of attention (from the
third sentence onwards). One might object to this analysis by arguing that the use
of the demonstrative at the beginning of the second sentence is motivated by the
fact that the child is selected out of a group of several potential topics. However,
the same strategy is used in contexts in which anaphoric demonstratives are not
selective. Consider, for instance, the following example.

(7)   To'aba'ita (Lichtenberk 1996: 385–7)
... keka soeto'o ta   ai   ura wela 'eri, ma
they ask   some woman for child that and
imole 'e-ki   keka sore'e: "Kamili'a 'e   a'i
person that-PL they say   we.EXCL it:FACT NEG
si   thaito'oma-na. "
NEG know-it
'... they asked some women about the child, and those people said:
"We don't know."'

According to Lichtenberk (1996: 387), the noun phrase *imole 'eki* 'those people'
is coreferential with *ta ai* 'some women' in the preceding clause, which intro-

duced a new discourse referent. As in all previous examples, the referent is marked by an anaphoric demonstrative when it is mentioned for the second time.

The use of anaphoric demonstratives after first mention is a common strategy to establish major discourse participants in the universe of discourse. Cyr (1993a, 1993b, 1996) notes the use of this strategy in Montagnais (Algonquian), and Himmelmann (1996) provides the following example from Tagalog (Austronesian).

(8)   Tagalog (Himmelmann 1996: 229)
        May   kasaysayan sa   isang manlalakbay; (0.7 sec)
        EXIST statement   LOC one   traveler   (0.7 sec)
        ang manlalakbay na ito   ay   si   Pepito.
        SPEC traveler   LK DEM PRED PROPER.NAME Pepito
        '(One incident) is told about a traveler; this traveler (his name) was Pepito.'

Example (8) includes the anaphoric demonstrative *na ito* after the noun *manlalakbay* 'traveler'. Similar to the demonstratives in previous examples, the demonstrative in (8) indicates that the focus of attention has been shifted to a new participant that was mentioned for the first time in the preceding sentence.

Himmelmann (1996: 229) points out that the use of anaphoric demonstratives after the first mention of a new discourse participant is especially common in languages that do not have a definite article; however, even in languages that employ a definite article, demonstratives are often preferred in this position (cf. Christophersen 1939: 29). Once a new discourse participant has been established as topic, it is usually tracked by third person pronouns, zero anaphors, definite articles, or pronominal affixes on the verb; but when a referent is mentioned for the second time, demonstratives are often the most common tracking device. The three steps that are involved in this strategy are summarized in Table 61.

Table 61. *The use of anaphoric demonstratives after first mention*

• 1st mention	• 2nd mention	• subsequent mentions
• (indefinite) NP	• anaphoric DEM	• 3.PRO, definite ART etc.
• new referent	• referent established as topic	• (topical) referent continued

Anaphoric demonstratives are not only used to establish new discourse topics. Lichtenberk (1988) observes, for instance, that in To'aba'ita demonstratives are also commonly used to reactivate a referent that occurred at some distance in the preceding discourse, while the referent of an immediately preceding clause is usually tracked by a third person pronoun or a pronominal affix on the verb.[29] What all anaphoric demonstratives have in common is that they do not just continue the focus of attention; rather, they indicate that the antecedent is not the referent that the hearer would expect in this context (i.e. the most topical NP). Anaphoric demonstratives are used when reference tracking is somewhat problematic, or as Himmelmann puts it: "demonstratives are used for tracking only if other tracking devices fail" (Himmelmann 1996: 227).[30]

Many languages have particular demonstratives that are specialized for the anaphoric use. Japanese, for instance, has three demonstrative roots: *ko-* 'near speaker', *so-* 'near hearer' and *a-* 'away from speaker and hearer', which combine with a category marker (e.g. *-ro* 'pronoun', *-no* 'determiner' etc.). All three demonstrative roots can be used exophorically, but only the *so-* demonstratives are commonly used as anaphors (cf. Imai 1996; see also Anderson and Keenan 1985: 285–6). Consider the following example.[31]

(9)   Japanese (Kuno 1973: 284)
      Kinoo   Yamada to yuu   hito   ni aimasita.
      yesterday Yamada as named person   met
      Sono (**kono* **ano*) *hito,   miti ni mayotte*
      that   person way in lose
      komatte.ita   node,   tasukete agemasita.
      was.in.trouble because helping gave (the favor of)
      'Yesterday, I met a man by the name of Yamada. Since he lost his way and was having difficulties, I helped him.'

The expression *sono hito* 'that person' is coreferential with a noun phrase in the preceding sentence. The only demonstrative that is acceptable in this context is *sono*.

Like Japanese, Wardaman and Finnish have three demonstratives, but only one of them is commonly used to track prior discourse participants. Wardaman uses the medial demonstrative *nana* for anaphoric reference (Merlan 1994: 138), and Finnish uses the distal demonstrative *se* (cf. Laury 1995, 1997). In both languages, anaphoric demonstratives can be used as independent pronouns and adjacent to a coreferential noun.

The anaphoric demonstratives in Japanese, Wardaman and Finnish can also be used exophorically, but some languages employ demonstratives that are exclusively used as anaphors. In Latin, for instance, the demonstrative *is* 'this/that' can only be used anaphorically, whereas *hic* 'near speaker', *iste* 'near hearer' and *ille* 'away from speaker and hearer' are primarily used with reference to entities in the surrounding situation. Note that *is* is not a third person pronoun:

continuing topics are tracked by zero anaphors in Latin; *is* is predominantly used to track topics that are discontinuitive, contrastive or emphatic.

Like Latin, Lezgian has three exophoric demonstratives and a special form for anaphoric reference, which Haspelmath (1993) glosses as 'the afore-mentioned'. Pronominal demonstratives are generally marked for number and case in Lezgian, while adnominal demonstratives are uninflected (cf. 4.1.1). In the following example the anaphoric demonstrative *ha* is used to indicate that the noun *universitet* is coreferential with the St. Petersburg University mentioned in the preceding sentence. Note that *ha* can also function as an independent pronoun.

(10)   Lezgian (Haspelmath 1993: 191)
        Zun   sifte Sankt=Peterburg.di-n universitet.di-z,
        I.ABS first St.=Petersburg-GEN   university-DAT
        fizika.di-n   fakul'tet.di-z, hax̂-na-j...   Axpa zun   ha
        physics-GEN faculty-DAT   enter-AOR-PAST then I.ABS that
        universitet.di-n juridičeskij *fakul'et.di-z hax̂-na.*
        university-GEN juridical   faculty-DAT enter-AOR
        'I first entered St. Petersburg University, faculty of physics. Then I entered the law faculty of that university.'

There are several other languages in my sample that have special anaphoric demonstratives: Hixkaryana (Derbyshire 1985: 7, 130), Ngiti (Kutsch 1994: 372–5), Urubu-Kaapor (Kakumasu 1986: 381), Maricopa (Gordon 1986: 55), and Koyra Chiini (Heath 1999: 62).

Finally, there are languages in which anaphoric demonstratives are marked by an additional affix. Anaphoric demonstratives in Tümpisa Shoshone, for instance, take the prefix *s-*, which is "used to signal given or definite information" (Dayley 1989: 136):

(11)   Tümpisa Shoshone (Dayley 1989: 142)
        S-a-tü   *s-a-kka*   *u*   *tukummahanningkünna.*
        ANA-DEM-NOM ANA-DEM-OBJ him cook.for
        'She cooked that for him.'

Similar anaphoric markers occur in Usan (Reesink 1987: 80), West Greenlandic (Fortescue 1984: 259), and Ngiyambaa (Donaldson 1980: 137).

5.3 The discourse deictic use

Like anaphoric demonstratives, discourse deictic demonstratives refer to elements of the surrounding discourse. Discourse deictic demonstratives are, however, not coreferential with a prior NP; rather, they refer to propositions (cf. Lyons 1977; Webber 1991; Canisius and Sitta 1991; Grenoble 1994; Herring 1994; Himmelmann 1996: 224–229; Fillmore 1997: 103–106).[32] More specifically, discourse deictic demonstratives focus the hearer's attention on aspects of meaning, expressed by a clause, a sentence, a paragraph, or an entire story. Consider the following example:

> (12)   English (Webber 1991: 111–2)
>
>   *A: Hey, management has reconsidered its position. They've promoted Fred to second vice president.*
>   *B: a. **That's** false.* (reference to proposition)
>   *b. **That's** a lie.* (reference to illocution)

The demonstratives in (12a–b) refer to an entire sentence. More precisely, the demonstrative in (12a) refers to the propositional content of the preceding utterance, while the demonstrative in (12b) focuses the hearer's attention on its illocutionary force (cf. Webber 1991: 112).

Discourse deictic demonstratives, like the ones in this example, must be distinguished from what Lyons calls "pure text deixis" (Lyons 1977: 668).[33] Pure text deictic demonstratives refer to the material side of language, as exemplified in the following sentences.

> (13)   English (Webber 1991: 108)
>   *I'm sorry. I didn't hear you. Could you repeat **that**?*

The demonstrative in (13) does not refer to a preceding proposition or speech act; rather, it refers to a string of speech sounds that the speaker could not interpret. Pure text deixis is a particular instance of the exophoric use. It refers to linguistic entities treated as an object of the surrounding situation. By contrast, discourse deictic demonstratives focus the hearer's attention on aspects of meaning evoked by the ongoing discourse. The referent of a discourse deictic demonstrative has no existence outside of the universe of discourse in the physical world.

Like anaphoric demonstratives, discourse deictic demonstratives serve a language-internal function. There are, however, a number of significant differences between the two uses. To begin with, anaphoric demonstratives are used to track prior discourse participants, while discourse deictic demonstratives function to establish an overt link between two propositions: the one in which they are embedded and the one to which they refer (cf. Grenoble 1994). Consider the following example:

(14)   English (USA Today page 25C, Dec. 12, 1997)
        "The object is to make fun", said Jon Butler, executive director of Pop
        Warner. "Teams have been working together since August to get here
        and we want them to have a good time."
        That's *why Pop Warner moved to the Disney complex three years*
        ago. With more than 5,000 players, coaches and parents attending in
        1994, it was growing.

The demonstrative at the beginning of the second paragraph summarizes the
information expressed in the preceding discourse, providing a thematic ground for
the sentences that follow. Being thematically associated with both the paragraph
that precedes and the paragraph that follows, the demonstrative creates an overt
link between two discourse units. It is similar to a sentence connective in that it
functions to combine two chunks of discourse. In the following chapter, I will
argue that discourse deictic demonstratives provide a common historical source
for the development of conjunctions and complementizers (cf. 6.3.3 and 6.3.4).

     Another difference between anaphoric and discourse deictic demonstratives
concerns the likelihood with which the referents of these demonstratives persist
in the ongoing discourse. Himmelmann (1996: 225) points out that the referents
of anaphoric demonstratives usually continue in the subsequent discourse, while
the referents of discourse deictic demonstratives normally do not persist. This is
a consequence of their discourse pragmatic function: anaphoric demonstratives are
commonly used to introduce a major discourse participant, which is often the
main topic of the sentences that follow, whereas discourse deictic demonstratives
function to provide a thematic link between two propositions (or speech acts) at
one particular point in the progressing discourse.

     Finally, discourse deictic demonstratives may refer to the discourse that
precedes as well as to the discourse that follows, while anaphoric demonstratives
can only be coreferential with a noun phrase in the previous discourse. That is,
anaphoric demonstratives are always anaphoric, while discourse deictic demonstratives can be both anaphoric and cataphoric.[34] This is illustrated in (15a–b).

(15)   English
        a.   A: *I've heard you will move to Hawaii?*
              B: *Who told you **that** (*this)?*
        b.   A: *Listen to **this** (*that): John will move to Hawaii.*

The distal demonstrative in (15a) refers back to the preceding proposition,
whereas the proximal demonstrative in (15b) anticipates upcoming information
expressed in the subsequent clause. Note that *this* and *that* are not interchangeable
with one another in these examples. The use of both demonstratives is limited to

certain contexts. Discourse deictic *that* is used only with anaphoric reference; that is, *that* may not refer to portions of the following discourse (cf. Fillmore 1997: 104–5; see also Halliday and Hasan 1976: 68). Discourse deictic *this*, on the other hand, can be both anaphoric and cataphoric, but it refers only to utterances produced by the same speaker; that is, *this* cannot refer to propositions or speech acts across speaker boundaries (cf. Chen 1990: 144; Gundel et al. 1993: 288).

Table 62 summarizes the major differences between the discourse deictic and anaphoric (tracking) uses.

Table 62. *Anaphoric and discourse deictic demonstratives*

Anaphoric demonstratives	Discourse deictic demonstratives
• they are coreferential with a prior NP	• they refer to propositions/speech acts
• they keep track of discourse participants	• they link two discourse units
• the referent commonly persists in the subsequent discourse	• the referent usually does not persist in the subsequent discourse
• only anaphoric	• anaphoric and cataphoric

Like anaphoric demonstratives, discourse deictic demonstratives are often formally distinguished from demonstratives serving other pragmatic functions. Usan, for instance, has two demonstratives, *ende* and *ete,* that are only used as discourse deictics (cf. Reesink 1987: 81; see also Himmelmann 1997: 128). *Ende* refers to propositions of the previous discourse; it consists of the demonstrative root *e* 'proximal', the anaphoric marker *-ng* 'given', the adposition *-t* 'locative', and a second demonstrative root at the end of the word. *Ete* is used to refer to subsequent propositions; it is formed from *e* 'proximal', *-t* 'locative' and *e* 'proximal' (cf. Reesink 1987: 81). In addition to *ende* and *ete,* Usan has four exophoric demonstratives and a special form for anaphoric reference: *eng*. The latter consists of the proximal demonstrative *e* and the anaphoric marker *-ng*. Table 63 shows the exophoric, anaphoric and discourse deictic demonstratives that occur in Usan. The use of *ende* and *ete* is exemplified in (16a–b).

Table 63. *Demonstratives in Usan (Reesink 1987: 76–81)*

PROXIMAL	*e*
UP.THERE	*ité*
DOWN.THERE	*úmo*
ACROSS.THERE	*iré*
ANAPHORIC	*eng*
DISCOURSE.DEICTIC (backward)	*ende*
DISCOURSE.DEICTIC (forward)	*ete*

(16)   Usan (Himmelmann 1997: 303, 309–10)

a.   *Âgin   amug igo namaibâ,   ...*
      sister.in.law bush be 2SG.OBJ.angry.SG.FUT.3SG ...
      wai   qeru me netinei.
      animal blood not 2SG.OBJ.give.1SG.FUT(UNCERTAIN)
      ***Ende** qâmâra bo   is   âin   erobon*
      DEM   say.3SG again descend bamboo under.cover
      igoai.
      be.3SG.PAST
      ' "My sister-in-law is in the bush and will be angry with you...
      I can't give the animal blood to you." When he said thus, (the
      moon) went down again and stayed inside the bamboo.'

b.   *End **ete**   qâmb igurei: ... "See inaun*
      DEM DEM   say   be.3PL.PAST   "now moon
      ag   et   igâma ende qi   eng in
      on.the.ground DEM be.3SG DEM 'or' DEM 1PL
      munangit wai   igumune ... ".
      human   animal be.1PL   ..."
      'Therefore they used to say thus: "If the moon were still here
      on the ground, we humans would have been animals,..." '

In (16a), *ende* summarizes the information of the preceding sentence, and in
(16b), *ete* is used to anticipate the information expressed in the subsequent quote.

As pointed out in Chapter 4, some languages have a particular class of
manner demonstratives, which are usually glossed as 'in this way', 'like this', or
'thus'. Manner demonstratives are frequently used as discourse deictics, as in the
following example from Ainu.

(17) Ainu (Refsing 1986: 98)

Ikoytupa   *an hi*   *kamuy nukar wa, pon*   *cep*
suffer.from.lack.of we NLZ gods   see   and be.small fish
poronno an   *eimekkar wa,* ***taa***   *e*   *se*   *ruwe ne.*
a.lot   PASS bestow   and in.this.way you bring ASS
'The gods saw our suffering and a lot of small fish were bestowed upon us, and in this way it is that you have brought them.'

The manner demonstrative in (17), *taa* 'in this way', is derived from the root of the proximal demonstrative *ta*. It functions as an anaphoric discourse deictic referring back to the preceding propositions. There are several other languages in my sample that use manner demonstratives as discourse deictics. In Chapter 2 we saw, for instance, that Ambulas uses the manner demonstratives *kéga* 'like this', *aga* 'like that', and *waga* 'like that' in order to refer to propositions: *kéga* and *aga* are cataphoric discourse deictics, while *waga* refers (anaphorically) to elements of the preceding discourse.

5.4 The recognitional use

The recognitional use has received much less attention in the literature than any of the other uses. Although this use is recognized in a number of studies (e.g. Lakoff 1974; Auer 1981, 1984; Chen 1990; Gundel et al. 1993), it has never been described in detail until recently. Himmelmann (1996, 1997) is the first to provide a systematic account of this use.

The recognitional use has two properties that distinguish it from all other uses. First, recognitional demonstratives are only used adnominally.[35] Second, recognitional demonstratives do not have a referent in the preceding discourse or the surrounding situation; rather, they are used to activate specific shared knowledge.[36] Consider the following example:

(18) English (Himmelmann 1996: 230)
... *it was filmed in California,* ***those*** *dusty kind of hills that they have out here in Stockton and all, ... so ...*

In (18) the *dusty hills* are mentioned for the first time. Although first mentions are usually marked by an indefinite article in English, the *dusty hills* occur with the distal demonstrative *those*. The demonstrative indicates that the following noun expresses information that is familiar to the hearer due to shared experience. Example (19) is similar in this respect.

(19)   English (Gundel et al. 1993: 278)
        I couldn't sleep last night. ***That*** *dog (next door) kept me awake.*

As in the previous example, example (19) includes a noun that occurs with a demonstrative at its first mention. The demonstrative does not refer to an entity in
the surrounding discourse or speech situation; rather, it indicates that the speaker
believes that the hearer knows the referent.

Recognitional demonstratives mark information that is *discourse new* and
hearer old. Prince (1992) introduces the terms "discourse new / discourse old"
and "hearer new / hearer old" in order to distinguish information that has been
evoked by the preceding discourse from information that is already in the hearer's
knowledge store (i.e. old with respect to the speaker's beliefs). Discourse old
information is also hearer old information, but hearer old information might be
discourse new: the hearer might know something although it was previously not
mentioned. Such information is *unactivated* (cf. Chafe 1987; 1994), but *pragmatically presupposed* (cf. Dryer 1996). Recognitional demonstratives are specifically
used to mark information that is discourse new (i.e. unactivated) and hearer old
(i.e. pragmatically presupposed). More precisely, recognitional demonstratives
mark information that is (i) discourse new, (ii) hearer old, *and* (iii) 'private'
(Himmelmann uses the term "specific" rather than private). Private information
is information that speaker and hearer share due to common experience in the
past. It is distinguished from *general cultural information* shared by all members
of the speech community. General cultural information is also hearer old at its
first mention, but unlike private hearer old information it is marked by a definite
article in English. Hawkins (1978: 115–122) refers to the use of definite articles
with nouns expressing general cultural information as the "larger situational use
of the definite article". Two examples are given in (20a–b).

(20)   English
        a.   *Last night I met* ***the*** *President.*
        b.   *I joined* ***the*** *navy for two years.*

The President and *the navy* express general cultural information which is familiar
to all speakers of the speech community including the current speaker and hearer.
Since *the President* and *the navy* do not convey private information, recognitional
demonstratives are not allowed in (20a–b). These examples show that the
recognitional use is restricted to nouns that encode private information.

The recognitional use often implies that speaker and hearer share the same
view or that they sympathize with one another. Consider the following examples
adapted from Lakoff (1974).

(21)   English (Lakoff 1974: 351, 352)
    a.   *How's **that** throat?*
    b.   ***That** Henry Kissinger sure knows his way around in Hollywood.*

The demonstrative in (21a) indicates that the speaker shares the hearer's concern about his or her throat, and the demonstrative in (21b) suggests that the interlocutors share the same view about Henry Kissinger. As in these examples, recognitional demonstratives are often used to indicate emotional closeness, sympathy, and shared beliefs and therefore Lakoff (1974) calls this use "emotional deixis".

Since the referent of a recognitional noun phrase was not previously activated, the speaker cannot be certain as to whether the hearer will indeed identify the referent. The information expressed by the noun following a recognitional demonstrative may not be sufficient for the hearer to find the referent in his or her knowledge store. In order to facilitate the identification task, the speaker may provide additional information about the referent in a relative clause, as in following example from German.

(22)   German (Auer 1984: 637)
    *Was isn eigentlich mit   **diesem** Haustelephon,   was*
    what is   MD   with that   house.telephone what
    mir (wir) immer   khabt ham;...
    we   used.to had   have...
    'What happened to that house telephone that we used to have?'

The *Haustelephon* 'house telephone' is a new discourse entity which is mentioned for the first time in this sentence. It is marked by an adnominal demonstrative in order to indicate that the hearer is familiar with the referent. However, since the *Haustelephon* was not previously activated the speaker cannot be certain as to whether the hearer will indeed identify the referent, and for that reason s/he provides additional information about the *Haustelephon* in a relative clause. Relative clauses are so frequently used after a recognitional mention that Himmelmann (1996: 230) considers the occurrence of relative clauses and other noun modifiers a secondary feature of this use. Furthermore, he notes that the noun marked by a recognitional demonstrative is often followed by a pause, providing a chance for the hearer to ask for clarification if s/he could not identify the referent (cf. Himmelmann 1997: 72–3). This is exemplified in (23).

(23)   German (Himmelmann 1997: 58)
        A: *Was hast n   (dann) gelesen?* (*0.2sec*)
              what have you (then) read   (0.2sec)
        B: (*Ja*)   **diesen** *Aufsatz von dem   Olson.* (*1.5sec*)
              (Yeah) that   essay   by the/that Olson (1.5sec)
        A: *Was is n   des für einer?* (*0.4sec*) *Ach so!* (*0.2sec*)
              what is PART that P   one   (0.4sec) INTJEC (0.2sec)
              Von   dem hab ich immer noch nix   mitgekriegt.
              About him have I   still   yet   anything heard
        A: 'What did you read next?' (0.2sec)
        B: 'That essay by Olson.' (1.5sec)
        A: 'What kind of person is he?' (0.4sec) 'Oh wait! Right!'(0.2 sec)
              'I still haven't heard anything about him.'

The 'essay by Olson', which speaker B mentions in line two, is a new discourse topic. Since speaker B believes that speaker A is familiar with the referent, *Aufsatz* 'essay' is marked by a recognitional demonstrative. Following this speech act, there is a pause of 1.5 seconds which allows the hearer to ask for clarification.

The recognitional use must be distinguished from the use of the demonstratives in the following examples:

(24)   English (Himmelmann 1997: 78)
        a.   *Similar payroll tax boosts would be imposed on **those** under the railroad retirement system.*
        b.   *The true artist is like one of **those** scientists who, from a single bone, can reconstruct an animal's entire body.*

Similar to the recognitional use, the demonstratives in (24a–b) occur with a subsequent relative clause. However, they do not appeal to private shared knowledge, nor do they focus the hearer's attention on entities in the speech situation or discourse. These demonstratives do not fit any of the uses discussed thus far. Himmelmann (1997: 78) characterizes them as semantically empty proforms that provide an anchorage point for the relative clauses that follow. In chapter 6, I will argue that the head of a relative clause is often marked by a grammatical item that developed from a recognitional demonstrative. I will refer to such grammatical items as *determinatives*. The demonstratives in (24a–b) can be seen as determinatives at an early stage of the grammaticalization process. They are formally indistinguishable from adnominal demonstratives, but they have lost the discourse pragmatic properties of a (recognitional) demonstrative and serve a purely grammatical function. In other languages, determinatives are further grammaticalized and formally distinguished from their historical source (cf. 6.4.4).

Apart from the recognitional use, there is one other context in which non-exophoric demonstratives are commonly used without a referent in the preceding discourse. In colloquial English, unstressed *this* is frequently used to introduce new discourse topics (cf. Prince 1981; Wald 1983; Wright and Givón 1987; Gernsbacher and Shroyer 1989). Consider the following example:

(25)   English (Prince 1981: 233)
        *A few years ago, there was **this** hippie, long-haired, slovenly. He confronted me...*

Like recognitional *that*, unstressed *this* precedes a noun that is mentioned for the first time, but it serves a very different discourse pragmatic function: recognitional *that* introduces hearer old information, while unstressed *this* marks information that is hearer new. Furthermore, while the referent of recognitional *that* is usually of low topicality and does not recur in the subsequent discourse (Himmelmann 1996: 230; 1997: 83), unstressed *this* marks important new topics that usually persists in the subsequent discourse (cf. Prince 1981; Wald 1983; Wright and Givón 1987; Givón 1990). Following Wright and Givón (1987), I assume that unstressed *this* is not just a different use of the proximal demonstrative; rather, it functions as an article used to mark specific indefinite information (cf. Gundel et al. 1993: 275). I will discuss specific indefinite *this* together with similar articles from other languages in the following chapter on grammaticalization (cf. 6.4.6).

Like anaphoric and discourse deictic demonstratives, recognitional demonstratives may have a particular form. Himmelmann (1996: 231–234, 1997: 62–71) reports that there are several Australian languages that employ a particular demonstrative in order to activate private hearer old knowledge. Yankunytjatjara, for instance, uses the demonstratives *panya* in order to "call the listener's attention to the fact that he or she is already familiar with the referent" (Goddard 1985: 107). Himmelmann (1996: 232) argues that *panya* is a recognitional demonstrative and he discusses further examples from Nunggubuyu and Mparntwe Arrernte.

5.5 The special status of exophoric demonstratives

The previous sections discussed four different pragmatic uses of demonstratives: the exophoric, anaphoric, discourse deictic, and recognitional uses. In the literature, it is often assumed that the exophoric use is the basic use from which all other uses derive (cf. Brugmann 1904: 7–8; Bühler 1934: 390; Lyons 1977: 671). This view has recently been questioned by Himmelmann (1996; see also Hanks 1990; Fuchs 1993; Laury 1997), who maintains that there is no evidence for the common assumption that the exophoric use is basic. Moreover, he argues that the four pragmatic uses discussed in the preceding sections must be of equal status because all four uses are universally attested. If the three endophoric uses were derived from the exophoric use, one would expect, according to Himmelmann (1996: 242), that the transpositions (or extensions) from the exophoric use to the three other uses would be less pervasive and less regular.

Himmelmann proposes this hypothesis based on very little data. In my view, it is still an open question whether all four uses are universally attested. And even if it turns out that all four uses are universal, it would not rule out that the exophoric use is basic and that the three other uses are derived from this use by regular transpositions. In the remainder of this chapter, I will argue, following previous work by Brugmann (1904), Bühler (1934), Lyons (1977), and many others, that the exophoric use is indeed the basic use from which all other uses derive. I present three arguments in support of this view. First, the exophoric use is prior in language acquisition. Second, exophoric demonstratives are morphologically and distributionally unmarked. And third, the grammaticalization of demonstratives originates from the anaphoric, discourse deictic and recognitional uses; that is, exophoric demonstratives are never immediately reanalyzed as grammatical markers. All three arguments suggest that the exophoric use has a special status. It is the prototypical use from which all other uses derive.

In a study on the acquisition of deictic words in English, Eve Clark (1978) has shown that gestures are crucial for young children to learn the use of deictic words such as *this* and *that* and *here* and *there*. She argues that the acquisition of deictic expressions occurs in four steps. At first, children use a pointing gesture without any words to focus the hearer's attention on entities in the surrounding situation. Then they begin to use an isolated demonstrative accompanied by a gesture. Next, they combine demonstratives with other linguistic expressions, producing utterances such as *this shoe* or *that mine*. And finally, they learn how to use demonstratives without a deictic gesture if the identification of the referent is sufficiently determined by situational clues (Clark 1978: 96–97; cf. Weissenborn 1988). The development is summarized in Table 64, which I adopted from Clark's paper (1978: 97).

Although Clark does not distinguish between different pragmatic uses, it is clear from her argumentation that the exophoric use is learned prior to the other

Table 64. *From deictic gesture to deictic word (Clark 1978: 97)*

Stage	Gesture	Utterance	Example
1	point		
2	point	+	'da' (= 'that')
3	point	+	'that shoe'
4			'that coat is mine'

uses because the exophoric use is the only use that is commonly accompanied by a pointing gesture. Children learn the use of exophoric demonstratives based on the directive force of deictic gestures, which in turn provides the ground for the acquisition of those uses that do not involve a gesture. The exophoric use of demonstratives is thus of central significance for the development of deictic words from deictic gestures, which suggests that the exophoric use plays a central role within the deictic system.[37]

Additional support for this view comes from markedness theory (cf. Greenberg 1966; Croft 1990: chap4). As shown in the preceding sections, many languages employ distinct demonstratives for different uses. In particular, anaphoric demonstratives are often marked by an affix that is added to a demonstrative root. I have given an example from Tümpisa Shoshone in Section 5.2. Three further examples from Usan, Ngiyambaa, and West Greenlandic are shown in (26) to (28).

(26) Usan (Reesink 1987: 80)
      Exophoric   *e*   'this'
      Anaphoric   *e-ng*   'this-GIVEN'

(27) Ngiyambaa (Donaldson 1980: 139)
      Exophoirc   *ŋilu*   'this.ERG'
      Anaphoric   *ŋilu-laː* 'this.ERG-GIVEN'

(28) West Greenlandic (Fortescue 1984: 261)
      Exophoric   *manna*   'this'
      Anaphoric   *ta-manna* 'ANA-this'

Like anaphoric demonstratives in Tümpisa Shoshone, anaphoric demonstratives in Usan, Ngiyambaa, and West Greenlandic are formed by adding an extra morpheme to a demonstrative root. The anaphoric demonstratives are thus morphologically more complex than their exophoric counterparts. Morphological complexity is one of the criteria that typologists use in order to determine the unmarked value of a grammatical category. Croft (1990) defines this criterion as follows:

> *Structure:* the marked value of a grammatical category will be expressed by at least as many morphemes as is the unmarked value of that category. (Croft 1990: 73)

Assuming this criterion, anaphoric demonstratives are *structurally* marked: in all languages included in my sample, anaphoric demonstratives involve at least as many morphemes as exophoric demonstratives, and in some languages they are distinguished from exophoric demonstratives by an additional morpheme. That is, if anaphoric and exophoric demonstratives do not have the same number of morphemes, anaphoric demonstratives are always more complex.

Like anaphoric demonstratives, discourse deictic and recognitional demonstratives may have a special form, but they are usually not more complex than exophoric demonstratives. Since they do not occur with an additional morpheme they are structurally unmarked. However, recognitional demonstratives have a marked distribution. As pointed out above, recognitional demonstratives are only used adnominally, while all other demonstratives occur in various syntactic contexts. Lexical items that occur in fewer syntactic contexts than other members of the same category are *distributionally* marked according to the following criterion:

> *Behavior (distributional):* if the marked value occurs in a certain number of distinct grammatical contexts (construction types), then the unmarked value will also occur in at least those contexts that the marked value occurs in. (Croft 1990: 82)

Thus, anaphoric demonstratives are morphologically (or structurally) marked vis-à-vis demonstratives of the exophoric use, and recognitional demonstratives have a marked distribution relative to the demonstratives of all other uses. Only discourse deictic demonstratives do not seem to be marked by any of the markedness criteria that typologists assume.

Finally, the exophoric use must be considered basic because the grammaticalization of demonstratives always originates from one of the three endophoric uses. Anaphoric demonstratives are, for instance, frequently reanalyzed as third person pronouns (cf. 6.3.1); discourse deictic demonstratives provide a common historical source for sentence connectives (cf. 6.3.4); and recognitional demonstratives may develop into determinatives (cf. 6.4.4). Anaphoric, discourse deictic and recognitional demonstratives serve language-internal functions; they are already to some extent grammaticalized in that they function to organize the information that is encoded in the ongoing discourse. Since exophoric demonstratives serve a language-external function, they cannot be immediately reanalyzed as grammatical markers. A demonstrative will always first go through a stage at which it is used with reference to linguistic entities in the surrounding discourse before it assumes a specific grammatical function. One can think of the grammaticalization of demonstratives as a continuum ranging from items that are used to orient the hearer in the outside world to items that are routinely used to organize the lexical material within the ongoing discourse. Exophoric demonstratives mark one end of this cline. The other is represented by grammatical items such as third person pronouns, sentence connectives, and determinatives. The three endophoric uses are somewhere in between the two ends of this cline, referring to linguistic entities within the universe of discourse. Figure 6 shows the cline of grammaticalization that I propose.

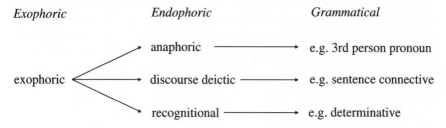

Figure 6. *The grammaticalization cline of demonstratives*

5.6 Summary

In this chapter, I have examined the pragmatic uses of demonstratives in discourse and face-to-face conversations. Following Himmelmann (1996, 1997), I have distinguished four different uses: the exophoric, anaphoric, discourse deictic, and recognitional uses. Exophoric demonstratives are primarily used to orient the hearer in the speech situation. They focus his or her attention on entities in the world outside of discourse and they are often accompanied by a pointing gesture. I have shown that the exophoric use is not restricted to concrete referents that are visible in the speech situation. Exophoric demonstratives are also commonly used with reference to abstract and removed objects, and they may indicate a referent in a fictive situation evoked by the ongoing discourse (Deixis 'am Phantasma'). Anaphoric demonstratives are coreferential with a noun or noun phrase in the previous discourse; they keep track of discourse participants that are contrastive, emphatic and somewhat unexpected. Very often, they occur after the first mention of a new referent in order to establish a new discourse topic. Discourse deictic demonstratives refer to an adjacent chunk of discourse. More specifically, they refer to aspects of meaning: the propositional content or illocutionary force of an utterance. Unlike anaphoric demonstratives, discourse deictic demonstratives do not track continuing topics; rather, they express an overt link between two propositions or speech acts. Finally, recognitional demonstratives activate private hearer old knowledge. They mark new discourse referents that speaker and hearer know from common experience in the past. Very often, recognitional demonstratives are accompanied by a relative clause (or a prepositional phrase) providing additional information about the referent. In the final section, I argued that the exophoric use of demonstratives is basic and unmarked. I presented three arguments in support of this view: first, the exophoric use is crucial for the acquisition of demonstratives by young children; second, exophoric demonstratives are morphologically unmarked relative to anaphoric demonstratives and distributionally unmarked vis-à-vis recognitional demonstratives; and third, the grammaticalization of demonstratives originates from the three endophoric uses.

CHAPTER 6

Grammaticalization

The previous chapters dealt with synchronic aspects of demonstratives: their morphological structures, semantic features, syntactic functions, and pragmatic uses. This chapter is concerned with the diachrony of demonstratives. More specifically, it investigates the development of demonstratives into grammatical markers. Crosslinguistically, demonstratives provide a common historical source for a wide variety of grammatical items such as definite articles, relative and third person pronouns, copulas, sentence connectives, complementizers, number markers, and possessives. The development of multiple grammatical markers from a single source item has been called *polygrammaticalization* (Craig 1991). It occurs when a single lexeme undergoes grammaticalization in several syntactic contexts (cf. Lehmann 1995b: 1258). Grammaticalization is often viewed as a process that involves isolated linguistic items, but it is the entire grammatical construction, rather than an isolated item, that is subject to grammaticalization (cf. Bybee, Perkins and Pagliuca 1994: 11). This chapter shows that the path-of-evolution that a demonstrative might take is crucially determined by the syntactic context in which it occurs. Specifically, it is argued that pronominal, adnominal, adverbial, and identificational demonstratives give rise to four different sets of grammatical markers which usually retain some of the syntactic properties that the demonstrative had in the source construction. Pronominal demonstratives develop into grammatical items that are either still used as pronouns (or have at least some of the properties of a pro-nominal). Adnominal demonstratives give rise to grammatical items that function as operators of nominal constituents. Adverbial demonstratives evolve into operators of verbs or verb phrases. And identificational demonstratives develop into grammatical markers that interact with nominal constituents derived from predicate nominals. There is thus a rather close correspondence between the syntactic function of the demonstrative in the source construction and the grammatical function of the target.

This chapter is organized as follows. Section 6.1 discusses some general principles of grammaticalization, providing the theoretical background for the following investigation. Section 6.2 defines the criteria that I will use in order to determine if and to what extent a demonstrative has undergone grammaticalization. Sections 6.3 to 6.6 describe the grammaticalization channels that originate from pronominal, adnominal, adverbial, and identificational demonstratives, respectively. Finally, Section 6.7 addresses the question: where do demonstratives come from — what is their historical source?

6.1 Some general principles of grammaticalization

Grammaticalization is usually defined as the process whereby lexical items develop into grammatical items and items that are already grammaticalized assume new grammatical functions (cf. Meillet 1921: 131–133; Kuryłowicz 1965: 52; Lehmann 1985: 303; Heine, Claudi and Hünnemeyer 1991a: 1–5; Hopper and Traugott 1993:xv; Bybee, Perkins and Pagliuca 1994: 4–5). Lexical items are content words, which encode the main semantic concepts of an utterance. Grammatical items, on the other hand, are function words, which organize the lexical material within a sentence. Lexical items comprise the major word classes — nouns, verbs, and adjectives — while grammatical items subsume such elements as prepositions, conjunctions, and auxiliaries. The former are always open classes (except for adjectives, which may be open or closed class; see Dixon 1982), while the latter are closed class items (cf. Talmy 1988).

Lexical and grammatical items form a *cline of grammaticality* ranging from free content words to bound grammatical morphemes (Hopper and Traugott 1993: 7). Between the two ends of this cline there is a wide variety of items that are more or less grammaticalized. Grammaticalization can be seen as the process by which an item moves towards the grammatical end of this cline. This process is *unidirectional* (cf. Hopper and Thompson 1993: 94–129). That is, lexical items develop into grammatical items and grammatical items may further grammaticalize, but grammatical items do not develop into lexical items or items that are less grammaticalized. A few counterexamples have been cited in the literature (cf. Jefferson and Zwicky 1980; Matsumoto 1988; Harris and Campbell 1995: 336–339), but most of them are controversial (cf. Bybee, Pagliuca and Perkins 1994: 13–14), and even if there are cases of "degrammaticalization" (Heine, Claudi and Hünnemeyer 1991b: 149) they would be so rare that they hardly undermine the claim that grammaticalization is basically a unidirectional process.

The development of grammatical items follows certain pathways, called *grammaticalization channels* (cf. Heine, Claudi and Hünnemeyer 1991a: 221). Grammaticalization channels are patterns of historical change leading time and again from the same source to the same target. Crosslinguistically, they are very similar and they tend to be stable over time. That is, new grammatical items may evolve through a certain grammaticalization channel at different times, giving rise to grammatical categories with different layers. Many Indo-European languages have, for instance, several layers of adpositions that represent different stages of a grammaticalization process, leading from constructions including a relational noun (e.g. *in front of*) to adpositions with highly abstract meanings (e.g. *of*) (cf. Lehmann 1985).

Grammaticalization may affect all aspects of a linguistic sign: its phonological form, its morphosyntactic features, and its meaning or function (cf. Heine and Reh 1984; Hopper and Traugott 1993; Lehmann 1993, 1995a, 1995b). At the phonological level, grammaticalization often involves a process of *phonological reduction* and *coalescence* (cf. Bybee, Pagliuca and Perkins 1994: 4–9). Items tend to shorten and to fuse with other elements in their environment when they grammaticalize; free forms lose some of their phonological substance, turn into clitics and then into affixes before they eventually disappear (cf. Heine and Reh 1984: 17–28). Phonological reduction and coalescence are perhaps the most obvious signs that grammaticalization has occurred, but they are not restricted to grammaticalization. Lehmann (1989) points out that *lexicalization* may also involve phonological reduction and coalescence. He defines lexicalization as a word formation process by which formerly independent items are combined into complex words with idiosyncratic semantic properties. Unlike lexicalization, grammaticalization gives rise to forms that are morphologically and semantically regular and transparent (cf. Lehmann 1995b: 1263–1264).[38]

At the morphosyntactic level, grammaticalization often restricts the distributional freedom of an item: more grammaticalized items tend to occur in a specific slot in a grammatical construction. Very often they are arranged in *paradigms* and their occurrence is *obligatory* in certain contexts (cf. Lehmann 1995a: 137–143). Moreover, lexical items may *lose the ability to inflect* when they grammaticalize. Although this is frequently accompanied by phonological reduction, it is in principle an independent process. Grammatical items may lose the ability to inflect even if they keep all of their phonological substance: they may occur with a *frozen* affix that has lost its meaning or function.

At the semantic level, grammaticalization involves a process of *semantic bleaching* or *fading* (Sweetser 1988, 1990): lexical items become semantically less concrete and pragmatically less significant (cf. Heine and Reh 1984: 15). At the same time, they gain new grammatical functions or meanings (cf. Sweetser 1988; Heine, Claudi and Hünnemeyer 1991a). According to Traugott (1989), linguistic signs become more *subjective* when they grammaticalize. She argues that the meaning of a grammatical item is often situated in the speaker's subjective belief toward the situation.

Heine, Claudi and Hünnemeyer (1991a) have shown that grammaticalization processes are commonly motivated by metaphorical extensions, metonymic transfers, and pragmatic inferences (cf. Claudi and Heine 1986; Traugott and König 1991). In their view, and in the view of many others, the initial stage of a grammaticalization process usually involves the metaphorical (or metonymic) use of a lexical expression or a conversational implicature that is triggered by a specific item.

6.2 Criteria for the grammaticalization of demonstratives

Having described the general principles of grammaticalization, I turn now to the features that characterize the grammaticalization of demonstratives. As pointed out at the end of Chapter 5, the grammaticalization of demonstratives is a continuous process leading from exophoric demonstratives used to orient the hearer in the outside world to grammatical items serving specific syntactic functions. This process involves a number of changes that one might summarize as follows:

Functional changes
1. Grammatical items that developed from demonstratives are no longer used to focus the hearer's attention on entities in the outside world.
2. They are deictically non-contrastive.

Syntactic changes
3. Their occurrence is often restricted to a particular syntactic context.
4. They are often obligatory to form a certain grammatical construction.

Morphological changes
5. They are usually restricted to the distal or, less frequently, the proximal form.
6. They may have lost their ability to inflect.

Phonological changes
7. They may have undergone a process of phonological reduction.
8. They may have coalesced with other free forms.

These are eight criteria that one might use in order to determine if and to what extent a demonstrative has grammaticalized. The two functional criteria apply to (almost) all demonstratives that have undergone grammaticalization: grammatical items that developed from demonstratives do not function to orient the hearer in the outside world and they are always non-contrastive (but see Section 6.5.2 for discussion of a notable exception). The other criteria may or may not apply, depending on the grammaticalization channel, the properties of the source item, and the stage that an emergent grammatical marker has reached. More grammaticalized demonstratives are more likely to have undergone any of the formal changes than less grammaticalized demonstratives. At the initial stage of a grammaticalization process, grammatical markers often have the same morphosyntactic and phonological properties as the source items (Hopper 1991).

Given the criteria I have suggested, one has to assume that anaphoric, discourse deictic, and recognitional demonstratives are already to some extent grammaticalized (as I have argued in Section 5.5). All three endophoric demonstratives serve language-internal functions and they are non-contrastive.[39] Moreover, anaphoric and recognitional demonstratives are usually restricted to the distal form, which suggests that they have undergone a morphological process, and recognitional demonstratives occur only in adnominal position, which indicates that they have changed syntactically. The division between grammatical items and endophoric demonstratives is strictly speaking an idealization. There is no clear-cut borderline that separates endophoric demonstratives from grammatical markers. There are only demonstratives that are more or less grammaticalized.

In the following four sections, I describe eighteen grammaticalization channels that commonly originate from a demonstrative. For each channel, I provide at least one example of a grammatical item that has undergone some morphosyntactic and/or phonological changes so that source and target are formally distinguished. Some of the grammaticalization processes that I examine have been discussed extensively in the literature on grammaticalization, but other changes have only been described in reference grammars or other special sources. I begin my investigation with the reanalysis of pronominal demonstratives, followed by the grammaticalization of adnominal and adverbial demonstratives, and I conclude with grammatical items that developed from identificational demonstratives in copular and nonverbal clauses.

6.3   The grammaticalization of pronominal demonstratives

6.3.1   *Third person pronouns*

In many languages, third person pronouns are historically derived from pronominal demonstratives.[40] Givón (1984: 353–360) has shown that the emergence of third person pronouns from demonstratives is part of a diachronic cline that one might describe as follows:

(1)   DEM PRO > third person PRO > clitic PRO > verb agreement

At the beginning of this cline we find anaphoric pronominal demonstratives tracking emphatic, contrastive and unexpected discourse topics. Anaphoric demonstratives that develop into third person pronouns become de-stressed and their use is gradually extended to all persisting topics. When third person pronouns continue to grammaticalize they may become clitics, which may eventually turn into agreement markers (cf. Givón 1984: 353; Lehmann 1995a: 39–42).

The entire cline is attested in the history of the French language. Modern standard French uses pronominal clitics to track continuing topics, but in certain nonstandard varieties the clitics are essentially used as agreement markers, which are commonly accompanied by a coreferential (pro)noun (cf. Lambrecht 1981). Historically, the clitics go back to free third person pronouns, which in turn developed from the demonstrative *ille* in Vulgar Latin (e.g. Harris 1978: 100–101).

6.3.2   Relative pronouns

Relative pronouns are often marked by a relativizer, which might be an (uninflected) particle or an (inflected) pronoun (cf. Keenan 1985). Though relative pronouns are widely used in European languages (both Indo-European and non-Indo-European such as Hungarian, Finnish and Georgian), they seem to be very uncommon in other parts of the world (cf. Comrie 1998). In my sample, there is only one non-European language that has a relativizer which one might consider a relative pronoun: Tümpisa Shoshone (Dayley 1989: 357–374). The relative pronoun in Tümpisa Shoshone is, however, rather different from the kind of relative pronoun that is commonly found in European languages. In European languages, relative pronouns tend to occur in the initial position of the relative clause and their case features are determined by their syntactic function within the embedded clause (cf. Comrie 1998). By contrast, relative pronouns in Tümpisa Shoshone may occur in any position in the relative clause and they have the same case features as the coreferential noun in the superordinate clause.

Relative pronouns have two common historical sources: (anaphoric) pronominal demonstratives and wh-question words (cf. Lehmann 1984). Consider the following examples from German:

(2)   German
  a.   *Er hat einen neuen Vorschlag gemacht, **der***
        he has a   new   suggestion made   REL
        mir besser gefallen hat.
        me better pleased has
        'He made a new suggestion, which I liked better.'
  b.   *Er hat einen neuen Vorschlag gemacht; **der** hat*
        he has a   new   suggestion made   REL has
        mir besser gefallen.
        me better pleased
        'He made a new suggestion; this one I liked better.'

The relative pronoun in (2a) occurs in a dependent clause, marked by the position of the finite verb at the end of the sentence. It has the same form as the pronominal demonstrative in (2b), which is embedded in an independent main clause (marked by a finite verb in second position). Relative pronouns and pronominal demonstratives are morphologically indistinguishable in German, but since their syntactic features are different they are commonly distinguished (cf. Eisenberg 1994: 200).[41] Relative pronouns are always fronted (i.e. they are always the first element in the relative clause), whereas pronominal demonstratives occur in the usual position of a (pro-)noun. That is, the relative pronoun in (2a) can only occur clause-initially, while the pronominal demonstrative in (2b) may also occur after the dative pronoun *mir* and the finite verb *hat* (cf. relative pronoun: **Mir der besser gefallen hat* vs. demonstrative pronoun: *Mir hat der besser gefallen*). Moreover, while relative pronouns are generally unstressed, anaphoric demonstratives may bear a contrastive accent.

The development of relative pronouns in German is controversial. Behaghel (1923–1932, III: 766) argues that they derive from an (anaphoric) pronominal demonstrative that continued a noun of the preceding sentence. However, Paul (1916–20, IV: 189–191) and Lockwood (1968: 242–244) contend that they evolved from a pronominal demonstrative that was originally governed by the verb in the main clause, as in (3):

(3)   Old High German (Lockwood 1968: 243)
       *enti aer antwurta **demo**   za imo sprah*
       but he answered DEM.DAT to him spoke
       'But he answered the one (who) spoke to him.'

In this example, *demo* is syntactically part of the main clause (i.e. it is governed by the main verb *antwurta* 'answer'), but semantically it belongs to both main and subordinate clause: it is an undergoer in the main clause and an actor in the subordinate clause. If main and subordinate clause require the same case, it is possible to interpret the demonstrative as a syntactic element of the subordinate clause:

(4)   Old High German (Lockwood 1968: 243)
       thô   liefun sâr   **thie**   *nan minnôtun meist*
       then ran   at.once DEM.NOM him loved   most
       'Then ran at once they who loved him most.'

The demonstrative in (4) is syntactically ambiguous: it occurs in nominative case and could be interpreted as the syntactic subject of the verb in either the main clause or the subordinate clause. According to Lockwood, the relative pronoun in German evolved from pronominal demonstratives that were ambiguous as in this example. The conversion was completed once the pivotal pronoun was represented twice, in main and subordinate clause, as in the following example from Early New High German:

(5)   Early New High German (Lockwood 1968: 244)
       *Wer ist **die**,   **die**   aufgehet aus   der Wüste wie*
       who is the.one who rises   from the desert like
       ein gerader Rauch?
       a   straight smoke
       'Who is the one who rises from the desert like smoke?'

Lehmann (1984: 378–383) suggests yet another developmental pathway along which the relative pronoun in German might have emerged. He argues that the German relative pronoun evolved from an adnominal demonstrative that preceded a postnominal attribute as in (6):

(6)   Old High German (Lehmann 1984: 378)
       *kuningin **thia** richun*
       queen   DEM mighty
       'the mighty queen'

Lehmann maintains that relative clauses in German are the result of a process whereby attributive adjectives like the one in (6) are expanded to attributive clauses in which the adnominal demonstrative is reinterpreted as a relative pronoun. A crucial stage of this process is marked by participial constructions like the one in (7), which are commonly found in Old High German:

(7)   Old High German (Lehmann 1984: 379)
       *ich bim Gabriel **thie** azstantu fora   gote*
       I   am   Gabriel DEM standing in.front.of god
       'I am Gabriel standing in front of God.'

Lehmann argues that the adnominal demonstrative in (7) establishes an overt link between the preceding noun and the participial construction, which it nominalizes. This construction has properties of both the attributive adjective in (6) and a full-fledged relative clause: like the attributive adjective in (6), the participial construction in (7) is a nominalized constituent that is linked to the preceding noun by an adnominal demonstrative; and like full-fledged relative clauses in Modern German, it is a clausal attribute that includes a verb, though the verb is nonfinite. Lehmann (1984: 379) argues that participial constructions of this sort developed into finite relative clauses by analogy to an older relative construction that included a finite verb and later disappeared.

Though Lehmann rejects the common assumption that the relative pronoun in German evolved from a pronominal demonstrative, he does not deny that there are languages in which relative pronouns can be traced back to pronominal demonstratives. On the contrary, he argues that the relative pronoun in Ancient Greek evolved from an anaphoric demonstrative pronoun. If Lehmann's analysis is accurate, relative pronouns may arise from two types of demonstratives: (i) pronominal demonstratives (which are either used as anaphors or as the pivot of a bi-clausal construction) and (ii) adnominal demonstratives that link a nominal attribute to the head noun.

6.3.3   *Complementizers*

Complementizers are frequently based on pronominal demonstratives that are used as discourse deictics (cf. Frajzyngier 1991). The complementizers of North and West Germanic languages, for instance, arose from a demonstrative that originally occurred in the main clause referring forward to the subsequent proposition. Harris and Campbell (1995: 287) provide the following example from Middle High German, which exemplifies the source construction.

(8)   Middle High German (Harris and Campbell 1995: 287)
       *joh gizalta in   sâr   **thaʒ,** thiu sâlida untar in   uuas*
       and told   them immediately that the luck   among them was
       'And he told them immediately that good fortune was among them.'

The initial clause in (8) includes the pronominal demonstrative *thaʒ,* which anticipates the information expressed in the following clause. When the cataphoric demonstrative was reanalyzed as a complementizer it became associated with the following subordinate clause where it occurs in Modern German.

The same process gave rise to the complementizer *that* in English (cf. Traugott 1992: 230–238). Hopper and Traugott (1993: 185–189) argue that the *that*-complementizer started out as a copy of a cataphoric pronominal demonstrative that occurred in the preceding main clause. Consider the following example from Old English:

(9)   Old English (Hopper and Traugott 1993: 186)
        þæt gefremede Diulius hiora consul, þæt þæt
        DEM arranged   Diulius their consul COMP DEM
        angin   wearð tidlice þurhtogen
        beginning was   in.time achieved
        'Their consul Diulius arranged (it) that it was started on time.'

The initial *þæt* in (9) is a fronted object pronoun used to anticipate the complement clause, which is introduced by a copy of the cataphoric demonstrative. Hopper and Traugott (1993: 186) point out that one could analyze the complement clause as an appositive of the object pronoun, rather than an argument of the verb in the preceding clause. The appositive clause turned into a complement clause when the cataphoric demonstrative was no longer used to anticipate its occurrence. The complementizers of North Germanic languages such as Swedish *att* and Icelandic *að* developed along the same pathway. Lockwood (1968: 222–223) provides the following two examples from Faroese, which show that the grammaticalization channel is still productive.

(10)   Faroese (Lockwood 1968: 223)
        a. *eg sigi, at   hann kemur*
            I say that he   comes
            'I say that he comes.'
        b. *eg sigi tað, hann kemur*
            I say that he   comes
            'I say that: he comes.'

The complement clause in (10a) is marked by the complementizer *at*, which introduces the embedded clause. Like the complementizers in English and German, the complementizer in Faroese can be traced back to a cataphoric demonstrative in the main clause. Example (10b) has the same structure as the construction from which the complement clause in (10a) developed. It includes a pronominal demonstrative that is used to anticipate the subsequent clause. This sentence exemplifies the source construction from which the complementizers in North and West Germanic languages evolved.

6.3.4 *Sentence connectives*

Sentence connectives are frequently formed from a pronominal demonstrative and some other element (e.g. an adverb or adposition) that indicates the semantic relationship between the conjoined propositions. Consider, for instance, the following example from Hixkaryana:

(11)   Hixkaryana (Derbyshire 1985b: 157)
       nomokyaknano tuna heno. ***ire ke*** *romararïn*
       it.was.coming rain QNT DEM because.of my.field
       hokohra wehxaknano
       NEG I.was
       'It was raining heavily. Therefore I did not work on my field.'

Example (11) shows two clauses linked by the pronominal demonstrative *ïre* and the causal postposition *ke*. Derbyshire (1985a: 57, 1985b: 157) treats *ïre ke* as a sentence connective, consisting of two words (cf. English *so that*), which are routinely used in combination to express a causal link between two propositions. Similar sentence connectives occur in many other languages in my sample. Epena Pedee, for instance, has a number of 'temporal relators' (Harms 1994: 144) formed from the distal demonstrative *ma* and a suffix that indicates the semantic relationship between the linked propositions. The most common temporal relator is *mapái* 'and/so then', consisting of *ma* and *-pái*, which Harms (1994: 144) glosses as 'only'. *Mapái* is used to express a link between two closely related events, as in (12):

(12)   Epena Pedee (Harms 1994: 144)
       tá-či náwe te čáa peečiadai-pá-ri ***ma-pái*** *či*
       our-REF mother house each dizzy-HAB-PRES that-only REF
       kʰari-pa-rí-pa kʰari-pá-ri kʰíra pa-ru-má-a
       sing-HAB-PRES-ERG sing-HAB-PRES face arrive-PRES-LOC-DAT
       'The shaman gets dizzy and loses her balance in each house. And then the singer sings until she (the shaman) revives.'

Sentence connectives are either based on pronominal demonstratives that are used as discourse deictics, or they involve a manner (adverbial) demonstrative. Epena Pedee, for instance, has a number of sentence connectives that consist of the manner demonstrative *maa* 'like that' and a morpheme that specifies the semantic relationship between the conjoined propositions. Example (13) includes the sentence connective *maap^héda* 'after that' formed from *maa* 'like that' and *-p^héda* meaning 'after':

(13) Epena Pedee (Harms 1994: 145)
      perõrá-pa   imáma wárra pee-t^haa-hí   maa-p^héda
      spotted.cavy-ERG tiger son   kill-OBJ-PAST like.that-after
      unu-hi-dá   ewári ába mée
      find-PAST-PL day one jungle
      'A spotted cavy killed a tiger's child. After that, one day they met in the jungle.'

Like Epena Pedee, Khasi has a set of sentence connectives that are formed from a distal demonstrative and a bound morpheme. Example (14) exhibits a complex sentence consisting of two clauses linked by *naŋta* 'then', which is formed from the adpositional marker *naŋ-* and the demonstrative root *-ta:*

(14) Khasi (Nagaraja 1985: 100)
      u   khla u   la   ba:m naŋ-ta u   la   thyú
      ART tiger ART PAST ate P-DEM ART PAST slept
      'The tiger ate then he slept.'

Finally, German employs a large number of pronominal adverbs that developed from an old oblique form of the pronominal demonstrative *das* (i.e. *dara, dar*) and an adposition:

Table 65. *Pronominal adverbs in German (Paul 1992)*

Modern form	Source	Gloss
damit	*da:r-mit(i)*	DEM.OBL-with
darüber	*dara ubiri*	DEM.OBL-above
darum	*da:r-umbi*	DEM.OBL-because.of
dabei	*da:r-bi:*	DEM.OBL-by
darin	*da:r-inne*	DEM.OBL-in
darauf	*da:r-u:f*	DEM.OBL-on.top.of
dazu	*da:ra-zuo*	DEM.OBL-to
dafür	*dara-fure*	DEM.OBL-for
dagegen	*dara-gegene*	DEM.OBL-against

The pronominal adverbs in Table 65 are either used to substitute for a prepositional phrase or they function to join two neighboring clauses. These forms are only weakly grammaticalized: the prepositions are still governed by the verb and the demonstratives establish an anaphoric link like discourse deictics but unlike fully grammaticalized conjunctions. In the following example, the pronominal adverb *darüber* 'about that/it' is used to indicate a link between the preceding question and the following clause.

(15) German
A: *Was machst du, wenn du fertig bist?*
what do   you when you finished are
'What are you going to do when you are finished?'
B: ***Darüber*** *habe ich noch nicht nachgedacht.*
DEM.OBL.about have I   yet not thought.about
'I haven't thought about it yet.'

Darüber is composed of the old oblique form of the pronominal demonstrative *das,* which is no longer used in Modern German, and the preposition *über* 'about', which is governed by the verb *nachdenken* at the end of the clause.

6.3.5 *Possessives*

Many languages do not have particular possessive markers, instead using personal or demonstrative pronouns (often in genitive case) in order to indicate the possessor. For instance, in Supyire a possessor may be realized by a pronominal demonstrative preceding the noun denoting the possessee. Possessive demonstratives have the same form as adnominal demonstratives, but unlike the latter, possessive demonstratives agree with their antecedent rather than with the head noun. The different agreement behavior of adnominal and possessive demonstratives is shown in (16a–b): the adnominal demonstrative in (16a) has the same noun class features as the following noun, while the noun class of the possessive demonstrative in (16b) corresponds to the noun class of its referent or antecedent.

(16) Supyire (Carlson 1994: 200, 201)
a. *ŋké ba-gé*
DEM(G2S) house-DEF(G2S)
'this/that house'
b. *ŋgé ba-gé*
DEM(G1S) house-DEF(G2S)
'that/this one'e house'

The possessive demonstratives in Supyire are ordinary pronominal demonstratives serving a particular semantic function in this construction. They may, however,

turn into possessive markers if they become disassociated from pronominal demonstratives that are used in other contexts. The development of possessive
markers from pronominal demonstratives is well attested. For instance, the French
possessive *leur* 'their' developed from the genitive masculine plural form of the
pronominal demonstrative *ille* in Vulgar Latin. Harris (1978: 87–95) describes the
development as follows. Classical Latin used the possessive pronoun *suus* in
order to indicate a possessor within the same sentence, and it used the genitive
forms of the anaphoric demonstrative *is* in order to indicate a possessor that is not
mentioned in the same clause. In other words, Classical Latin distinguished
reflexive from non-reflexive possessives: *suus* was used as a reflexive possessive,
and *eius* SG.M, *eorum* PL.M and *earum* PL.F functioned as non-reflexive possessives. The latter were later replaced by *illius* SG.M/F, *illorum* PL.M and *illarum*
PL.F when the demonstrative *ille* took over the function of *is*. Old French lost the
distinction between reflexive and non-reflexive possessives and restricted the use
of *suus* to singular while the former masculine plural form of the non-reflexive
possessives, *illorum,* was adopted as the corresponding plural form. The singular
and plural feminine forms, *illius* and *illarum,* disappeared. As the grammaticalization process continued, *illorum* was shortened to *leur* (*il-**lor**-um*) and by
analogy it developed a new plural form, *leurs,* used to indicate multiple possess-
ees.

6.4   The grammaticalization of adnominal demonstratives

6.4.1   *Definite articles and noun class markers*

Adnominal demonstratives provide a common historical source for definite
articles. The development has been described in numerous studies including
Christophersen (1939), Heinrichs (1956), Krámský (1972), Ultan (1978a), Harris
(1978, 1980), Greenberg (1978, 1991), Lüdtke (1991), Vogel (1993) Cyr (1993a,
1993b, 1996), Leiss (1994), Epstein (1994, 1995), Lehmann (1995a), Laury
(1995, 1997), and Himmelmann (1997, 1998). This section summarizes the
central findings discussed in these works.

Most of the studies that I have cited assume that definite articles arise from
anaphoric adnominal demonstratives (e.g. Greenberg 1978: 69; see Himmelmann
1997 for a different view). The use of anaphoric demonstratives is usually
confined to non-topical antecedents that tend to be somewhat unexpected,
contrastive or emphatic (cf. 5.2). When anaphoric demonstratives develop into
definite articles their use is gradually extended from non-topical antecedents to

all kinds of referents in the preceding discourse. In the course of this development, demonstratives lose their deictic function and turn into formal markers of definiteness. An example of such a definite marker is the article *the* in English.

The semantic reanalysis of adnominal demonstratives as markers of definiteness is usually accompanied by certain formal changes. Since articles are generally unstressed they often lose some of their phonological substance and cliticize to an element in their environment. The definite articles in Swedish, Rumanian and Basque, for instance, are bound morphemes (i.e. enclitics or suffixes) that evolved from free forms.

Furthermore, as we have seen in Chapter 4, adnominal demonstratives are often independent pronouns that are only loosely adjoined to a coreferential noun in apposition. Since articles are in general syntactically dependent, one has to assume that adnominal demonstratives often lose their status as free nominals when they become reanalyzed as definite markers (cf. Himmelmann 1997: 144–157).

Finally, Plank and Moravcsik (1996) report (based on unpublished work by Siewierska and Bakker 1992) that, at least in European languages, demonstratives are significantly more often inflected than articles, which suggests that adnominal demonstratives often lose the ability to inflect when they grammaticalize as definite markers.

Once demonstratives have turned into definite markers, their use may spread from definite nouns to nouns expressing specific indefinite information (cf. Greenberg 1978). When this happens, articles occur with (almost) every noun, definite and indefinite, unless the noun is (i) non-specific (i.e. generic), (ii) inherently definite (e.g. proper names), or (iii) otherwise marked for definiteness (e.g. by a demonstrative). Greenberg (1978) mentions several Bantu languages having articles of this type (Bemba, Zulu, Xhosa). When such articles continue to grammaticalize they often turn into gender or noun class markers before they eventually disappear (cf. Schuh 1990). Table 66 shows three nouns from Turkana marked by three different gender prefixes whose historical relationship to the distal demonstratives is still reflected in their phonological form:

Table 66. *Noun class markers in Turkana (Dimmendaal 1983: 307)*

NC-NOUN		DEM	
(ŋ)a-bɛr-ʋ`	'woman'	*ya´*	'that.F'
(ŋ)e-kìle	'man'	*ye´*	'that.M'
(ŋ)i-ìŋok	'dog'	*yi´*	'that.N'

6.4.2   *Linkers*

Definite articles are used to indicate the information status of a nominal expression. They must be distinguished from linking articles, or linkers, which function to establish an overt link between the elements of a complex noun phrase. Unlike definite articles, which tend to occur at the margin of an NP, linkers are usually placed between the head noun and the associated modifiers. Consider, for instance, the following examples from Tagalog, in which the noun modifiers (i.e. an adjective in (17a), a relative clause in (17b), a numeral in (17c), a demonstrative in (17d), and an interrogative pronoun in (17e)) are linked to the following noun by the linking article *na* (allomorph *-ng*).

(17)   Tagalog (Himmelmann 1997: 160, 161, 161, 162; Foley 1980: 181)
   a.   *ang   malíít na langgám*
        SPEC small LK ant
        'the little ant'
   b.   *ang paa ng   mama... na bàbaríl sa   kanyá*
        SPEC foot GEN man   LK gun   LOC 3SG.DAT
        'the feet of the man who was going to shoot at him'
   c.   *sa   isa-ng   mànlalakbáy*
        LOC one-LK traveler
        'about a traveler'
   d.   *ay   yuu-ng   mama*
        PRED DEM-LK man
        'when that man'
   e.   *ano-ng   puno*
        what-LK tree
        'what tree'

Similar constructions occur in many other Austronesian languages, in which the linker has often the same or a very similar form as the linker in Tagalog (cf. Foley 1980). Examples from Toba Batak, Tolai, Wolio, and Ilokano are given in (18) to (21).

(18)   Toba Batak (Foley 1980: 186)
   huta   na leban
   village LK another
   'another village'

(19)   Tolai (Foley 1980: 189)
        a   mamat na vat
        ART heavy LK stone
        'a/the heavy stone'

(20)   Wolio (Foley 1980: 192)
        heqgane na be-a-umba-mo
        time   LK INTENTION-3SG-COME-DEF
        'the time he will come'

(21)   Ilokano (Foley 1980: 185)
        ti   kuarta nga in-gatang-mo
        ART money LK PERF-buy-2SG
        'the money with which you bought'

Himmelmann (1997: 172–188) argues that the linkers in Tagalog and other
Austronesian languages developed from adnominal demonstratives. He points out
that *na* (and *nga*) is not only a common form of the Austronesian linker; the
same form is also frequently used as a medial or distal demonstrative (e.g. *na*
'that' Sichule, *nana* 'that' Kambera) (Himmelmann 1997: 164). Table 67 shows
the Proto-Oceanic demonstratives as reconstructed by Ross (1988; adopted from
Himmelmann 1997: 164). Note that the medial demonstrative *na* has the same
form as the linkers in Tagalog, Toba Batak, Tolai, and Wolio, which probably
emerged from this form.

Table 67. *Proto-Oceanic demonstratives (Ross 1988: 100)*

PROXIMAL	*e/ne*
MEDIAL	*a/na*
DISTAL	*o/no*

Linkers are not only found in the Austronesian language family. There are also
linkers in Chadic (Schuh 1983a, 1990), Cushitic (Hetzron 1995), and Albanian
(Sasse 1991). In Chadic and Cushitic, the linker is a genitive suffix that evolved
from a (demonstrative) determiner (cf. Schuh 1990: 601–607). Schuh (1983a,
1990) presents two possible scenarios for the development of the "genitive-linking
morphemes" in Bade, Hausa, Kera, and other Chadic languages, without commit-
ting himself to either one. Either they evolved from a determiner of the possessed
noun, as in (22a), or they developed from a pronoun that functioned as the head
of the possessor, as in (22b).

(22)   The evolution of genitive-linking morphemes in Chadic (cf. Schuh
        1990: 605–6)
        a.   [[possessee DET] possessor] >   possessee-GEN possessor
              [[horse that] of John's]
        b.   possessee [PRO possessor]   >   possessee-GEN possessor
              [horse [that of John's]]

If (22b) is the right scenario the genitive linkers would not derive from determiners (i.e. adnominal demonstratives) but rather from (demonstrative) pronouns
that occurred with a possessor NP in apposition.

The Albanian linker is a free morpheme, which is obligatory with adjectives
(23a) and genitive nouns (23b), but does not occur with demonstratives (23c) and
other noun operators.

(23)   Albanian (Himmelmann 1997: 167, 171, 171)
        a.   (një) shok   i   mirë
              one   friend.INDEF.M LK.NOM.SG.M good
              'a good friend'
        b.   nën-a   e   vajz-ë
              mother.DEF.NOM.SG.F LK.NOM.SG.F girl-INDEF.GEN.SG.F
              'a girl's mother'
        c.   ky   libër
              this.NOM.SG.M book.INDEF.M
              'this book'

Himmelmann (1997: 172–183) shows that linkers occur more frequently with
lexical attributes such as adjectives, genitives and relative clauses than with noun
operators such as demonstratives and interrogative pronouns (cf. Foley 1980).
Based on this finding, he argues that the grammaticalization of linkers originates
in constructions that involve a noun and a lexical attribute and that the use of
linkers with noun operators is due to later extensions. If Himmelmann's hypothesis is correct the linker in Tagalog is further grammaticalized than the linker in
Albanian. The former is used with both attributes and operators, while the use of
the latter is restricted to certain types of lexical attributes and does not occur with
noun operators.

6.4.3   *Boundary markers of postnominal relative clauses/attributes*

Relative pronouns are only one of several relative markers that may arise from
a demonstrative. Many African languages have relative clauses in which the head
of the relative construction is marked by an adnominal demonstrative that is

repeated at the end of the relative clause.[42] Consider, for instance, the following example from Izi:

(24)   Izi (Meier, Meier and Bendor-Samuel 1975: 165)
        kèbé ndú   ònó   !nwé né   ngú ònó ré
        keep people DEM own mother your DEM well
        'Keep your mother's relatives well.'

The relative construction in (24) includes two adnominal demonstratives: one that occurs after the head noun, and one that occurs at the end of the relative clause (which is a nonverbal clause in this case). The initial demonstrative can be analyzed as a modifier of the head noun, but the final demonstrative does not have an obvious function. Meier, Meier and Bendor-Samuel (1975: 165) argue that the final instance of *ònó* serves as a boundary marker of the relative clause: it "gives cohesion to what otherwise would be a rather loose construction". In their perspective, the final *ònó* is not an ordinary demonstrative, but rather a grammatical marker used to form relative clauses. The same type of relative construction occurs in Sango:

(25)   Sango (Samarin 1967: 73)
        á.famille só   ahé   mbi só, mbi yí   ála   pɛpɛ
        relatives that laugh 1SG that 1SG like them NEG
        'Relatives who make fun of me, I don't like them.'

Like relative clauses in Izi, relative clauses in Sango are often marked by a copy of the demonstrative that accompanies the head noun at the end of the relative clause. According to Samarin (1967: 73), the final demonstrative is used to tie the whole construction together; it is a specific grammatical marker used to indicate the final boundary of the relative clause.

Sankoff and Brown (1976) describe the emergence of a similar relative construction in Tok Pisin. Like relative clauses in Izi and Sango, relative clauses in Tok Pisin occur with an adnominal demonstrative at the final boundary of the relative clause.

(26)   Tok Pisin (Sankoff and Brown 1976: 632)
        meri ia,   em i   yangpela meri, draipela meri ia,
        girl REL 3SG PRED young   girl big   girl REL
        em   harim istap
        3SG listen ASP
        'This girl, who was a young girl, big girl, was listening.'

The relative clause in (26) is marked by the particle *ia,* which is etymologically related to the adverbial demonstrative *here* in English. *Ia* was first reanalyzed as an adnominal demonstrative before it assumed the function of a boundary marker in relative clauses (e.g. *man ia* 'this guy'; Sankoff and Brown 1976: 639–641). Sankoff and Brown (1976: 657) point out that *ia* is often omitted when the relative clause occurs at the end of a sentence, where the final boundary of the relative clause is sufficiently marked by intonation. They characterize the two instances of *ia* in (26) as a "bracketing device" used to mark relative clauses and other postnominal attributes (Sankoff and Brown 1976: 631); that is, both instances of *ia* serve a grammatical function in this construction. Example (27) shows that the *ia...ia* construction is not only used to mark relative clauses; it also occurs with nominal attributes that follow a preceding noun.

(27)   Tok Pisin (Sankoff and Brown 1976: 642)
        ... na em, man ia,   lapun man ia,   stap   autsait ia
                    man this old   man this stayed outside here
        '... and this man, this old man, stayed outside.'

In this example, *ia* "brackets" the noun phrase in apposition to *man.* Sankoff and Brown maintain that *ia...ia* has basically the same function in this construction as in relative clauses. In both contexts, it is used to mark lexical material that provides necessary information for the identification of the preceding noun (Sankoff and Brown 1976: 640).[43]

Finally, Ewe has relative clauses that are marked by two relative particles, *si* and *lá,* which seem to have the same function as the two *ias* in Tok Pisin.

(28)   Ewe (Heine and Reh 1984: 251)
        nyɔ́nu si vá étsɔ lá mé-ga-le o
        woman REL come yesterday REL NEG-yet-be NEG
        'The woman who came yesterday is no longer here.'

Sentence (28) includes a relative construction that is marked by two relative particles: *si* and *lá. Si* follows the head noun and *lá* occurs at the end of the relative clause. Historically, *si* is related to the proximal demonstrative *sia,* which is composed of a demonstrative root and a definite marker, and *lá* can be traced back to a definite article, which in turn may have developed from an adnominal demonstrative. Heine and Reh (1984: 251) consider *si* and *lá* a "discontinuous morpheme" used to mark relative clauses. According to their analysis, *si...lá* has basically the same function as *ia...ia* in Tok Pisin. In both languages, relative clauses are framed by two relative markers that derive from adnominal demonstratives (cf. Benveniste 1966).[44] Heine and Reh (1984: 251) argue that relative clauses in Ewe might have developed from an afterthought construction that was used to clarify the meaning of the preceding noun, which has now become the head of the relative construction.

6.4.4 Determinatives

In Chapter 5 it was pointed out that a recognitional demonstrative may turn into a relative marker that indicates the nominal head of a relative clause. Himmelmann (1997: 77–78) argues that English has such a relative marker at an early stage of the grammaticalization process.

(29) English (Himmelmann 1997: 78)
... *provision was made for payment for unemployment relief by nationwide taxation rather than by a levy only on **those** states afflicted with manpower surplus.*

The distal demonstrative in this example does not indicate a referent in the preceding discourse or speech situation, nor is it used to activate private hearer old knowledge; rather, it functions to mark the nominal head of a relative clause. Demonstratives of this sort are sometimes called *determinatives* (cf. Quirk et al. 1972: 217; Himmelmann 1997: 77–80). They are not only used adnominally, but also as independent pronouns functioning as the head of the subsequent relative clause:

(30) English (Himmelmann 1997: 77)
***Those** who backed a similar plan last year hailed the message.*

Like English, Swedish has determinatives, which serve the same grammatical function. They are morphologically indistinguishable from adnominal demonstratives, but their syntactic properties are different. While adnominal demonstratives always cooccur with a definite article that is attached as a suffix to the following noun, adnominal determinatives precede a noun that is not marked by a definite article. Consider the following examples:

(31) Swedish (Holmes and Hinchliffe 1994: 167, 168; Viberg et al. 1991: 144)
a. *De turist-er-na fick mycket sol.*
DEM tourist-PL-DEF got lot.of sun
'Those tourists got a lot of sun.'

b. *De* turist-er *som åkte till Island fick mycket sol,*
    DTM tourist-PL REL went to Island got lot.of sun
    medan **de** *turist-er som åkte till Italien fick*
    while DTM tourist-PL REL went to Italy got
    regn varje dag.
    rain every day
    'Those tourists who went to Iceland got a lot of sun, while
    those tourists who went to Italy had rain every day.'
c. *Jag vill ha tillbaka bok-en som du lånade*
    I want have back book-DEF REL you borrowed
    i förra veckan.
    in last week
    'I'd like the book back that you borrowed last week.'

Example (31a) shows an adnominal demonstrative modifying a noun that is
marked for definiteness by the suffix *-na*. Sentence (31b), on the other hand,
includes two adnominal determinatives that precede a noun without a definite
article (i.e. without the suffix *-na*). Note that the nominal head of a relative
clause is not generally used without a definite article. The definite article is only
omitted if the head noun is accompanied by a determinative as in (31b). Example
(31c) shows that the head noun of a relative construction *does* occur with a
definite article if it is not marked by a determinative.

Like determinatives in English, determinatives in Swedish can be used
pronominally, as in the following example:

(32)   Swedish (Holmes and Hinchliffe 1994: 169)
        Island har mycket att bjuda **dem** *som gillar äventyr.*
        Iceland has a.lot to offer DTM REL like adventure
        'Iceland has a lot to offer those who like adventures.'

German has a determinative that developed from the definite article *der* and the
demonstrative *jener* (Lockwood 1968: 73). *Derjenige* and its inflected forms are
primarily used as the head of a relative clause as in the following example (cf.
Drosdowski 1995: 336):

(33)   German
        Derjenige*, der das gemacht hat, wird bestraft.*
        the.one   who this/it did   has will be.punished
        'The one who has done this will be punished.'

In colloquial German, *derjenige* may also occur with a subsequent prepositional
phrase (e.g. *Wir nehmen* **denjenigen** *mit dem besten Angebot.* 'We will take the

one with the best offer.'), and occasionally it is used as a plain pronoun (e.g. *Derjenige soll kommen.* 'That one is supposed to come.'). However, according to Lockwood (1968: 73), these are extensions of the use of *derjenige* with a following relative clause; originally, *derjenige* was used only as a determinative pronoun.[45]

6.4.5 Number markers

In a recent study, Frajzyngier (1997) has shown that demonstratives may be the historical source for plural markers. He discusses data from several Chadic languages in which plural markers and demonstratives are morphologically related.[46] Consider the following examples from Mupun, Hona and Podoko:

(34) Mupun (Frajzyngier 1997: 201)
      saar   'hand'
      saar mo   'hands'
      mo   'these/they'

(35) Hona (Frajzyngier 1997: 204)
      kwàlàmbá   'bottle'
      kwàlàmbá-yà   'bottles'
      dí-yà   'this'

(36) Podoko (Frajzyngier 1997: 207–8)
      dǝya   'bird'
      dǝya-kaki   'birds'
      ʸma-ká   'that'

In all three examples, the plural marker has the same form as a demonstrative or one of its components. Based on these and parallel data from several other Chadic languages, Frajzyngier maintains that the plural markers in Chadic developed from former demonstratives. His analysis appears to be straightforward in the case of plural markers that evolved from plural demonstratives: the latter are readily reinterpreted as plural markers if they lose their deictic function. However, Frajzyngier maintains that plural markers also arose from singular demonstratives. He discusses several factors that may have contributed to the grammaticalization of singular demonstratives as plural markers. Most importantly, he points out that plural marking in Chadic is often confined to definite nouns marked by an adnominal demonstrative or a related noun modifier. Due to the cooccurrence of definiteness and plural marking, adnominal demonstratives may become associated with the semantic feature of plurality and then they are immediately reanalyzed as plural markers if they lose their deictic function. Plural marking is not confined to nouns in Chadic. Verbs are also commonly marked by a plural affix. As in many other languages, the plural affixes of verbs are often similar to the plural markers of nouns in Chadic. Frajzyngier attributes the morphological resemblance of verbal and nominal plural markers to a common historical origin. He claims that both plural markers developed from demonstratives. I suspect, however, that nominal and verbal plural markers originate from demonstratives in two different source constructions: nominal plural markers are probably derived from adnominal demonstratives that accompany a juxtaposed noun, while verbal plural markers develop from pronominal demonstratives that cliticize to a verb stem.

Frajzyngier's study is primarily concerned with Chadic languages, but he points out that there are also many other languages in which plural markers and demonstratives are morphologically related (cf. Dryer 1989b). It is thus conceivable that the development of plural markers from demonstratives is a widespread phenomenon and by no means restricted to Chadic.

6.4.6   Specific indefinite articles

Wright and Givón (1987) have shown that many languages distinguish between two different indefinite nouns: indefinite nouns having a specific referent and indefinite nouns denoting a non-specific entity. Specific indefinites are often used to introduce a major discourse participant that will persist in the subsequent discourse, whereas non-specific indefinites do not usually recur in the sentences that follow. Many languages mark specific indefinites by an article based on the numeral 'one' and non-specific indefinites by zero (cf. Wright and Givón 1987; Givón 1995). Standard English does not distinguish between the two indefinites; both specific and non-specific indefinites occur with the article *a*. However, in colloquial English, unstressed *this* and *these* are commonly used to mark specific indefinite information that will persist in the subsequent discourse (cf. Wright and Givón 1987: 15–28; cf. also Prince 1981; Wald 1983; Gernsbacher and Shroyer 1989). A typical example is shown in (37):

(37)   English (Givón 1990: 921)
        *...So next he passes **this** bum and boy, the guy was real ragged, run down and all, was not even begging, just sitting there; so he stops and gives him a dollar and the next thing you know the guy is screaming...*

The noun phrase *this bum* introduces a new discourse participant, which is one of the main topics in the sentences that follow. Following Wright and Givón

(1987), I assume that unstressed *this* is a particular indefinite article, strictly distinct from the adnominal demonstrative from which it descended. Unlike the demonstrative, indefinite *this* is generally non-deictic; that is, indefinite *this* does not function to orient the hearer in the speech situation or in the universe of discourse; rather, it provides particular processing instructions. As Givón (1990: 921) puts it, indefinite *this* is a "grammatical signal" that "instructs the hearer to open and activate a file for the referent".[47]

There is, at least, one other language in my sample that seem to have a specific indefinite article derived from an adnominal demonstrative. Like English, Urim uses a former demonstrative to introduce new discourse topics. In this function, demonstratives are often accompanied by the indefinite article *ur,* as in the following example.

(38)   Urim (Hemmilä 1989: 46)
        kin   ur pa   ekg naren ampen   tukgwan
        woman a that two gather breadfruit ripe
        'Two women were gathering ripe breadfruits.'

6.5 The grammaticalization of adverbial demonstratives

6.5.1 *Temporal adverbs*

Time is an abstract concept that is often metaphorically structured in spatial terms (e.g. Lakoff and Johnson 1980). Mapping spatial expressions onto the temporal dimension provides a common historical source for the development of temporal markers (cf. Bybee and Dal 1989; Bybee, Pagliuca and Perkins 1991; Lichtenberk 1991; Haspelmath 1997). Since temporal expressions are semantically more abstract and subjective than spatial terms, it is commonly assumed that the development of temporal markers from spatial expressions is a case of grammaticalization (cf. Heine, Claudi and Hünnemeyer 1991a: 156–157; Haspelmath 1997).

Temporal adverbs such as *now* and *then* in English are frequently derived from adverbial demonstratives (cf. Anderson and Keenan 1985: 297–299). Very often, adverbial demonstratives are directly imported into the temporal domain. Anderson and Keenan (1985: 298) cite, for instance, the examples in Table 68 from Wik-Munkan (Pama-Nyungan), which are used both as locational and temporal deictics. They consist of three deictic stems, *in-* 'proximal', *an-* 'medial' and *nan-* 'distal', and two suffixes, *-pal,* which indicates movement from a certain direction, and *-man,* which denotes a stationary referent.[48]

Table 68. *Spatial–temporal deictics in Wik-Munkan (Anderson and Keenan 1985: 298)*

Form	Spatial sense	Temporal sense
inman	'right here'	'right now, today'
inpal	'from here'	'from now'
anpal	'from there (distant)'	'from then (on)'
anman	'around there'	'around now'
nanpal	'from there (near)'	'from then (recent)'
nanman	'there (close), that place'	'now (general), any near time'

Anderson and Keenan (1985: 298) point out that some of the terms in Table 68 have acquired special meanings so that the temporal senses are not always predictable from the corresponding spatial terms. This is a clear indication that the temporal expressions have become independent of the spatial demonstratives from which they derive.

According to Anderson and Keenan (1985: 298), it is fairly uncommon for a language to employ temporal deictics that are completely independent of the demonstrative system. However, temporal and spatial deictics do not always have the same morphological form as in Wik-Munkan. Consider, for instance, the following forms from Kannada:

Table 69. *Demonstratives and temporal adverbs in Kannada (Schiffmann 1983: 38–9)*

	DEM DETS	DEM PROS	DEM ADVS	TEMP ADVS
PROXIMAL	*iː*	*ivanu*	*illa*	*iːga*
DISTAL	*aː*	*avanu*	*alla*	*aːga*

The temporal adverbs, *iːga* 'now' and *aːga* 'then', involve the same deictic roots as all other elements of the deictic system, but they are clearly distinguished from adnominal, pronominal and identificational demonstratives. There are many other languages in my sample in which temporal adverbs are formally distinguished from demonstratives, but involve the same deictic roots.[49]

6.5.2   Directional/locational preverbs

Preverbs are elements such as *con-, re-* and *dis-* in Latin that are affixed to the verb stem. According to Lehmann (1995a: 97–104), preverbs are commonly derived from relational adverbs that indicate the semantic relationship between a verb and a noun. Lehmann shows that a language may have several layers of preverbs whose syntactic and semantic properties can be quite different. For instance, the oldest layer of preverbs in German includes inseparable prefixes of the verb (e.g. *be-, er-* and *ver-*). Their semantic contribution to the verb is vague and the meaning of the resulting forms is usually quite idiosyncratic. Preverbs that developed more recently (e.g. *aus-, auf-* and *ab-*) tend to be semantically more transparent and they are separable from the verb stem in certain contexts.

Directional preverbs are often derived from adverbial demonstratives.[50] German, for instance, has two directional preverbs, *hin* 'hither' and *her* 'thither', which developed from an old demonstrative root, *hi*, which only survived in a few forms such as *hin* and *her* and *hier* 'here' and *heute* 'today' (cf. Lockwood 1968: 36, 72). *Hin* and *her* are still sometimes used as independent adverbs, but more frequently they function as preverbs. Lehmann maintains that preverbation in German and other Indo-European languages is not an instance of grammaticalization but rather of lexicalization.[51] He argues that the use of preverbs in these languages is usually not fully productive and that most verbs including a preverb are semantically irregular. These are typical properties of a word formation process rather than grammaticalization (cf. Lehmann 1989).

Although I would not dispute Lehmann's general conclusion, it seems to me that the formation of complex verbs including a directional preverb are usually more regular and productive than other instances of preverbation. The two directional preverbs in German, for instance, combine fully productively with all verbs expressing a directional process and the resulting forms are semantically regular and transparent. Some examples are shown in Table 70.

The verbs shown in this table express a process or activity that is directed toward a specific location. The meanings of these verbs are completely regular and their formation is fully productive. Verbs that do not fit this pattern such as *hindeuten* 'to indicate', *hinrichten* 'to execute', or *hinweisen* 'to point out' developed from verbs that were at one point semantically regular. It is thus essential to distinguish between the development by which the demonstrative adverbs *hin* and *her* turned into directional preverbs and subsequent changes that affected the entire verb form. The former is an instance of grammaticalization, giving rise to verbs that are semantically regular and transparent. Only the latter is a lexicalization process whereby a verb including *hin* and *her* may assume a new meaning that diverges from the original pattern.

There are several other languages in my sample in which directional preverbs developed from demonstratives. Papago, for instance, has two directional

Table 70. *Directional preverbs in German*

hin-/her-kommen	'to come hither / thither'
hin-/her-fahren	'to go by vehicle hither / thither'
hin-/her-laufen	'to run hither / thither'
hin-/her-rennen	'to run hither / thither'
hin-/her-schwimmen	'to swim hither / thither'
hin-/her-kriechen	'to crawl hither / thither'
hin-/her-fliegen	'to fly hither / thither'
hin-/her-jagen	'to chase hither / thither'
hin-/her-bringen	'to take hither / thither'
hin-/her-holen	'to get hither / thither'
hin-/her-ziehen	'to drag hither / thither'
hin-/her-tragen	'to carry hither / thither'
hin-/her-hören	'to listen to s.th. or s.o. / to me'
hin-/her-sehen	'to look at s.th. or s.o. / at me'

preverbs, *ʔi-* 'toward' and *ʔa(m)-* 'away', which are based on the adverbial demonstratives *ʔia* 'here' and *ʔam* 'there' (Mason 1950: 42, 65).

(39)   Papago (Mason 1950: 42)

    a.   *ʔi-ʔgebeɩ*
       TOWARD-take.it
       'Take it there.'

    b.   *ʔam-hihiʔ*
       AWAY-they.went
       'They went there.'

Two further examples from Mojave and Inuktitut are shown in (40) and (41)
respectively. In both languages, preverbs have the same form as some of the demonstratives that are used as independent words in other contexts. Note that the
preverb in (40) does not indicate the direction of a motion verb; rather, it is used
to mark the location expressed by a positional verb. Apart from motion verbs,
verbs denoting a location or existence provide a common context for the occurrence of a directional/locational preverb.

(40)   Mojave (Munro 1976: 35)

    v-ʔ-uwaː-k
    DEM-1–be.at-TNS
    'I am around.' (or 'Here I am.')

(41)   Inuktitut (Denny 1982: 373)
        pa-una-ar-puq
        up.there.RESTRICTED-via-move-3SG
        'He is going via around up there.'

6.6 The grammaticalization of identificational demonstratives

6.6.1 *Nonverbal copulas*

In a frequently cited paper, Li and Thompson (1977) have shown that copulas often arise from demonstratives and third person pronouns. More specifically, they argue that nonverbal copulas derive from anaphoric pronouns, either from anaphoric personal pronouns or from anaphoric demonstrative pronouns. Subsequent studies by Schuh (1983b), Eid (1983), Gildea (1993), and Devitt (1994) supported their finding (see Stassen 1997: 76–91 for a crosslinguistic overview of nonverbal copula constructions).

In this section, I argue that Li and Thompson's analysis is only partially correct. Though I agree with their hypothesis that nonverbal copulas often develop from anaphoric third person pronouns, I disagree with their claim that copulas may develop along the same path from anaphoric pronominal demonstratives. Challenging their view, I maintain that the development of nonverbal copulas from third person pronouns and from demonstratives follow two different pathways. Before I discuss the demonstrative-to-copula path-of-evolution I will briefly describe the mechanism whereby personal pronouns develop into copulas. The mechanism is shown in (42), which I adapted from Devitt (1994: 144):

(42)   [NP   NP]   /   [NP$_i$ [PRO$_i$ NP]]   ⇒   [NP$_i$ COP$_i$ NP]
        SUBJ PRED   TOP SUBJ PRED   SUBJ PRED
        nonverbal clause   topicalization   copular clause

Li and Thompson maintain that the reanalysis of anaphoric pronouns as nonverbal copulas originates from a topic-comment construction in which the topical NP is resumed by an anaphoric subject pronoun. Since the topic and the pronominal subject are coreferential they will agree if there is any agreement marking in the language. When such a topic-comment construction is routinely used to express an identity relation between the topic and the predicate nominal, the topicalized NP is eventually reanalyzed as the subject of an equational sentence in which the anaphoric pronoun assumes the function of a copula. Li and Thompson support their analysis by data from several languages including Modern Hebrew, where the reanalysis of third person pronouns as copulas is due to a very recent development; so recent, indeed, that their status as copulas is not immediately obvious. Consider the following examples:

(43) Modern Hebrew (Glinert 1989: 189, 188)
a. *ha-sha'on$_i$* **hu$_i$** *matana*
    the-clock.M.SG is/he.M.SG present.F.SG
    'The clock is a present.'
b. *hevrat$_i$* *bóing* **hi$_i$** *taagid* *anaki*
    company.F.SG Boeing is/she corporation.M.SG giant
    'The Boeing company is a giant corporation.'

In both sentences *hu* 3SG.M and *hi* 3SG.F agree with the sentence-initial NP, which one might interpret either as the topicalized noun phrase of a nonverbal clause or as the subject of a copular construction. If the initial NP is the subject of a copular clause, *hu* and *hi* would be nonverbal copulas; but if it is the topic of a topic-comment construction, *hu* and *hi* would function as anaphoric pronouns. Following Berman and Grosu (1976), Li and Thompson argue that *hu* and *hi* are nonverbal copulas in this context. They present three arguments in support of their view. First, they point out that the NP preceding *hu* and *hi* can be a first or second person pronoun, as in (44).

(44) Modern Hebrew (Berman and Grosu 1976: 271)
ani/ata/hu **hu** *hašoter*
I/you/he 3SG.M the.policeman
'I am / you are / he is the policeman.'

If *hu* were a pronoun in this example, the sentence would be ungrammatical because pronominal *hu* and *hi* have to agree with their antecedent.

Second, a topicalized noun phrase is usually separated from the following clause by an intonational break. Since *hu* and *hi* follow the sentence-initial constituent without a pause, the latter must be the subject of a copular clause, rather than a topicalized noun phrase of a nonverbal clause.

And finally, while the predicate nominal of an identificational sentence can be questioned (45a–b), it is impossible to question the postverbal NP of a topic-comment construction (46a–b), as illustrated by the following examples adopted from Berman and Grosu (1976):

(45)   Modern Hebrew (Berman and Grosu 1976: 277, 277)
  a.   *moše* **hu** *xayal*
       Moshe he/is soldier
       'Moshe is a soldier.'
  b.   *ma* **hu** *moše*
       what he/is Moshe
       'What is Moshe?'

(46)   Modern Hebrew (Berman and Grosu 1976: 277, 277)
  a.   *moše,* **hu** *ohev et rivka*
       Moshe he/is loves ACC Rivka
       'Moshe, he loves Rivka.'
  b.   **et mi moše,* **hu** *ohev*
       ACC whom Moshe he loves
       *'Who is such that Moshe, he loves her?'

Thus far, I agree with Li and Thompson's analysis. I challenge, however, their claim that the development of nonverbal copulas from demonstratives involves the same mechanism as the development of copulas from third person pronouns. More precisely, I disagree with their hypothesis that nonverbal copulas derive from anaphoric pronominal demonstratives that resume a topicalized noun phrase. Questioning this part of their analysis, I maintain that nonverbal copulas that are based on demonstratives develop from identificational demonstratives in nonverbal clauses. Crucial evidence for my hypothesis also comes from Modern Hebrew.

Modern Hebrew has not only copulas that are derived from personal pronouns, but also a set of nonverbal copulas that developed from the demonstratives *ze* M.SG, *zot* F.SG and *éle* PL. Like *hu* and *hi*, the demonstratives are still used with their original function; that is, apart from their use as copulas, they are still used as demonstratives. When *ze, zot* and *éle* are used as demonstratives they may function as pronominal demonstratives or as identificational demonstratives in nonverbal clauses. Pronominal and identificational demonstratives have the same form, but they differ in their agreement behavior: anaphoric pronominal demonstratives agree in gender and number with their antecedent, while identificational demonstratives agree with the predicate nominal that follows. This is exemplified in (47a–b).

(47)   Modern Hebrew (Glinert 1989: 100, Informant)
   a.   *ten   li   kasda$_i$ aHéret, ani sone et   zot$_i$*
        give me helmet.F.SG other   I   hate ACC DEM.F.SG
        'Give me another helmet, I hate this (one).'
   b.   *ze$_i$ aba$_i$ sheli*
        DEM.M.SG father.M.SG mine
        'This is my father.'

The demonstrative in (47a) is an anaphoric pronominal demonstrative. It agrees in gender and number with the noun *kasda* 'helmet' in the preceding clause (both demonstrative and noun are feminine singular). Example (47b), on the other hand, shows an identificational demonstrative in a nonverbal clause. In this sentence, the demonstrative agrees in gender and number with the following predicate nominal *aba (sheli)* '(my) father' (both demonstrative and noun are masculine singular). In order to determine whether the nonverbal copula developed from a pronominal or identificational demonstrative, one has to examine the agreement properties of the copula:

(48)   Modern Hebrew (Glinert 1989: 189)
       ha-báyit   shelHa zot$_i$ dugma$_i$ tova
       the-house.M.SG your   COP/DEM.F.SG example.F.SG good
       'Your house is a good example.'

Example (48) includes two noun phrases of different genders and the feminine singular demonstrative *zot*, which Glinert (1989: 189) analyzes as a copula in this example. The copula agrees in gender and number with the predicate nominal at the end of the sentence, rather than with the sentence initial NP. The plural copula in (49) exhibits the same kind of agreement.

(49)   Modern Hebrew (Glinert 1989: 190)
       ha-músika   she-baHárti éle$_i$ (ze)   ktaim$_i$
       the-music.M.SG SUB-I.picked COP/DEM.PL pieces.PL
       she-kulam ohavim
       SUB-love   everyone
       'The music I picked is pieces everyone loves.'

Like *zot* in (48), the plural copula *éle* agrees with the predicate nominal rather than the preceding subject. Note that in casual speech, the copual *ze* may occur instead of *éle* (or *zot*) regardless of the gender and number features of the coreferential noun. Since the copulas in (48) and (49) show the same agreement behavior as the demonstratives in nonverbal clauses, I assume that they derive from identificational demonstratives rather than anaphoric demonstrative pronouns, as Li and Thompson have argued. (50) shows the mechanism that I suggest for the developmental pathway from demonstratives to copulas.

(50)   [NP] [DEM$_i$ NP$_j$]   ⇒   [NP COP$_i$ NP$_j$]

There are two crucial differences between the grammaticalization path shown in (50) and the mechanism described by Li and Thompson (which I believe is only appropriate for nonverbal copulas derived from third person pronouns). First, the agreement features of copulas derived from demonstratives are determined by the predicate nominal rather than the subject; and second, copular clauses including a former demonstrative develop from two intonation units, a topical NP and a nonverbal clause, that merge into a single construction, whereas copular clauses that include a former third person pronoun emerge from a construction that is expanded by left-dislocation.[52]

Additional support for my analysis comes from Kilba. Kilba has three nonverbal copulas which have the same form as identificational demonstratives in nonverbal clauses, while they differ from demonstrative pronouns. The demonstrative pronouns are complex free forms whereas the identificational demonstratives and nonverbal copulas are monosyllabic enclitics. Consider the forms in Table 71, which is repeated from Section 4.3.1.

Table 71. *Demonstrative pronouns — identifiers in Kilba (Schuh 1983b: 315–317)*

	DEM PROS/DETS	DEM IDENTS
PROXIMAL	*(nə́)nə́nnà*	*=ná*
DISTAL	*(nà)ndándà*	*=ndá*
REMOVED	*(ŋgə̀)ŋgə́ŋgà*	*=ŋgá*

Schuh (1983b) shows that the identificational demonstratives have turned into copulas that mark three different tenses: *=ná* has been reanalyzed as a present tense copula, *=ndá* indicates past tense, and *=ŋgá* is used in copular clauses whose subject is out of sight (a similar development occurred in Panare; cf. Gildea 1993):

(51)   Kilba (Schuh 1983b: 321)
        a.   *ùsmân hə̀bà **ná***
              Usman Kilba is
              'Usman is a Kilba.' (Usman is present)

b. *ùsmân hə́bà* **ndá**
Usman Kilba was
'Usman was a Kilba.'

c. *ùsmân hə́bà* **ŋgá**
Usman Kilba was
'Usman is a Kilba.' (Usman is not present)

6.6.2 *Focus markers*

In a recent study, Luo (1997) has shown that focus markers often have the same or a very similar morphological form as copulas and/or demonstratives. The morphological resemblance among these categories suggests that in such cases they are historically related. Givón (1979: 246–248) and Heine and Reh (1984: 147–182) have shown that in many African languages focus markers emerged from former copulas (see McWhorter 1994 for an alternative analysis of the evolution of the focus marker *ni* in Swahili). More specifically, they have argued that focus markers frequently arise from copulas in cleft constructions. The mechanism is shown in (52):

(52)   [[Ø COP NP]$_S$ [REL CL]$_S$]$_S$ ⇒ [[FOC NP]$_{NP}$ ...]$_S$

The source construction consists of two clauses: a copula clause (with zero subject) providing focal information and a relative clause providing presupposed information. In the target construction, the copula clause has been reanalyzed as a focal NP of the former relative clause. Given that demonstratives are a common historical source for nonverbal copulas (see above), one might posit that the morphological relationship between demonstratives and focus markers is due to the development of focus markers from nonverbal copulas that in turn evolved from identificational demonstratives in nonverbal clauses:

(53)   IDENT DEM > COPULA > FOCUS MARKER

Though (53) appears to be a likely pathway for the development of focus markers (cf. Luo 1997), it is conceivable that focus markers may also develop directly from identificational demonstratives in nonverbal clauses. (54) shows the mechanism by which they would thus emerge.

(54)   [[DEM Ø NP]$_S$ [REL CL]$_S$]$_S$ ⇒ [[FOC NP]$_{NP}$:]$_S$

Note that the source construction in (54) has the same structure as the one in (52) except that the focal part of the cleft construction includes an identificational demonstrative in a nonverbal clause rather than a copula with zero subject. The mechanism in (54) may account for the development of focus markers in languages such as Ambulas and Mokilese, where demonstratives and focus markers are morphologically related but show no obvious relationship to a copula. As shown in 2.1.2, Ambulas has two demonstrative identifiers, *kén* 'proximal' and *wan* 'distal', which are frequently used as focus markers:

(55)　Ambulas (Wilson 1980: 157)
　　　*véte　dé wak a　[**wan** méné] kaapuk yéménén*
　　　see.and he said ah FOC you　not　　you.went
　　　'He saw him and said, "Ah, so *you* did not go."'

Similarly, Mokilese (Austronesian) employs a focus marker (*ioar*) which, according to Harrison (1976: 309), can be traced back to an old deictic form that is cognate to a demonstrative identifier in Ponapean (see 4.3.1).

(56)　Mokilese (Harrison 1976: 311)
　　　ioar　Wilson ma pwehng ih　mehu
　　　FOCUS Wilson REL told　　him that
　　　'It was Wilson who told him that.'

Since there is no evidence that the focus markers in Ambulas and Mokilese developed from a copula, it is at least a plausible hypothesis that they emerged directly from a demonstrative identifier in a nonverbal clause.

6.6.3　*Expletives*

Expletives are semantically empty pro-forms that some languages require to form certain syntactic constructions. Two examples from French and Modern Hebrew are given in (57) and (58) respectively.

(57)　French (Calvez 1993: 332)
　　　C'est toi　que je connais le　mieux.
　　　it.is　you that I　know　the best
　　　'You are the one I know best.'

(58)   Modern Hebrew (Glinert 1989: 63)
        (*ze*) *tov*   [*she-bat*]
        it   good SUB-you.came
        'It's good (that) you came.'

In these examples, *ce* and *ze* function as dummy pro-forms (the use of *ze* is optional): they do not have a referent and serve a purely grammatical function. Historically, *ce* and *ze* are derived from identificational demonstratives in copular clauses. In other syntactic contexts, expletives developed from demonstratives that were originally used as pronouns or adverbs (cf. Traugott 1992: 216–219). An example of the former is English *it* in *It rained;* and an example of the latter is the existential *there* in sentences like *There was an old man who lived in Western New York.*

6.7 The diachronic origin of demonstratives

Having described the grammaticalization of demonstratives, I now address the question: where do demonstratives come from — what is their historical source?

Demonstratives are usually considered grammatical items (for a different view see Woodworth 1991: 285). Grammaticalization theory holds that all grammatical items are eventually derived from lexical expressions (cf. Hopper and Traugott 1993: 104), but there is no evidence from any language that demonstratives developed from a lexical source or any other source, for that matter, that is non-deictic. Demonstratives are sometimes reinforced by lexical items such as *ecce* 'behold' in Vulgar Latin, which strengthened the weakened demonstrative *ille* (VL *ecce ille* > OFr *cest cel* > Fr *ce;* Harris 1978: 70–77). In such a case, the lexical item may become part of the demonstrative, and if the original demonstrative subsequently disappears the lexical item may assume a deictic function (cf. Brugmann 1904).[53] This might be, however, the only mechanism by which a non-deictic term may evolve into a demonstrative. Frajzyngier (1987, 1996) claims that the demonstratives in Mupun and several other Chadic languages developed from motion verbs and verbs of saying, but his analysis is very speculative and the suggested development appears to be unmotivated.[54] As Himmelmann (1997: 20) notes, apart from those cases where a demonstrative developed from a lexical item that functioned to reinforce a weakened demonstrative, there is no convincing evidence from any language that demonstratives may have evolved from a lexical source (cf. Traugott 1982: 245; Hopper 1991: 31; Hopper and Traugott 1993: 129). A number of studies have therefore suggested that demonstratives might present an exception to the hypothesis that all grammatical expressions are eventually derived from lexical items (cf. Plank 1979a; Traugott 1982).[55] Demonstratives, or the deictic elements on which they are based, might belong to the basic vocabulary of every language. This is not only suggested by the absence of any positive evidence for a lexical source, it is also supported by the fact that demonstratives belong to the very few items that display a non-arbitrary relationship between phonetic form and meaning. Based on a representative sample of 26 languages, Woodworth (1991) has shown "that there is a systematic relationship between vowel quality and distance such that the vowel quality of the form with proximal meaning has a higher pitch than that of the form with distal meaning." This confirms earlier studies by Sapir (1949) and Ultan (1978b) who cast the same finding in articulatory terms: the vowels of proximal demonstratives tend to be higher and more advanced than the vowels of the corresponding medial and distal forms. Plank (1979a) argues that the iconic relationship between phonetic shape and meaning might indicate that demonstratives are newly created words (cf. also Plank 1979b). Questioning the hypothesis that all grammatical items are either derived from lexical items or from grammatical items that previously developed from a lexical source, he argues:

> doch möchte ich bei meiner Konzeption von lexikalisch und grammatisch nicht a priori ausschliessen, dass bestimmte grammatische Mittel ihren historischen Ursprung nicht in lexikalischen oder ehemals funktionsverschiedenen grammatischen Ausdrucksmitteln haben. Zumindest bei grammatischen Kategorien aus Bereichen, in denen Form-Bedeutungszuordnungen tendentiell auf ikonischer statt auf rein symbolischer Basis erfolgen, sollte auch das erste Verfahren der "Urschöpfung" von Ausdrücken in unmittelbar grammatischer Funktion im Auge behalten werden. Zu denken wäre dabei an zwei- oder mehrstufige Systeme der Ortsdeixis (hier — dort), deren Vokalmuster in vielen Sprachen frappante Ähnlichkeiten aufweisen, ... (Plank 1979a: 331–332)

> [but for my conception of lexical and grammatical I do not want to exclude a priori that certain grammatical items do not originate from lexical items or items that previously served another grammatical function. At least for those grammatical categories for which the pairing of form and meaning is partially iconic rather than purely symbolic, the first strategy of creating new terms that are immediately used to serve a grammatical function should also be considered. Place deictic systems including two or more terms show, for instance, a pattern of vowel alternation that is strikingly similar in many languages, ...]

The iconic relationship between sound shape and meaning could, of course, also be the result of a phonological process that is involved in the grammaticalization of demonstratives. But given that sound symbolism is usually associated with newly created words, the systematic relationship between vowel quality and distance seems to support the hypothesis that demonstratives are new creations. This would also be in accordance with the fact that demonstratives are not ordinary grammatical items. Grammatical items function to organize the lexical material in discourse, while demonstratives serve a language-external function (at least in their most basic use). A number of scholars, including Peirce (1955) and Bühler (1934), have argued that demonstratives and other deictics form a particular class of items that is distinct from all other linguistic expressions (see also Ehlich 1979, 1982, 1983, 1987). Demonstratives are used to orient the hearer in the speech situation, focusing his or her attention on objects of interest. This is one of the most basic functions of human communication for which there might be a particular class of linguistic expressions that emerged very early in the evolution of language. In this connection, it is interesting to note that demonstratives are also among the very first items in language acquisition. According to Eve Clark (1978: 95), demonstratives often appear in the first ten words of English-speaking children, and they are always among the first fifty. Apart from demonstratives there are hardly any other closed class items that English-speaking children learn before they begin to construct their first simple sentences (Brown 1973). All this suggests that demonstratives are not ordinary grammatical markers, and hence it would make sense if they do not derive from lexical items as all other grammatical markers.

If demonstratives are not derived from lexical items, there would be two different sources from which grammatical markers may emerge: lexical expressions and demonstratives. The grammaticalization of items from both domains would be unidirectional. That is, grammatical items develop from lexical expressions and demonstratives but never vice versa. Furthermore, there would be no transitions between the two source domains — demonstratives do not develop into lexical items, nor is there evidence that lexical items have ever been reanalyzed as demonstratives. These considerations are summarized in Figure 7.

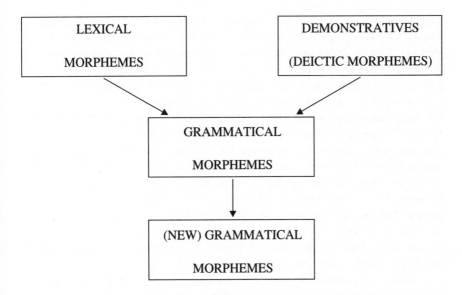

Figure 7. *The two source domains of grammatical items*

According to Figure 7, grammatical markers evolve from two different sources: lexical items and demonstratives. The grammaticalization processes that originate from these two sources differ significantly. The grammaticalization of lexical items involves such mechanisms as metaphorical extension, metonymic transfer and conversational implicature (cf. Sweetser 1990; Heine, Claudi and Hünnemeyer 1991a; Traugott and König 1991; Hopper and Traugott 1993; Bybee, Perkins and Pagliuca 1994). These mechanisms are irrelevant to the grammaticalization of demonstratives, which is based on the extension of the exophoric use to the three endophoric uses (cf. 5.5). Endophoric demonstratives serve a language-internal function, providing a natural starting point for the development of grammatical markers. It seems that grammatical morphemes always emerge from a secondary use of the source expression: lexical items that are used in a metaphorical (or metonymic) sense or that trigger a conversational implicature and demonstratives that function to indicate a referent in the universe of discourse or to activate private shared knowledge.

6.8 Summary

In this chapter, I have shown that demonstratives provide a common historical source for a wide variety of grammatical items. I have examined the grammatica-lization path of eighteen grammatical markers that frequently arise from demon-stratives. I have shown that the path-of-evolution that a demonstrative takes is largely determined by the syntactic context in which it undergoes grammaticali-zation. Pronominal, adnominal, adverbial, and identificational demonstratives provide input into different grammaticalization channels giving rise to grammati-cal items that usually retain some of the syntactic properties of their historical source. There are, however, a few grammatical items that may arise from more than one source. Sentence connectives, for instance, derive from pronominal de-monstratives that are used as discourse deictics and from manner demonstratives, which are commonly classified as adverbs. Also, expletives may originate from demonstratives in three different contexts: (i) identificational demonstratives in copular and nonverbal clauses, (ii) pronominal demonstratives functioning as subjects of an impersonal verb, and (iii) adverbial demonstratives in existential constructions. Table 72 provides an overview of the grammaticalization channels that I have examined in this chapter.

The list of grammatical items hown in Table 72 is by no means exhaustive. Other grammaticalization processes starting from a demonstrative have been suggested in the literature. For instance, Vries (1995) has argued that a number of Papuan languages have topic markers that are based on pronominal demonstra-tives, and Ehlich (1986, 1987) has shown that interjections and discourse markers may evolve from deictics (i.e. demonstratives).[56] Finally, it is well known that in many languages demonstratives are commonly used as hesitation signals (e.g. Korean, Japanese, Mandarin Chinese, Finnish, Passamaquoddy-Maliseet).

In the final section of this chapter, I have considered the hypothesis that de-monstratives (or the deictic roots on which demonstratives are based) belong to the basic vocabulary of every language. I presented three arguments that seem to support this view. First, there is no positive evidence that demonstratives derive from lexical items. Second, demonstratives exhibit an iconic relationship between phonetic shape and meaning, which is usually associated with newly created words. And third, demonstratives do not serve a language-internal function like ordinary grammatical markers; rather, they are used for one of the most basic functions of human communication, for which there might be a class of linguistic items that is distinct from both lexical and grammatical expressions.

Table 72. *The grammaticalization of demonstratives*

Source	Target
Pronominal demonstratives:	third person pronouns relative pronouns complementizers sentence connectives possessives adnominal determinatives verbal number markers expletives (linkers)
Adnominal demonstratives:	nominal number markers definite articles/noun class markers linkers boundary markers of attributes pronominal determinatives specific indefinite articles (relative pronouns)
Adverbial demonstratives:	directional preverbs temporal adverbs expletives
Identificational demonstratives:	nonverbal copulas focus markers expletives

CHAPTER 7

Conclusion

It has been the purpose of this study to provide a comprehensive overview of the form, function and grammaticalization of demonstratives in the world's languages. This final chapter summarizes the major results of my investigation and discusses some of the areas that merit further examination.

7.1 Major findings

Chapter 2 examined the morphological features of demonstratives: the occurrence of demonstrative clitics, the inflectional properties of demonstratives in different syntactic contexts, and the formation of demonstrative stems. It was shown that the occurrence of demonstrative clitics is largely restricted to adnominal demonstratives; pronominal, adverbial and identificational demonstratives are almost always unbound. The inflectional properties of demonstratives vary with their syntactic function. Pronominal demonstratives are more often inflected than adnominal and identificational demonstratives, which in turn are more likely to inflect than adverbial demonstratives; the latter are usually uninflected unless they occur with a set of locative case markers. The stem of most demonstratives is monomorphomemic. If it consists of more than one morpheme, pronominal demonstratives are often formed from a demonstrative root and a nominalizing suffix, a third person pronoun or a classifier, and adverbial demonstratives may be composed of a demonstrative root and a locative marker or a locational noun. Adnominal and identificational demonstratives have either the same stems as pronominal demonstratives or they consist solely of a deictic root.

Chapter 3 examined the semantic features of demonstratives. It was argued that demonstratives have two kinds of semantic features: deictic features, which indicate the location of the referent in the speech situation, and qualitative features, which characterize the referent. The deictic features indicate whether the referent is near or away from the deictic center, whether it is at a higher or lower elevation, whether the referent is visible or out of sight, uphill or downhill, upriver or downriver, or whether it is moving toward or away from the deictic center or across the speaker's line of vision. I argued that although pronominal and adnominal demonstratives are not always deictically contrastive, all languages have at least two (adverbial) demonstratives that indicate a contrast on a distance scale: a proximal demonstrative, which refers to a location near the deictic center, and a distal demonstrative, which indicates a referent at greater distance. The qualitative features of demonstratives are subsumed under six semantic categories: (i) ontological status, (ii) animacy, (iii) humanness, (iv) sex, (v) number, and (vi) boundedness. The features of these categories classify the referent, which provides important clues for its identification by the hearer.

Chapter 4 investigated the distribution and the categorial status of demonstratives. I argued that demonstratives occur in four syntactic contexts: (i) they are used as independent pronouns in argument position of verbs and adpositions, (ii) they are used together with a cooccurring noun or (iii) a cooccurring verb, and (iv) they may occur in copular and nonverbal clauses. Some languages employ the same demonstratives in all four contexts, but most languages have several series of demonstratives that serve specific syntactic functions in particular environments. If the demonstratives being used in one of these four contexts are phonologically distinguished or if they have different morphosyntactic properties, they belong to different grammatical categories, which I call (i) demonstrative pronouns, (ii) demonstrative determiners, (iii) demonstrative adverbs, and (iv) demonstrative identifiers. I used the corresponding adjectives — pronominal, adnominal, adverbial, and identificational — in order to refer to the use of a demonstrative in a specific syntactic context regardless of its categorial status. It was shown that some languages do not have a particular class of demonstrative determiners, instead, using a demonstrative pronoun with a coreferential noun in apposition. Other languages lack a particular class of demonstrative pronouns and use demonstrative determiners together with a classifier, a third person pronoun, or a nominal particle where most languages use a demonstrative pronoun. Adnominal demonstratives in English are phonologically and morphologically indistinguishable from demonstrative pronouns, but since they are associated with two different word classes one must assume that pronominal and adnominal *this* and *that* belong to distinct categories. In Old English, adnominal demonstratives had the status of independent pronouns that were adjoined to a coreferential noun in apposition, but in Modern English, adnominal demonstratives are determiners and categorially distinguished from demonstrative pronouns. Adverbial demonstratives are usually distinct from demonstrative pronouns and determiners. There are only a few languages in my sample in which adverbial demonstratives belong to the same category as pronominal and adnominal demonstratives. Finally, identificational demonstratives are usually considered demonstrative pronouns, but my investigation showed that the demonstratives in copular and nonverbal clauses are often formally (i.e. categorially) distinguished from pronominal demonstratives in other contexts: they may have a particular phonological form or they may differ in their inflection.

Chapter 5 was concerned with the pragmatic uses of demonstratives. Following a recent study by Himmelmann (1996), I distinguished four different uses: (i) the exophoric, (ii) anaphoric, (iii) discourse deictic, and (iv) recognitional uses. Exophoric demonstratives function to orient the hearer in the speech situation; they serve a language-external function. The other three uses function to refer to linguistic elements in the surrounding discourse or to activate private shared knowledge; they serve a language-internal function enhancing discourse coherence. I used the notion of endophoric demonstrative in order to distinguish these three uses from the exophoric use. Anaphoric demonstratives are co-referential with a prior NP; they keep track of discourse topics. Discourse deictic demonstratives refer to a chunk of the surrounding discourse; they express an overt link between two discourse units. Finally, recognitional demonstratives activate information that is already in the hearer's knowledge store. The exophoric use is the most basic use from which all other uses derive: exophoric demonstratives are prior in language acquisition, they are morphologically and distributionally unmarked (vis-à-vis anaphoric and recognitional demonstratives), and the grammaticalization of demonstratives originates from one of the three endophoric uses. One can think of the grammaticalization of demonstratives as a cline ranging from exophoric demonstratives that are used to orient the hearer in the outside world to grammatical markers that serve a specific syntactic function. Anaphoric, discourse deictic, and recognitional demonstratives are somewhere in between the two ends of this cline.

In Chapter 6 I showed that the grammaticalization of demonstratives is largely determined by the syntactic context in which a demonstrative occurs. Pronominal, adnominal, adverbial, and identificational demonstratives are associated with grammatical items that usually retain some of the syntactic properties of their historical source. Pronominal demonstratives are frequently reanalyzed as third person pronouns, relative pronouns, complementizers, sentence connectives, possessives, expletives, and verbal number markers; adnominal demonstratives may develop into definite articles (noun class markers), linkers, adnominal determinatives, nominal number markers, boundary markers of postnominal attributes, and, perhaps, relative pronouns; adverbial demonstratives are often reanalyzed as temporal adverbs and in some languages they developed into directional preverbs, sentence connectives, and expletives; and identificational demonstratives are the source for nonverbal copulas, focus markers, and expletives.

Finally, I considered the hypothesis that demonstratives might not derive from lexical items, as commonly assumed, but rather from a class of genuine deictics that belong to the basic vocabulary of every language. I presented three arguments in support of this view. First, there is no convincing evidence from any language that would indicate that demonstratives evolve from a lexical source. Second, demonstratives are among the very few items that exhibit an iconic relationship between form and meaning, which is characteristic of newly created words. And third, demonstratives serve one of the most fundamental functions of human communication for which all languages use a set of deictics that might have developed very early in the evolution of language.

7.2 Future research

My findings raise a number of questions that deserve further investigation. In this final section, I outline some areas of future research that would thematically continue the current work.

In Chapter 4, I discussed the semantic values of demonstratives as described in reference grammars. The vast majority of grammars that I consulted use semantic labels such as 'proximal' or 'near speaker' in order to characterize the meanings of demonstratives. These labels are, however, only rough approximations. The meaning of a demonstrative is often more complex. It would be a very interesting project to study the semantic values of demonstratives in greater detail. One issue that requires special attention is the distinction between distance-oriented and person-oriented systems, as suggested by Anderson and Keenan. Are these really two different systems, or is a person-oriented system just a variant of a distance-based system with a special deictic term for entities near the hearer, as I have argued in my discussion of the deictic system in Quileute?

Another interesting question that could not be addressed in this work is why languages differ as to the number and kind of deictic terms that they employ. It has been repeatedly argued that the cultural environment of a speech community determines, at least to some extent, the size of a deictic system (cf. Frei 1944; Denny 1978; Perkins 1992). Specifically, it has been claimed that the size of a deictic system decreases "as the degree to which the spatial environment is man-made increases" (e.g. Denny 1978: 80). This claim has been put forward based on crosslinguistic comparison: the deictic systems of many aboriginal languages are much more complex than the deictic systems of languages that are spoken by people in modern societies. This hypothesis presupposes that the deictic systems of languages such as English, French or Japanese were more complex at an earlier stage in their history. In order to test the hypothesized correlation between the size of a deictic system and the cultural environment of the speech community one has to study the historical development of deictic systems. In particular, it is necessary to examine the deictic systems of languages spoken in societies that underwent significant socioeconomic changes.[57]

Another topic that would be worthwhile to investigate is whether the distinction between different demonstrative categories correlates with other syntactic features of a language. What motivates, for instance, the categorial distinction between demonstrative pronouns and demonstrative determiners, which occurs in some languages but not in others? And why do most languages employ a spearate class of demonstrative adverbs? I suspect that the existence of different demonstrative categories correlates with the existence of more general word classes. For instance, if a language has a class of determiners, I would expect that adnominal demonstrative will be distinguished from pronominal, adverbial and identificational demonstratives. If, on the other hand, a language does not have a class of determiners (like Old English), it is quite likely that adnominal demonstratives belong to the same category as demonstratives that occur in other contexts. In other words, my hypothesis is that the distinction between demonstrative pronouns, determiners, adverbs, and identifiers is motivated by the devision between more general word class that occur in a particular language.

In the chapter on grammaticalization, I did not consider the question of whether the distance features of demonstratives might have an effect on their path-of-evolution. Greenberg (1978: 61) and Givón (1984: 226) argued that definite articles are almost always derived from distal demonstratives. There might be similar correlations between other grammatical markers and certain distance categories. My impression is that most grammatical markers derive from distal demonstratives, but this needs thorough investigation.

Finally, it is left for future research to decide whether demonstratives are derived from lexical expressions, as most previous studies assumed, or whether they are based on a set of genuine deictics, as I suggested. Although it is, of course, impossible to *prove* that demonstratives form a genuine class of deictics that did not evolve from lexical expressions, this hypothesis will become increasingly convincing if future studies fail to find evidence for a non-deictic source from which demonstratives might have emerged.

Notes

1. An overview of some of the philosophical literature on deixis and demonstratives is given in Levinson (1983: 55–61).

2. Rijkhoff and Bakker (1998) provide an overview of various sampling methodologies. See also Bell (1978), Dryer (1989c), Nichols (1992), Rijkhoff, Bakker, Hengeveld, and Kahrel (1993), and Bybee, Perkins and Pagliuca (1994).

3. Note that some of the forms in Table 8 end in a long vowel (e.g. *milíí*). The final vowel is only lengthened when the demonstratives are used pronominally; in adnominal position, the final vowel is always short.

4. In "extremely limited non-colloquial situations" the demonstratives *ku* and *i* can occur without a defective noun, *ku* meaning 'he' and *i* 'this fact' (cf. Sohn 1994: 294).

5. Note that adverbial demonstratives may attach to a noun when they are used adnominally, as in French *cette maison-là* 'that house there' (cf. 4.2).

6. In some studies, clitics are defined in phonological terms: clitics are usually unstressed and they are not affected by phonological rules that are sensitive to word boundaries. However, Anderson (1992: 200) shows that phonological criteria are insufficient to define clitics. He argues that clitics can only be defined in syntactic terms. Clitics are "phrasal affixes" (Klavans 1985: 95), which may attach to various elements of a phrase: (i) the initial word, (ii) the final word, (iii) the head etc. (cf. Anderson 1992: 202).

7. The case markers of demonstratives have probably a different origin. As pointed out above, the case endings of demonstratives are usually very similar to the case endings of nouns and therefore it is reasonable to assume that they developed from the same source. As Lehmann (1985, 1995a), Lord (1993) and others have shown, case markers are frequently derived from adpositions or serial verbs.

8. Himmelmann does not consider the categorial status of *das*. While some German linguists consider *das* a demonstrative when it is stressed (e.g. Engel 1988), others assume that stressed *das* is not distinguished from the (unstressed) definite article of the same form (e.g. Bisle-Müller 1991).

9. The same argument applies, of course, to person-oriented systems with three deictic terms, which can be seen as variants of two-term systems.

10. Dixon (1972: 48) points out that the suffixes of the 'river' series refer to 'water' features in general, and that the 'hill' suffixes may also refer to 'cliff', 'tree' etc.

11. The use of demonstrative determiners and demonstrative identifiers is usually not restricted to a certain kind of referent: they refer to whatever is denoted by the noun or predicate nominal with which they cooccur.

12. Some of my sources use the notion *intensive* instead of *emphatic* (cf. Redden 1980: 70; Dixon 1972: 48). I assume that emphatic and intensive markers have basically the same pragmatic function.

13. Note that 'precision' is different from 'boundedness'. The features of the category 'precision' indicate whether the speaker draws the hearer's attention to a specific location or whether the location of the referent is not made precise, while the features of the category 'boundedness' indicate how the referent is conceptualized.

14. See Moravcsik (1997) for an interesting discussion of adnominal demonstratives in Hungarian, which behave in some ways like independent pronouns and in others like "satellites of the noun" (cf. 6.4.1).

15. Note that under Abney's analysis determiners are the only functional elements that are subcategorized like verbs (and other lexical elements). All other functional elements require a complement, i.e. they cannot be intransitive (cf. Abney 1987: 285).

16. Further theory internal support for the Det-as-head analysis comes from the following consideration. Jackendoff (1977) has shown that there can be two specifiers in the English noun phrase: *[The]₁ [many]₂ good men*. The traditional NP analysis cannot accommodate such structures because X-bar theory does not allow for more than one specifier per phrase. The Det-as-head analysis provides room for an additional specifier by treating one of them as the head of DP and the other as its specifier (cf. Abney 1987: 287–295). This argument relies, of course, crucially on the assumption that *many* and other adnominal elements that may occur in the 'second determiner slot' are in fact determiners.

17. Abney points out that this is a possible interpretation, but his discussion suggests that there is also a non-restrictive reading (which I don't get).

18. I use the term 'construction' in the sense of Construction Grammar, in which constructions are defined as conventional pairings of form and meaning (cf. Fillmore, Kay and O'Connor 1988; Fillmore and Kay 1993; Goldberg 1995; Lakoff 1987; Diessel 1997b).

19. The French forms are less grammaticalized in that the adverbial intensifiers *ci* and *là* are not obligatory like their counterparts in Afrikaans and Swedish.

20. Temporal deictics such as English *now* and *then* are also sometimes classified as demonstrative adverbs (cf. Anderson and Keenan 1985: 297), but I will keep them separate from demonstratives. In Section 6.5.1, I argue that temporal deictics are grammatical markers that frequently develop from adverbial demonstratives.

21. There is, however, a semantic difference between pronominal and identificational demonstratives in English: in copular clauses, *this* and *that* may refer to a person as in *This is my friend*. In all other syntactic contexts, pronominal *this* and *that* cannot denote a human referent (cf. Halliday and Hasan 1976: 62–63).

22. Schuh (1977) does not decompose the demonstrative in Table 51, but they seem to consist of a deictic root (*m-*), a gender/number affix (*-s* MASC, *-c* FEM, *-d* PL), and a distance/category marker (*-o* 'proximal pronoun', *-aa(ni)* 'proximal identifier'; *ii* 'distal pronoun/identifier', *-əno* 'particular pronoun', *-ənaa(ni)* 'particular identifier').

23. Schuh (1977) does not indicate morpheme boundaries, but the plural forms of the demonstrative pronouns are apparently formed from a demonstrative root and the plural marker *-aw-*, which is inserted into the root before the final mid back vowel.

24. The *ce* in copular clauses must be kept separate from the masculine singular form of the demon-

strative determiners; cf. *C'est Pascal* 'This is Pascal' vs. *ce cadeau* 'this gift'.

25. In Durie's grammar (1985), there are only examples of adnominal demonstratives that cliticize to a preceding element, but his description suggests that adnominal demonstratives can also be free forms.

26. In addition to the forms in Table 60, Pangasinan has two further series of demonstratives, which Benton (1971: 91–93) calls "demonstratives of similarity" and "independent demonstratives". The demonstratives of similarity are manner demonstratives; they belong to the category of demonstrative adverbs. The independent demonstratives occur in a variety of contexts: (i) in equational sentences, (ii) after the marker *ed* (which seems to function as an adposition), and (iii) linked to a noun phrase by the particle *ya*. They appear to be similar to sentential demonstratives such as French *voilà*, but this needs further investigation.

27. Since the out-of-sight demonstratives that we saw in Chapter 3 are anchored in the speech situation and are deictically contrastive, they can be viewed as exophoric demonstratives despite the fact that they refer to entities that are not present in the speech situation.

28. Himmelmann (1996) refers to the anaphoric use as the "tracking use", emphasizing the discourse pragmatic function of demonstratives that are coreferential with a prior NP.

29. The average referential distance of third person pronouns is 1.7 in Lichtenberk's data. The referential distance of demonstratives is much higher: it is 3.4 for the proximal demonstrative *'eri*, and 8.6 for the distal demonstrative *baa*. These are the figures for adnominal demonstratives. Lichtenberk does not consider the pronominal use of *'eri* and *baa*.

30. An exception to this might occur in languages that do not have third person pronouns and/or definite articles (or languages in which the use of third person pronouns is restricted to human/animate referents). These languages frequently employ anaphoric demonstratives to track major discourse participants (Nikolaus Himmelmann p.c.).

31. Kuno (1973: 282–290) argues that *ano* can also be used anaphorically. He points out, however, that unlike *sono, ano* only occurs when the antecedent denotes an entity that speaker and hearer know personally from previous experience. This suggests that *ano* functions as a recognitional demonstrative rather than an anaphor.

32. Demonstratives referring to an event or situation are often subsumed under the discourse deictic use (cf. Webber 1991; Himmelmann 1996).

33. Lyons (1977: 668) refers to discourse deictic demonstratives as "impure text deixis". The notion of text deixis is sometimes used as a synonym of the notion discourse deixis or as a cover term subsuming both text and discourse deixis.

34. In the literature, the notion anaphoric is used in two different ways: on the one hand it refers to the tracking use of demonstratives, and on the other hand it indicates that a pronoun, noun (phrase) or adverb refers to an element of the preceding discourse. In the former sense, 'anaphoric' contrasts with the terms 'exophoric', 'discourse deictic' and 'recognitional'; in the latter sense, it contrasts with the term 'cataphoric'.

35. According to Nikolaus Himmelmann (p.c.), recognitional demonstratives in Nunggubuyu can also be used pronominally, but in all languages with which I am familiar recognitional demonstratives are used only adnominally.

36. Himmelmann (1996: 236–9) points out that a recognitional demonstrative may be coreferential with a distant NP that is no longer activated.

37. In accordance with the data from language acquisition, Brugmann (1904) and Bühler (1934)

argue that the exophoric use of demonstratives is prior in the evolution of language. That is, they claim that the more abstract uses of demonstratives developed phylogenetically from demonstratives that were used to focus the hearer's attention on concrete objects in the speech situation. If this is correct, it would strengthen my hypothesis that the exophoric use is basic.

38. Note that the notion of lexicalization is also used to denote the (uncommon) process by which grammatical items develop into lexical forms (cf. Hopper and Traugott 1993: 104).

39. Discourse deictic demonstratives may indicate a contrast between anaphoric and cataphoric reference, but they do not indicate two different locations on a distance scale.

40. First and second person pronouns are usually not derived from demonstratives. But see Humboldt (1832) for some examples.

41. There is one minor difference in genitive plural. The genitive plural of the relative pronoun is *deren*. The pronominal demonstrative, on the other hand, has two forms: *deren* and *derer* (Drosdowski 1995: 335–336). *Deren* is used to indicate the possessor in a possessive noun phrase (e.g. *die Schüler und deren Eltern* 'the pupils and their parents'), while *derer* is used either to refer to a subsequent relative clause (e.g. *das Schicksal derer, die...* 'the fate of those who...'), or as a free standing pronoun functioning as the object of verbs that take an argument in genitive case (e.g. *Wir gedenken derer nicht mehr.* 'We don't commemorate those (people) any more') (cf. Drosdowski 1995: 334).

42. I use the following terminology: a 'relative clause' is an embedded clause that is used to modify a noun phrase in the main clause, which I refer to as the 'head of the relative construction'. The 'relative construction' comprises the embedded clause and the head noun.

43. According to Verhaar (1995: 215–6), the *ia...ia* construction occurs only in one particular dialect and is almost entirely absent in "standard or received Tok Pisin". It is one of several relative constructions used "by speakers when they do not know immediately how to continue what they are saying...". (Verhaar 1995: 216).

44. Like Heine and Reh, Benveniste (1966) argues that *si* and *lá* "frame" the relative clause in Ewe. However, in contrast to Heine and Reh, Benveniste does not consider *si* ... *lá* a discontinuous morpheme; rather, he contends that *si* and *lá* serve two separate functions in this construction.

45. To be precise, Lockwood only considers *derjenige* plus prepositional phrase. That is, he does not mention the use of *derjenige* as a plain pronoun and he also ignores the occasional use of *derjenige* with a subsequent noun (e.g. *Diejenigen Leute, die das gesagt haben,...* ' 'Those people who said that...').

46. Frajzyngier uses the notion of demonstrative as a cover term for demonstratives, definite articles and anaphoric pronouns. I only cite examples that Frajzyngier glosses as demonstratives.

47. Himmelmann (1996: 222) argues that unstressed *this* is an extension of the use of Deixis am Phantasma (cf. 5.1) and therefore should not be considered a grammatical marker. If indefinite *this* was just another use of the proximal demonstrative, one would expect that it occurred in contrast to the distal form *that* and that it is stressed in certain contexts. Since indefinite *this* is always unstressed and non-contrastive, I assume, with Wright and Givón, that unstressed *this* does not represent a particular use but rather a specific grammatical marker.

48. The latter contrasts with a third suffix (not shown in this table) which indicates a "location in a time-dependent fashion: that is, location at some fixed point in time" (Anderson and Keenan 1985: 298).

49. Wari' has three demonstratives that combine spatial and temporal reference. They indicate how

long the referent, which is either a person or object, has been absent from the current speech situation: *paca'* 'that just occurred (always heard but never seen)', *cara ne* 'that recently absent', and *cara pane* 'that long absent' (these are the adnominal forms). While *ne* and *pane* are sentence-final temporal deictics, it is unclear whether *paca'* and *cara* can be traced back to any other form; in particular, it is unclear if they derived from locational deictics.

50. Turkish has two locational preverbs, *bu* 'proximal' and *o* 'distal', that have the same morphological form as the adnominal demonstratives while they differ from demonstrative adverbs and pronouns; the latter two are morphologically more complex. At first glance, these data seem to suggest that the preverbs in Turkish originated from adnominal demonstratives. It is, however, difficult to conceive how a preverb might have developed from an adnominal demonstrative, given that preverbs and adnominal demonstratives occur in very different syntactic contexts. Following Himmelmann (1997: 21), I assume that demonstratives are historically based on deictic particles with no specific syntactic function. Given that all demonstratives in Turkish include the deictic roots, *bu* and *o*, it is quite likely that *bu* and *o* are the direct descendants of such particles. I suspect that the preverbs of Modern Turkish developed from these particles. More specifically, I make the following claim (which is subject to future investigation): the preverbs *bu* and *o* evolved from deictic particles that were used adverbially before the demonstratives of the current system emerged.

51. Lehmann (1995a: 101–3) examines another type of preverbation in Totonac and Abkhaz which, in his view, might be an instance of grammaticalization.

52. Li and Thompson do not use the term left-dislocation and thus one cannot be certain as to whether they mean that the topical NP is a left-dislocated constituent of a nonverbal clause. This is, however, how subsequent studies have interpreted their analysis (cf. Gildea 1993; Devitt 1994).

53. Brugmann (1904: 123) discusses a similar case in Swiss German, where the identity pronoun *selb* 'ipse', which many German dialects use to strengthen the weakened demonstrative *der*, assumed a deictic function.

54. Williams (1976: 33) claims that Tuscarora has a demonstrative (*kyé:nv:* 'this') that is derived from the verb: *k-yenv:* 'I am holding it'. She does not explain, however, how this might have happened. It seems that her hypothesis is solely based on the morphological similarity between the two forms, which could simply be an accident.

55. Traugott (1982: 245) says, for instance: "However, it is dubious whether we can trace all grammatical markers derived by processes of grammaticalization to lexical items rather than to certain seemingly fundamental grammatical items, such as demonstrative pronouns and interrogatives. The Indo-European *t*-demonstrative and *kU*-interrogative, for example, have been remarkably resistant to change over several thousand years, and no lexical source seems reconstructable for them."

56. Wilkins (1992) argues that interjections and deictics have many features in common, which might suggest that there is a common diachronic relationship between interjections and deictics (i.e. demonstratives).

57. Fuchs (1996) shows that standard Croatian (spoken in the city of Zagreb) has (almost) lost the middle term of a three-term deictic system, which most rural dialects of Croatian have preserved. Her discussion implies that the change in the Zagreb dialect has been caused by changes in the socioeconomic environment of the speakers. According to Frei (1944: 123) two-term deictic systems are in general derived from three-term systems by reduction of the middle term as in the Zagreb dialect of Croatian.

APPENDIX A

Data sources

Acehnese	Durie (1985)
Ainu	Refsing (1986), Dettmar (1989)
Alamblak	Bruce (1984)
Ambulas	Wilson (1980)
Ao	Gowda (1975)
Apalai	Koehn and Koehn (1986)
Barasano	Jones and Jones (1991)
Basque	Saltarelli (1988)
Burushaski	Lorimer (1935), Berger (1998)
Byansi	Trivedi (1991)
Canela-Krahô	Popjes and Popjes (1986)
Czech	Harkins (1953)
Duwai	Schuh (1977)
Dyirbal	Dixon (1972)
Epena Pedee	Harms (1994)
Ewondo	Redden (1980)
Finnish	Sulkala and Karjalainen (1992), Laury (1995, 1997)
French	Calvez (1993)
Georgian	Hewitt (1995)
German	Eisenberg (1994)
Gulf Arabic	Holes (1990, 1995)
Guugu Yimidhirr	Haviland (1979)
Halkomelem	Galloway (1993)
Hixkaryana	Derbyshire (1985a, 1985b)
Hua	Haiman (1980)
Izi	Meier, Meier and Bendor-Samuel (1975)
Japanese	Kuno (1973), Imai (1996)
Kannada	Schiffmann (1983), Sridhar (1990)
Karanga	Marconnès (1931)
Khasi	Rabel (1961), Nagaraja (1985)
Kiowa	Watkins (1984)
Korean	Lee (1989), Sohn (1994)
Koyra Chiini	Heath (1999)
Kunuz Nubian	Abdel-Hafiz (1988)
Kusaiean	Lee (1975)
Lahu	Matisoff (1973)
Lango	Noonan (1992)
Lealao Chinantec	Rupp (1989)

Lezgian	Haspelmath (1993)
Logbara	Crazzolara (1960)
Mam	England (1983)
Manam	Lichtenberk (1983)
Mandarin Chinese	Chao (1968), Lin (1981), Li and Thompson (1981)
Margi	Hoffmann (1963)
Modern Hebrew	Glinert (1989)
Mojave	Munro (1976)
Mulao	Wang and Guoqiao (1993)
Nama	Hagman (1977)
Nandi	Creider and Tapsubei Creider (1989)
Ngiti	Kutsch (1994)
Ngiyambaa	Donaldson (1980)
Nùng	Saul and Freiberger Wilson (1980)
Nunggubuyu	Heath (1980, 1984)
Oneida	Michelson (1996), Diessel (1999b)
Pangasinan	Benton (1971)
Passamaquoddy-Maliseet	Leavitt (1996), Ng (1999)
Picurís	Zaharlick (1977)
Ponapean	Rehg (1981)
Punjabi	Bhatia (1993)
Quileute	Andrade (1933)
Santali	Bodding (1929)
Slave	Rice (1989)
Supyire	Carlson (1994)
Swazi	Ziervogel (1952)
Swedish	Viberg et al. (1995), Holmes and Hinchliffe (1994)
Tauya	MacDonald (1990)
Tok Pisin	Verhaar (1995)
Tümpisa Shoshone	Dayley (1989)
Turkana	Dimmendaal (1983)
Turkish	Lewis (1967), Underhill (1976), Kornfilt (1997)
Tuscarora	Mithun (1987)
Tzutujil	Dayley (1985)
Urim	Hemmilä (1989)
Urubu-Kaapor	Kakumasu (1986)
Usan	Reesink (1987)
Ute	Givón (1980)
Vietnamese	Thompson (1965), Phú Phong (1992)
Wardaman	Merlan (1994)
Wari'	Everett and Kern (1997)
Western Bade	Schuh (1977)
West Futuna-Aniwa	Dougherty (1983)
West Greenlandic	Fortescue (1984)
Yagua	Payne and Payne (1990)
Yankunytjatjara	Goddard (1985)
Yimas	Foley (1991)

APPENDIX B

The inflectional features of pronominal demonstratives[1]

	Number	Gender	Case	None[2]
Acehnese				+
Ainu	+			
Alamblak	+	+		
Ambulas	+	+		
Ao	+	+		
Apalai	+	+		
Barasano	+	+		
Basque	+	+	+	
Burushaski	+	+	+	
Byansi	+		+	
Canela-Krahô	+			
Czech	+	+	+	
Duwai	+			
Dyirbal		+	+	
Epena Pedee	+	+	+	
Ewondo	+	+		
Finnish	+		+	
French	+	+		
Georgian	+		+	
German	+	+	+	
Gulf Arabic	+	+		
Guugu Yimidhirr	+		+	
Halkomelem	+	+		
Hixkaryana	+	+		
Hua			+	
Izi				+
Japanese	+			
Kannada	+	+	+	
Karanga	+	+		
Khasi	+	+		
Kiowa	+	+		
Korean				*
Koyra Chiini				+
Kunuz Nubian	+			
Kusaiean				*

Lahu				*
Lango	+			
Lealao Chinantec		(+)		
Lezgian	+		+	
Logbara	+			
Mam	+			
Manam	+			
Mandarin Chinese				*
Margi	+			
Modern Hebrew	+	+		
Mojave	+		+	
Mulao				+
Nama	+	+		
Nandi	+			
Ngiti	+			
Ngiyambaa	+		+	
Nùng				*
Nunggubuyu	+	+	+	
Oneida				+
Pangasinan	+			
Passamaquoddy-Maliseet	+	+		
Picurís	+	+		
Ponapean	+			
Punjabi	+	+	+	
Quileute	+	+		
Santali	+	+	+	
Slave	+			
Supyire	+	+		
Swazi	(+)	+		
Swedish	+	+		
Tauya			+	
Tok Pisin				+
Tümpisa Shoshone	+		+	
Turkana	+	+		
Turkish	+		+	
Tuscarora				+
Tzutujil	+			
Urim				+
Urubu-Kaapor				+
Usan				+
Ute	+	+	+	
Vietnamese				*
Wardaman	+		+	
Wari'	+	+		
Western Bade	+	+		
West Futuna-Aniwa				*
West Greenlandic	+		+	

Yagua	+	+		
Yankunytjatjara	+		+	
Yimas	+	+		
Total	**64**	**38**	**25**	**17**

1. Some of the sources that I consulted do not explicitly discuss the inflectional features of pronominal demonstratives. In particular, in grammars of languages in which demonstratives are not marked for gender, number and/or case, it is often not stated that pronominal demonstratives are uninflected. Moreover, there are several grammars in my sample that do not distinguish between (inflectional) affixes and clitics (cf. 2.2.1). The reader would therefore be advised to check the original sources before citing information from this appendix.

2. The star * indicates that the language does not have pronominal demonstratives.

References

Abdel-Hafiz, A. S. 1988. A Reference Grammar of Kunuz Nubian. Buffalo, New York: SUNY Buffalo dissertation.

Abney, S. P. 1987. The English Noun Phrase in its Sentential Aspect. Cambridge, Massachusetts, MIT dissertation.

Andersen, H. (ed.) 1995. Historical Linguistics 1993. Amsterdam: John Benjamins.

Anderson, S. R. 1992. A-Morphous Morphology. Cambridge: Cambridge University Press.

Anderson, S. R. and Keenan, E. L. 1985. "Deixis." In Shopen (ed.) 3, 259–308.

Andrade, M. J. 1933. "Quileute." In Handbook of American Indian Languages, F. Boas (ed.), 149–292. New York: Augustin.

Ariel, M. 1990. Accessing Noun-Phrase Antecedents. London: Routledge.

Auer, J. C. P. 1981. "Zur indexikalitätsmarkierenden Funktion der demonstrativen Artikelform in deutschen Konversationen." In Sprache: Verstehen und Handeln, G. Hindelang and W. Zillig (eds.), 301–311. Tübingen: Niemeyer.

Auer, J. C. P. 1984. "Referential Problems in Conversation." Journal of Pragmatics 8: 627–648.

Baker, M. C. 1996. The Polysynthesis Parameter. New York: Oxford University Press.

Bhatia, T. K. 1993. Punjabi: A Cognitive-Descriptive Grammar. London: Routledge.

Behaghel, O. 1923–32. Deutsche Syntax: Eine geschichtliche Darstellung. 4 vols. Heidelberg: Winter.

Bell, A. 1978. "Language Samples." In Greenberg et al. (eds.) 1, 123–156.

Benton, R. A. 1971. Pangasinan Reference Grammar. Honolulu: University of Hawaii Press.

Benveniste, E. 1966. "La phrase relative: Problème de syntaxe générale." In E. Benveniste, Problèmes de linguistique générale, 208–222. Paris: Gallimard.

Berger, H. 1998. Die Burushaski-Sprache von Hunza und Nager. Teil 1: Grammatik. Wiesbaden: Harrassowitz.

Berman, R. A. and Grosu, A. 1976. "Aspects of the Copula in Modern Hebrew." In *Studies in Modern Hebrew Syntax and Semantics: The transformational-generative approach*, P. Cole (ed.), 265–285. Amsterdam: North-Holland.

Bisle-Müller, H. 1991. *Artikelwörter im Deutschen.* Tübingen: Niemeyer.

Bloomfield, L. 1933. *Language.* New York: Holt, Rinehart, and Winston.

Bodding, P. O. 1929. *Materials for a Santali Grammar.* Dunka: Santal Mission of the Northern Churches.

Borsley, R. D. 1996. *Modern Phrase Structure Grammar.* Oxford: Blackwell.

Brown, C. 1985. "Polysemy, Overt Marking, and Function Words." *Language Sciences* 7: 283–332.

Brown, R. 1973. *A First Language.* Harvard: Harvard University Press.

Bruce, L. 1984. *The Alamblak Language of Papua New Guinea (East Sepik).* Canberra: Australian National University.

Brugmann, K. 1904. *Demonstrativpronomina der indogermanischen Sprachen.* Leipzig: Teubner.

Brugmann, K. and Delbrück, B. 1911. *Grundriss der vergleichenden Grammatik der indogermanischen Sprachen.* 2 vols. Strassburg: Teubner.

Bühler, K. 1934. *Sprachtheorie: Die Darstellungsfunktion der Sprache.* Jena: Fischer.

Bybee, J. L. and Dahl, Ö. 1989. "The Creation of Tense and Aspect Systems in the Languages of the World." *Studies in Language* 13: 51–103.

Bybee, J. L., Pagliuca, W. and Perkins, R. D. 1991. "Back to the Future." In Traugott and Heine (eds.) 2, 17–58.

Bybee, J. L., Perkins, R. D. and Pagliuca, W. 1994. *The Evolution of Grammar: Tense, aspect, and modality in the languages of the world.* Chicago: University of Chicago Press.

Calvez, D. J. 1993. *French Reference Grammar.* Lincolnwood: National Textbook.

Canisius, P. and Sitta, G. 1991. "Textdeixis: Zum Verhältnis von Deixis, Substitution und Anaphora." In *Betriebslinguistik und Linguistikbetrieb: Akten des 24. Linguistischen Kolloquiums Bremen 1989*, E. Klein, F. Pouradier Duteil and K. H. Wagner (eds.), 143–152. Tübingen: Niemeyer.

Carlson, R. 1994. *A Grammar of Supyire.* Berlin: Mouton de Gruyter.

Chafe, W. L. 1987. "Cognitive Constraints on Information Flow." In *Coherence and Grounding in Discourse*, R. S. Tomlin (ed.), 21–52. Amsterdam: John Benjamins.

Chafe, W. L. 1994. *Discourse, Consciousness, and Time: The flow and displacement of conscious experience in speaking and writing.* Chicago: University of Chicago Press.

Channon, R. 1985. "Anaphoric *that*: A friend in need." *Chicago Linguistic Society* 11: 98–109.

Chao, Y. R. 1968. *A Grammar of Spoken Chinese*. Berkeley: University of California Press.

Chen, R. 1990. "English Demonstratives: A case study of semantic expansion." *Language Sciences* 12: 139–153.

Chomsky, N. 1981. *Lectures on Government and Binding*. Dordrecht: Foris.

Christophersen, P. 1939. *The Articles: A study of their theory and use in English*. Copenhagen: Munksgaard.

Clark, E. V. 1978. "From Gesture to Word: On the natural history of deixis in language acquisition." In *Human Growth and Development*, J. S. Bruner and A. Garton (eds.), 85–120. Oxford: Oxford University Press.

Claudi, U. and Heine, B. 1986. "On the Metaphorical Base of Grammar." *Studies in Language* 10: 297–335.

Comrie, B. 1998. "Rethinking the Typology of Relative Clauses." *Language Design* 1: 59–86.

Comrie, B. Forthcoming. "Pragmatic Binding: Demonstratives as anaphors in Dutch." *Berkeley Linguistics Society* 23.

Craig, C. G. 1991. "Ways to Go in Rama: A case study in poly-grammaticalization." In Traugott and Heine (eds.) 2, 455–492.

Crazzolara, J. P. 1960. *A Study of the Logbara (Ma'di) Language*. London: Oxford University Press.

Creider, C. A. and Tapsubei Creider, J. 1989. *A Grammar of Nandi*. Hamburg: Buske.

Croft, W. 1990. *Typology and Universals*. Cambridge: Cambridge University Press.

Cyr, D. E. 1993a. "Cross-linguistic Quantification: Definite articles vs. demonstratives." *Language Sciences* 15: 195–229.

Cyr, D. E. 1993b. "Definite Articles and Demonstratives in Plains Cree." In *Papers from the Twenty-Fourth Algonquian Conference*, W. Cowan (ed.), 64–80. Ottawa: Carleton University.

Cyr, D. E. 1996. "Nikotwâsik iskwâhtêm, pâskihtêpayih!" In *Studies in Honour of H. C. Wolfart*, J. D. Nichols and A. C. Ogg (eds.), 77–111. Winnipeg: Memoir.

Dayley, J. D. 1985. *Tzutujil Grammar*. Berkeley: University of California Press.

Dayley, J. D. 1989. *Tümpisa (Panamint) Shoshone Grammar*. Berkeley: University of California Press.

De Mulder, W. 1996. "Demonstratives as Locating Expressions." In Pütz and Dirven (eds.), 29–47.

178   REFERENCES

Denny, J. P. 1978. "Locating the Universals in Lexical Systems for Spatial Deixis." *Chicago Linguistic Society: Papers from the Parasession on the Lexicon:* 71–84.

Denny, J. P. 1982. "Semantics of the Inuktitut (Eskimo) Spatial Deictics." *International Journal of American Linguistics* 48: 359–384.

Derbyshire, D. C. 1985a. *Hixkaryana.* Amsterdam: North-Holland.

Derbyshire, D. C. 1985b. *Hixkaryana and Linguistic Typology.* Dallas: Summer Institute of Linguistics and University of Texas at Arlington Press.

Derbyshire, D. C. and Pullum, G. K. (eds.) 1986–1998. *Handbook of Amazonian Languages.* 4 vols. Berlin: Mouton de Gruyter.

Dettmar, H. A. 1989. *Ainu-Grammatik.* 2 vols. Wiesbaden: Harrassowitz.

Devitt, D. 1994. Copula Constructions in Crosslinguistic and Diachronic Perspective. Buffalo, New York: SUNY Buffalo dissertation.

Diessel, H. 1997a. "The Diachronic Reanalysis of Demonstratives in Crosslinguistic Perspective." *Chicago Linguistic Society* 33: 83–98.

Diessel, H. 1997b. "Verb-first Constructions in German." In *Lexical and Syntactical Constructions and the Construction of Meaning,* M. Verspoor, K. D. Lee and E. Sweetser (eds.), 51–68. Amsterdam: John Benjamins.

Diessel, H. 1998. Demonstratives in Crosslinguistic and Diachronic Perspective. Buffalo, New York: SUNY Buffalo dissertation.

Diessel, H. 1999a. "The Morphosyntax of Demonstratives in Synchrony and Diachrony." *Linguistic Typology* 3: 1–49.

Diessel, H. 1999b. "The Use of Demonstratives in Oneida Narratives." In *Buffalo Papers in Linguistics,* K. Michelson (ed.). Buffalo, New York: SUNY Buffalo.

Diessel, H. Forthcoming. "Predicative Demonstratives." *Berkeley Linguistics Society* 23.

Dimmendaal, G. J. 1983. *The Turkana Language.* Dordrecht: Foris.

Dixon, R. M. W. 1972. *The Dyirbal Language of North Queensland.* Cambridge: Cambridge University Press.

Dixon, R. M. W. 1982. *Where Have All the Adjectives Gone.* Berlin: Mouton.

Donaldson, T. 1980. *Ngiyambaa: The language of the Wangaaybuwan.* Cambridge: Cambridge University Press.

Dougherty, J. W. D. 1983. *West Futuna-Aniwa: An introduction to a Polynesian outlier language.* Berkeley: University of California Press.

Drosdowski, G. (ed.) 1995. *Duden. Grammatik der deutschen Gegenwartssprache.* Mannheim: Dudenverlag.

Dryer, M. S. 1989a. "Article-Noun Order." *Chicago Linguistic Society* 25: 82–97.

Dryer, M. S. 1989b. "Plural Words." *Linguistics* 27: 865–895.

Dryer, M. S. 1989c. "Large Linguistic Areas and Language Sampling." *Studies in Language* 13: 257–292.

Dryer, M. S. 1992a. "The Greenbergian Word Order Correlations." *Language* 68: 81–138.

Dryer, M. S. 1992b. "SVO Languages and the OV: VO Typology." *Linguistics* 27: 443–482.

Dryer, M. S. 1996. "Focus, Pragmatic Presupposition, and Activated Propositions." *Journal of Pragmatics* 26: 475–523.

Durie, M. 1985. *A Grammar of Acehnese on the Basis of a Dialect of North Aceh.* Dordrecht: Foris.

Ehlich, K. 1979. *Verwendungen der Deixis beim sprachlichen Handeln.* 2 vols. Bern: Lang.

Ehlich, K. 1982. "Anaphora and Deixis: Same, similar, or different?" In Jarvella and Klein (eds.), 315–338.

Ehlich, K. 1983. "Deixis und Anapher." In Rauh (ed.), 79–98.

Ehlich, K. 1986. *Interjektionen.* Tübingen: Narr.

Ehlich, K. 1987. *"so*–Überlegungen zum Verhältnis sprachlicher Formen und sprachlichen Handelns, allgemein und an einem widerspenstigen Beispiel." In *Sprache und Pragmatik. Lunder Symposium 1986,* I. Rosengren (ed.), 279–298. Stockholm: Almqvist and Wiksell.

Ehrich, V. 1992. *Hier und Jetzt: Studien zur lokalen und temporalen Deixis im Deutschen.* Tübingen: Niemeyer.

Eid, M. 1983. "The Copula Function of Pronouns." *Lingua* 59: 197–207.

Eisenberg, P. 1994. *Grundriss der deutschen Grammatik.* [Third edition]. Stuttgart: Metzler.

Engel, U. 1988. *Deutsche Grammatik.* Heidelberg: Groos.

England, N. C. 1983. *A Grammar of Mam: A Mayan language.* Austin: University of Texas Press.

Epstein, R. 1994. "The Development of the Definite Article in French." In *Perspectives on Grammaticalization,* W. Pagliuca (ed.), 63–80. Amsterdam: John Benjamins.

Epstein, R. 1995. "The Later Stages in the Development of the Definite Article: Evidence from French." In Andersen (ed.), 159–175.

Everett, D. L. and Kern, B. 1997. *Wari': The Pacaas Novos language of Western Brazil.* London: Routledge.

Fillmore, C. J. 1982. "Towards a Descriptive Framework for Spatial Deixis." In Jarvella and Klein (eds.), 31–59.

Fillmore, C. J. 1997. *Lectures on Deixis.* Stanford: CSLI Publications.

180 REFERENCES

Fillmore, C. J. and Kay, P. 1993. *Construction Grammar.* Berkeley, University of California, Ms.

Fillmore, C. J., Kay, P. and O'Connor, C. 1988. "Regularity and Idiomaticity in Grammatical Constructions: The case of *let alone.*" *Language* 64: 501–538.

Foley, W. A. 1980. "Toward a Universal Typology of the Noun Phrase." *Studies in Language* 4: 171–199.

Foley, W. A. 1991. *The Yimas Language of New Guinea.* Stanford: Stanford University Press.

Fortescue, M. 1984. *West Greenlandic.* London: Croom Helm.

Fox, B. A. (ed.) 1996. *Studies in Anaphora.* Amsterdam: John Benjamins.

Frajzyngier, Z. 1987. "From Verb to Anaphora." *Lingua* 72: 155–168.

Frajzyngier, Z. 1991. "The *de dicto* Domain in Language." In Traugott and Heine (eds.) 1, 219–251.

Frajzyngier, Z. 1996. "On Sources of Demonstratives and Anaphors." In Fox (ed.), 169–203.

Frajzyngier, Z. 1997. "Grammaticalization of Number: From demonstratives to nominal and verbal plural." *Linguistic Typology* 1: 193–242.

Frei, H. 1944. "Systèmes de déictiques." *Acta Linguistics* 4: 111–129.

Fuchs, A. 1993. *Remarks on Deixis.* Heidelberg: Groos.

Fuchs, Ž. M. 1996. "*Here* and *There* in Croatian: A case study of an urban standard variety." In Pütz and Dirven (eds.), 49–62.

Galloway, B. D. 1993. *A Grammar of Upriver Halkomelem.* Berkeley: University of California Press.

Gernsbacher, M. A. and Shroyer, S. 1989. "The Cataphoric Use of the Indefinite *this* in Spoken Narratives." *Memory and Cognition* 17: 536–540.

Gildea, S. 1993. "The Development of Tense Markers from Demonstrative Pronouns in Panare (Cariban)." *Studies in Language* 17: 53–73.

Givón, T. 1979. *On Understanding Grammar.* New York: Academic Press.

Givón, T. 1980. *Ute Reference Grammar.* Ignacio: Ute Press.

Givón, T. (ed.) 1983. *Topic Continuity in Discourse: Quantified Cross-Language Studies.* Amsterdam: John Benjamins.

Givón, T. 1984. *Syntax. A Functional-Typological Introduction,* vol. 1. Amsterdam: John Benjamins.

Givón, T. 1990. *Syntax. A Functional-Typological Introduction,* vol. 2. Amsterdam: John Benjamins.

Givón, T. 1995. *Functionalism and Grammar.* Amsterdam: John Benjamins.

Glinert, L. 1989. *The Grammar of Modern Hebrew.* Cambridge: Cambridge University Press.

Goddard, C. 1985. *A Grammar of Yankunytjatjara*. Alice Springs: Institute of Aboriginal Development.

Goldberg, A. E. 1995. *A Construction Grammar Approach to Argument Structure*. Chicago: University of Chicago Press.

Gordon, L. 1986. *Maricopa Morphology and Syntax*. Berkeley: University of California Press.

Gowda, K. S. G. 1975. *Ao Grammar*. Mysore: Central Institute of Indian Languages.

Greenberg, J. H. 1963. "Some Universals of Language, with Particular Reference to the Order of Meaningful Elements." In *Universals of Grammar*, J. H. Greenberg (ed.), 73–113. Cambridge: MIT Press.

Greenberg, J. H. 1966. *Language Universals, With Special Reference to Feature Hierarchies*. The Hague: Mouton.

Greenberg, J. H. 1978. "How Does a Language Acquire Gender Markers." In Greenberg et al. (eds.) 3, 47–82.

Greenberg, J. H. 1985. "Some Iconic Relationships among Place, Time, and Disourse Deixis." In *Iconicity in Syntax*, J. Haiman (ed.), 271–287. Amsterdam: John Benjamins.

Greenberg, J. H. 1991. "The Last Stages of Grammatical Elements: Contractive and expansive desemanticization." In Traugott and Heine (eds.) 1, 301–314.

Greenberg, J. H., Ferguson, C. A. and Moravcsik, E. A. (eds.) 1978. *Universals of Human Language*. 4 vols. Stanford: Stanford University Press.

Grenoble, L. 1994. "Discourse Deixis and Information Tracking." *Berkeley Linguistics Society* 20: 208–219.

Grimes, B. F. (ed.) 1997. *Ethnologue: Languages of the world*. [Thirteenth edition]. Dallas: Summer Institute of Linguistics.

Gundel, J. K., Hedberg, N. and Zacharski, R. 1993. "Cognitive Status and the Form of Referring Expressions in Discourse." *Language* 69: 274–307.

Hagman, R. S. 1977. *Nama Hottentot Grammar*. Bloomington: Indiana University Press.

Haiman, J. 1980. *Hua: A Papuan Language of the Eastern Highlands of New Guinea*. Amsterdam: John Benjamins.

Haiman, J. and Thompson, S. A. (eds.) 1988. *Clause Combining in Grammar and Discourse*. Amsterdam: John Benjamins.

Hale, K. 1983. "Walpiri and the Grammar of Nonconfigurational Languages." *Natural Language and Linguistic Theory* 1: 5–47.

Halliday, M. A. K. and Hasan, R. 1976. *Cohesion in English*. London: Longman.

Hanks, W. F. 1989. "The Indexical Ground of Deictic Reference." *Chicago Linguistic Society: Parasession on Language in Context*: 104–122.

Hanks, W. F. 1990. *Referential Practice*. Chicago: University of Chicago Press.

Harkins, W. E. 1953. *A Modern Czech Grammar.* New York: King's Crown Press.

Harms, P. L. 1994. *Epena Pedee Syntax.* Dallas: Summer Institute of Linguistics and University of Texas at Arlington Press.

Harris, A. C. and Campbell, L. 1995. *Historical Syntax in Cross-Linguistic Perspective.* Cambridge: Cambridge University Press.

Harris, M. 1978. *The Evolution of French Syntax: A comparative approach.* London: Longman.

Harris, M. 1980. "The Marking of Definiteness in Romance." In *Historical Morphology,* J. Fisiak (ed.), 141–156. The Hague: Mouton.

Harrison, S. P. 1976. *Mokilese Reference Grammar.* Honolulu: University of Hawaii Press.

Haspelmath, M. 1993. *A Grammar of Lezgian.* Berlin: Mouton de Gruyter.

Haspelmath, M. 1997. *From Space to Time: Temporal adverbials in the world's languages.* Unterschleissheim: Lincom Europa.

Haviland, John 1979. "Guugu Yimidhirr." In *Handbook of Australian Languages,* R. M. W. Dixon and B. J. Blake (eds.) 1, 27–180.

Hawkins, J. A. 1978. *Definiteness and Indefiniteness.* London: Croom Helm.

Heath, J. 1980. "Nunggubuyu Deixis, Anaphora, and Culture." *Chicago Linguistic Society: Parasession on Pronouns and Anaphora:* 151–165.

Heath, J. 1984. *Functional Grammar of Nunggubuyu.* Canberra: Australian Institute of Aboriginal Studies.

Heath, J. 1986. "Syntactic and Lexical Aspects of Nonconfigurationality in Nunggubuyu (Australia)." *Natural Language and Linguistic Theory* 4: 375–408.

Heath, J. 1999. *A Grammar of Koyra Chiini: The Songhay of Timbuktu.* Berlin: Mouton de Gruyter.

Heine, B. 1997. *Cognitive Foundations of Grammar.* New York: Oxford University Press.

Heine, B. and Reh, M. 1984. *Grammaticalization and Reanalysis in African Languages.* Hamburg: Buske.

Heine, B., Claudi, U. and Hünnemeyer, F. 1991a. *Grammaticalization: A conceptual framework.* Chicago: University of Chicago Press.

Heine, B., Claudi, U. and Hünnemeyer, F. 1991b. "From Cognition to Grammar: Evidence from African languages." In Traugott and Heine (eds.) 1, 149–187.

Heinrichs, H. M. 1954. *Studien zum bestimmten Artikel in den germanischen Sprachen.* Giessen: Schmitz.

Hemmilä, R. 1989. "The Demonstrative Pronouns *pa* and *ti* in Urim Discourse." *Language and Linguistics in Melanesia* 20: 41–63.

Hengeveld, K. 1990. "A Functional Analysis of Copula Constructions in Mandarin Chinese." *Studies in Language* 14: 291–323.

Hengeveld, K. 1992. *Non-Verbal Predication: theory, typology, diachrony.* Berlin: Mouton de Gruyter.

Herring, S. C. 1994. "Discourse Functions of Demonstrative Deixis in Tamil." *Berkeley Linguistics Society* 20: 246–259.

Hetzron, R. 1995. "Genitival Agreement in Awngi: Variation on an Afroasiatic theme." In *Double Case: Agreement by Suffixaufnahme,* F. Plank (ed.), 325–335. New York: Oxford University Press.

Hewitt, B. G. 1995. *Georgian: A structural reference grammar.* Amsterdam: John Benjamins.

Himmelmann, N. 1996. "Demonstratives in Narrative Discourse: A taxonomy of universal uses." In Fox (ed.), 205–254.

Himmelmann, N. 1997. *Deiktikon, Artikel, Nominalphrase: Zur Emergenz syntaktischer Struktur.* Tübingen: Niemeyer.

Himmelmann, N. 1998. "Regularity in Irregularity: Article use in adpositional phrases." *Linguistic Typology* 2: 315–353.

Hoffmann, C. 1963. *A Grammar of the Margi Language.* London: Oxford University Press.

Holes, C. 1990. *Gulf Arabic.* London: Routledge.

Holes, C. 1995. *Modern Arabic: Structures, functions and varieties.* London: Longman.

Holmes, P. and Hinchliffe, I. 1994. *Swedish: A comprehensive grammar.* London: Routledge.

Hopper, P. J. 1987. "Emergent Grammar." *Berkeley Linguistics Society* 13: 139–157.

Hopper, P. J. 1991. "On Some Principles of Grammaticalization." In Traugott and Heine (eds.) 1, 17–35.

Hopper, P. J. and Traugott, E. C. 1993. *Grammaticalization.* Cambridge: Cambridge University Press.

Hudson, R. 1984. *Word Grammar.* Oxford: Blackwell.

Humboldt, W. von 1832 (1807). "Ueber die Verwandtschaft der Ortsadverbien mit dem Pronomen in einigen Sprachen." In *Abhandlungen der historisch-philologischen Klasse der Königlichen Akademie der Wissenschaften zu Berlin aus dem Jahre 1829,* 1–26. Reprinted in *Wilhelm von Humboldts Gesammelte Schriften,* 1. Abteilung, Band 6, 304–330. Berlin: Behr.

Imai, S. 1996. Space Divisions in Terms of Japanese Deictic Demonstratives. Buffalo, SUNY Buffalo, Ms.

Jackendoff, R. S. 1977. *X-Bar Syntax.* Cambridge: MIT Press.

Jakobson, R. 1971 (1957). "Shifters, Verbal Categories, and the Russian Verb."
In *Roman Jakobson, Selected Writings*, vol. 2, 130–147. The Hague: Mouton.

Jarvella, R. J. and Klein, W. (eds.) 1982. *Speech, Place, and Action*. Chichester:
John Wiley.

Jefferson, R. J. and Zwicky, A. M. 1980. "The Evolution of Clitics." In *Papers
from the Fourth International Conference on Historical Linguistics*, E. C.
Traugott, R. La Brum and S. Shepherd (eds.), 221–231. Amsterdam: John
Benjamins.

Jones, W. and Jones, P. 1991. *Barasano Syntax*. Dallas: Summer Institute of
Linguistics and University of Texas at Arlington Press.

Kakumasu, J. 1986. "Urubu-Kaapor." In Derbyshire and Pullum (eds.) 1, 326–403.

Keenan, E. L. 1985. "Relative Clauses." In Shopen (ed.) 2, 147–170.

Klavans, J. L. 1985. "The Independence of Syntax and Phonology in Clitici-
zation." *Language* 61: 95–120.

Koehn, E. and Koehn, S. 1986. "Apalai." In Derbyshire and Pullum (eds.) 1,
33–127.

Kornfilt, J. 1997. *Turkish*. London: Routledge.

Koshal, S. 1979. *Ladakhi Grammar*. Delhi: Motilal Banarsidass.

Krámský, J. 1972. *The Article and the Concept of Definiteness in Language*. The
Hague: Mouton.

Kuno, S. 1973. *The Structure of the Japanese Language*. Cambridge: MIT Press.

Kuryłowicz, J. 1965. "The Evolution of Grammatical Categories." Reprinted in
J. Kuryłowicz, 1976, *Esquisses Linguistiques*, vol. 2, 38–54. Munich: Fink.

Kutsch Lojenga, C. 1994. *Ngiti: A Central-Sudanic language of Zaire*. Köln:
Köppe.

Lakoff, R. 1974. "Remarks on *this* and *that*." *Chicago Linguistic Society* 10:
345–356.

Lakoff, G. 1987. *Women, Fire, and Dangerous Things*. Chicago: University of
Chicago Press.

Lakoff, G. and Johnson, M. 1980. *Metaphors We Live By*. Chicago: University
of Chicago Press.

Lambrecht, K. 1981. *Topic, Antitopic and Verb Agreement in Non-Standard
French*. Amsterdam: John Benjamins.

Laury, R. 1995. "On the Grammaticalization of the Definite Article SE in Spoken
Finnish." In Andersen (ed.), 239–250.

Laury, R. 1997. *Demonstratives in Interaction: The emergence of a definite article
in Finnish*. Amsterdam: John Benjamins.

Leavitt, R. M. 1996. *Passamaquoddy-Maliseet*. Munich: Lincom Europa.

Lee, K. D.1975. *Kusaiean Grammar*. Honolulu: University of Hawaii Press.

Lee, H. H. B. 1989. *Korean Grammar.* Oxford: Oxford University Press.

Lehmann, C. 1984. *Der Relativsatz: Typologie seiner Strukturen, Theorie seiner Funktionen, Kompendium seiner Grammatik.* Tübingen: Narr.

Lehmann, C. 1985. "Grammaticalization: Synchronic variation and diachronic change." *Lingua e Stile* 20: 303–318.

Lehmann, C. 1989. "Grammatikalisierung und Lexikalisierung." *Zeitschrift für Phonetik, Sprachwissenschaft und Kommunikationsforschung* 42: 11–19.

Lehmann, C. 1993. "Theoretical Implications of Grammaticalization Phenomena." In *The Role of Theory in Language Description*, W. A. Foley (ed.), 315–340. Berlin: Mouton de Gruyter.

Lehmann, C. 1995a. *Thoughts on Grammaticalization.* Munich: Lincom Europa.

Lehmann, C. 1995b. "Synsemantika." In *Syntax: Ein internationales Handbuch*, J. Jacobs, A. von Stechow, W. Sternefeld, and T. Vennemann (eds.), 1251–1266. Berlin: Mouton de Gruyter.

Leiss, E. 1994. "Die Entstehung des Artikels im Deutschen." *Sprachwissenschaft* 19: 307–319.

Levinson, S. C. 1983. *Pragmatics.* Cambridge: Cambridge University Press.

Lewis, G. L. 1967. *Turkish Grammar.* Oxford: Oxford University Press.

Li, C. N. and Thompson, S. A. 1977. "A Mechanism for the Development of Copula Morphemes." In *Mechanisms of Syntactic Change,* C. N. Li (ed.), 419–444. Austin: University of Texas Press.

Li, C. N. and Thompson, S. A. 1981. *Mandarin Chinese: A functional reference grammar.* Berkeley: University of California Press.

Lichtenberk, F. 1983. *A Grammar of Manam.* Honolulu: University of Hawaii Press.

Lichtenberk, F. 1988. "The Pragmatic Nature of Nominal Anaphora in To'aba'ita." *Studies in Language* 12: 299–344.

Lichtenberk, F. 1991. "On the Gradualness of Grammaticalization." In Traugott and Heine (eds.) 1, 37–80.

Lichtenberk, F. 1996. "Patterns of Anaphora in To'aba'ita Narrative Discourse." In Fox (ed.) 1996, 379–411.

Lin, H. T. 1981. *Essential Grammar for Modern Chinese.* Boston: Cheng and Tsui.

Linde, C. 1979. "Focus of Attention and the Choice of Pronouns in Discourse." In *Discourse and Syntax* [Syntax and Semantics 12], T. Givón (ed.), 337–354. New York: Academic Press.

Linde, C. and Labov, W. 1975. "Spatial Networks as a Site for the Study of Language and Thought." *Language* 51: 924–939.

Lockwood, W. B. 1968. *Historical German Syntax.* Oxford: Clarendon.

Lord, C. 1993. *Historical Change in Serial Verb Constructions.* Amsterdam: John Benjamins.

Lorimer, D. L. R. 1935. *The Burushaski Language. Vol. 1: Introduction and Grammar.* Oslo: Instituttet for Sammenligende Kulturforskning.

Lüdtke, H. 1991. "Überlegungen zur Entstehung des bestimmten Artikels im Romanischen." *Linguistica* 31: 81–97.

Luo, C. 1997. "Iconicity or Economy? Polysemy between demonstratives, copulas and contrastive focus markers." *Chicago Linguistic Society* 33: 273–286.

Lyons, J. 1977. *Semantics.* 2 vols. Cambridge: Cambridge University Press.

Lyons, J. 1979. "Deixis and Anaphora." In *The Development of Conversation and Discourse*, T. Myers (ed.), 88–103. Edinburgh: Edinburgh University Press.

MacDonald, L. 1990. *A Grammar of Tauya.* Berlin: Mouton de Gruyter.

MacNeill, D., Cassell, J. and Levy, E. T. 1993. "Abstract Deixis." *Semiotica* 95: 5–19.

Marconnès, F. S. J. 1931. *A Grammar of Central Karanga: The language of Old Monomotapa as at present spoken in Central Mashonaland, Southern Rhodesia* [Supplement to *Bantu Sudies*, 5]. Johannesburg: Witwatersrand University Press.

Mason, J. A. 1950. *The Language of the Papago of Arizona.* Philadelphia: University Museum, University of Pennsylvania.

Matisoff, J. A. 1973. *The Grammar of Lahu.* Berkeley: University of California Press.

Matsumoto, Y. 1988. "From Bound Grammatical Markers to Free Discourse Markers: History of some Japanese connectives." *Berkeley Linguistics Society* 14: 340–351.

McWhorter, J. 1994. "From Focus Marker to Copula in Swahili." *Berkeley Linguistics Society: Special Session on Historical Issues in African Languages:* 57–66.

Meier, P., Meier, I. and Bendor-Samuel, J. 1975. *A Grammar of Izi: An Igbo language.* Norman: Summer Institute of Linguistics and University of Oklahoma Press.

Meillet, A. 1921 (1912). "L'évolution des formes grammaticales." In *A. Meillet, Linguistique historique et linguistique générale,* vol. 1, 130–148. Paris: Klincksieck.

Merlan, F. C. 1994. *A Grammar of Wardaman: A language of the Northern Territory of Australia.* Berlin: Mouton de Gruyter.

Michelson, K. 1996. Oneida Grammar. Buffalo, SUNY Buffalo, Ms.

Mithun, M. 1987. "The Grammatical Nature and Discourse Power of Demonstratives." *Berkeley Linguistics Society* 13: 184–194.

Moravcsik, E. 1997. "Parts and Wholes in the Hungarian Noun Phrase — a Typological Study." In *Proceedings of LP '96. Typology — Prototypes, Item Orderings and Universals*, B. Palek (ed.), 307–324. Prague: Charles University Press.

Munro, P. 1976. *Mojave Syntax*. New York: Garland.

Nagaraja, K. S. 1985. *Khasi: A descriptive analysis*. Pune: Deccan College.

Ng, E. 1999. When Words with the Same Forms Have Different Functions: Demonstratives and their derivatives in Maliseet-Passamaquoddy. Buffalo, SUNY Buffalo, Ms.

Nichols, J. 1992. *Linguistic Diversity in Space and Time*. Chicago: University of Chicago Press.

Noonan, M. 1992. *A Grammar of Lango*. Berlin: Mouton de Gruyter.

Paul, H. 1916–1920. *Deutsche Grammatik*. 5 vols. Halle an der Saale: Niemeyer.

Paul, H. 1920. *Prinzipien der Sprachgeschichte*. Tübingen: Niemeyer.

Paul, H. 1992. *Deutsches Wörterbuch*, H. Henne and G. Objartel (eds.) [Ninth, revised edition], Tübingen: Niemeyer.

Payne, D. L. and Payne, T. E. 1990. "Yagua." In Derbyshire and Pullum (eds) 2, 249–474.

Peirce, C. S. 1955. *Philosophical Writings of Peirce* J. Buchler (ed.). New York: Dover.

Perkins, R. D. 1992. *Deixis, Grammar, and Culture*. Amsterdam: John Benjamins.

Phú Phong, N. 1992. "Vietnamese Demonstratives Revisited." *Mon-Khmer Studies* 20: 127–136.

Plank, F. 1979a. "Ikonisierung und De-Ikonisierung als Prinzipien des Sprachwandels." *Sprachwissenschaft* 4: 121–158.

Plank, F. 1979b. "Exklusivierung, Reflexivierung, Identifizierung, relationale Auszeichnung. Variationen zu einem semantisch-pragmatischen Thema." In *Sprache und Pragmatik. Lunder Symposium 1978*, I. Rosengren (ed.), 330–354. Lund: Gleerup.

Plank, F. and Moravcsik, E.1996. "The Maltese Article: Language-particulars and universals." *Rivista di Linguistica* 8: 183–212.

Pollard, C. and Sag, I. A. 1994. *Head-Driven Phrase Structure Grammar*. Chicago: University of Chicago Press.

Popjes, J. and Popjes, J. 1986. "Canela-Krahô." In Derbyshire and Pullum (eds.) 1, 128–199.

Postal, P. M. 1969. "On So-called 'Pronouns' in English." In *Modern Studies in English: Readings in transformational grammar*, D. A. Reibel and S. A. Schane (eds.), 201–224. Englewood Cliffs: Prentice-Hall.

Prince, E. F. 1981a. "On the Inferencing of Indefinite-*this* NPs." In *Elements of Discourse Understanding*, A. K. Joshi, B. L. Webber and I. A. Sag (eds.), 231–250. Cambridge: Cambridge University Press.

Prince, E. F. 1981b. "Towards a Taxonomy of Given-new Information." In *Radical Pragmatics*, P. Cole (ed.), 223–255. New York: Academic Press.

Prince, E. F. 1992. "The ZPG letter: Subjects, definiteness and information-status." In *Discourse Description: Diverse analyses of a fundraising text*, S. A. Thompson and W. Mann (eds.), 295–325. Amsterdam: John Benjamins.

Pushpa, K. 1976. *Kokborok Grammar.* Mysore: Central Institute of Indian Languages.

Pütz, M. and Dirven, R. (eds.) 1996. *The Construal of Space in Language and Thought.* Berlin: Mouton de Gruyter.

Quirk, R., Greenbaum, S., Leech, G. and Svartvik, J. 1972. *A Grammar of Contemporary English.* London: Longman.

Rabel, L. 1961. *Khasi: A language of Assam.* Baton Rouge: Louisiana State University Press.

Raidt, E. H. 1993. "Linguistic Variants and Language Change: Deictic variants in some German and Dutch dialects vis-à-vis Afrikaans." In *Historical Linguistics 1991*, J. van Marle (ed.), 281–293. Amsterdam: John Benjamins.

Rauh, G. (ed.) 1983. *Essays on Deixis.* Tübingen: Narr.

Rauh, G. 1983. "Aspects of Deixis." In Rauh (ed.), 9–60.

Redden, J. E. 1980. *A Descriptive Grammar of Ewondo.* Carbondale, Illinois: Department of Linguistics.

Reed, L. 1994. "An Aspectual Analysis of French Demonstrative *ce*." *Berkeley Linguistics Society* 20: 300–312.

Reesink, G. P. 1987. *Structures and their Function in Usan: A Papuan language of Papua New Guinea.* Amsterdam: John Benjamins.

Refsing, K. 1986. *The Ainu language.* Århus: Aarhus University Press.

Rehg, K. L. 1981. *Ponapean Reference Grammar.* Honolulu: University of Hawaii Press.

Renck, G. L. 1975. *A Grammar of Yagaria.* Canberra: Australian National University.

Rice, K. 1989. *A Grammar of Slave.* Berlin: Mouton de Gruyter.

Rijkhoff, J. and Bakker, D. 1998. "Language Sampling." *Linguistic Typology* 2: 263–314.

Rijkhoff, J., Bakker, D., Hengeveld, K, and Kahrel, P. 1993. "A Method of Language Sampling." *Studies in Language* 17: 169–203.

Ross, M. D. 1988. *Proto Oceanic and the Austronesian Languages of Western Melanesia.* Canberra: Australian National University.

Ruhlen, M. 1991. *A Guide to the World's Languages. Vol. 1: Classification.* [Second edition]. Stanford: Stanford University Press.

Rupp, J. E. 1989. *Lealao Chinantec Syntax.* Dallas: Summer Institute of Linguistics and University of Texas at Arlington Press.

Saltarelli, M. 1988. *Basque.* London: Croom Helm.

Samarin, W. J. 1967. *A Grammar of Sango.* The Hague: Mouton.

Sankoff, G. and Brown, P. 1976. "The Origins of Syntax in Discourse: A case study of Tok Pisin relatives." *Language* 52: 631–666.

Sapir, E. 1949. "A Study in Phonetic Symbolism." In *Selected Writings of Edward Sapir,* D. G. Mandelbaum (ed.), 61–72. Berkeley: University of California Press.

Sasse, H-J. 1991. *Arvanitika: Die albanischen Sprachreste in Griechenland,* vol. 1. Wiessbaden: Harrassowitz.

Saul, J. E. and Freiberger Wilson, N. 1980. *Nùng Grammar.* Dallas: Summer Institute of Linguistics and University of Texas at Arlington Press.

Schachter, P. 1985. "Parts-of-speech systems." In Shopen (ed.) 1, 3–61.

Schiffmann, H. F. 1983. *A Reference Grammar of Spoken Kannada.* Seattle: University of Washington Press.

Schuh, R. G. 1977. "Bade/Ngizim determiner system." *Afroasiatic Linguistics* 4–3: 1–74.

Schuh, R. G. 1983a. "The Evolution of Determiners in Chadic." In *Studies in Chadic and Afroasiatic Linguistics,* E. Wolff and H. Meyer-Bahlburg (eds.), 157–210. Hamburg: Buske.

Schuh, R. G. 1983b. "Kilba Equational Sentences." *Studies in African Linguistics* 14: 311–326.

Schuh, R. G. 1990. "Re-Employment of Grammatical Morphemes in Chadic: Implications for language history." In *Linguistic Change and Reconstruction Methodology,* P. Baldi (ed.), 599–618. Berlin: Mouton de Gruyter.

Shetter, W. Z. 1994. *Dutch: An essential grammar.* London: Routledge.

Shopen, T. ed. 1985. *Language Typology and Syntactic Description.* 3 vols. Cambridge: Cambridge University Press.

Sidner, C. L. 1983. "Focusing in the Comprehension of Definite Anaphora." In *Computational Models of Discourse,* M. Brady and R. C. Berwick (eds.), 267–330. Cambridge: MIT Press.

Siewierska, A. and Bakker, D. 1992. Data from Word Order Database. Handout at Joint Meeting of NP and Constituent Order Groups of Eurotype, Donostia.

Sitta, G. 1991. *Deixis am Phantasma: Versuch einer Neubestimmung.* Bochum: Brockmeyer.

Sohn, H-M. 1994. *Korean.* London: Routledge.

190

REFERENCES

Sridhar, S. N. 1990. *Kannada*. London: Routledge.
Stassen, L. 1997. *Intransitive Predication*. Oxford: Clarendon.
Sulkala, H. and Karjalainen, M. 1992. *Finnish*. London: Routledge.
Sweetser, E. 1988. "Grammaticalization and Semantic Bleaching." *Berkeley Linguistics Society* 14: 389–405.
Sweetser, E. 1990. *From Etymology to Pragmatics: Metaphorical and cultural aspects of semantic structure*. Cambridge: Cambridge University Press.
Talmy, L. 1988. "The Relation of Grammar and Cognition." In *Topics in Cognitive Linguistics*, B. Rudzka-Ostyn (ed.), 165–205. Amsterdam: John Benjamins.
Thompson, L. C. 1965. *A Vietnamese Grammar*. Seattle: University of Washington Press.
Traugott, E. C. 1982. "From Propositional to Textual Meanings: Some semantic-pragmatic aspects of grammaticalization." In *Perspectives on Historical Linguistics*, W. P. Lehmann and Y. Malkiel (eds.), 245–271. Amsterdam: John Benjamins.
Traugott, E. C. 1989. "On the Rise of Epistemic Meanings in English: An example of subjectification in semantic change." *Language* 65: 31–55.
Traugott, E. C. 1992. "Syntax." In *The Cambridge History of the English Language. Vol. 1: The Beginnings to 1066*, R. M. Hogg (ed.), 168–289. Cambridge: Cambridge University Press.
Traugott, E. C. and König, E. 1991. "The Semantics-pragmatics of Grammaticalization Revisited." In Traugott and Heine (eds.) 1, 189–218.
Traugott, E. C. and Heine, B. (eds.) 1991. *Approaches to Grammaticalization*. 2 vols. Amsterdam: John Benjamins.
Trivedi, G. M. 1991. *Descriptive Grammar of Byansi. A Bhotiya language*. Calcutta: Anthropological Survey of India, Government of India, Department of Culture.
Ullmer-Ehrich, V. 1978. "Wohnraumbeschreibungen." *Zeitschrift für Literaturwissenschaft und Linguistik* 9: 58–84.
Ultan, R. 1978a. "On the Development of a Definite Article." In *Language Universals. Papers from the Conference held at Gummersbach/Cologne, Germany, October 3–8, 1976*, H. Seiler (ed.), 249–265. Tübingen: Narr.
Ultan, R. 1978b. "Size-sound Symbolism." In Greenberg et al. (eds.) 2, 525–568.
Underhill, R. 1976. *Turkish Grammar*. Cambridge: MIT Press.
Van Valin, R. D. Jr. and LaPolla, R. J. 1997. *Syntax: Structure, meaning, and function*. Cambridge: Cambridge University Press.
Vennemann, T. and Harlow, R. 1977. "Categorial Grammar and Consistent Basic XV Serialization." *Theoretical Linguistics* 4: 227–254.

Verhaar, J. W. M. 1995. *Toward a Reference Grammar of Tok Pisin: An experiment in corpus linguistics.* Honolulu: University of Hawaii Press.

Viberg, Å., Ballardini, K. and Stjärnlöf, S. 1995. *Essentials of Swedish Grammar.* Lincolnwood, Illinois: Passport.

Vogel, P. M. 1993. "Über den Zusammenhang von definitem Artikel und Ferndeixis." *Sprachtypologie und Universalienforschung* 46: 222–233.

Vries, L. de 1995. "Demonstratives, Referent Identification and Topicality in Wambon and Some Other Papuan Languages." *Journal of Pragmatics* 24: 513–533.

Wald, B. 1983. "Referents and Topic Within and Across Discourse Units: Observations from current vernacular English." In *Discourse-Perspectives on Syntax,* F. Klein-Andreu (ed.), 91–116. New York: Academic Press.

Wang, C. and Guoqiao, Z. 1993. *An Outline of Mulao.* Canberra: Australian National University.

Watkins, L. J. 1984. *A Grammar of Kiowa.* Lincoln: University of Nebraska Press.

Webber, B. L. 1991. "Structure and Ostension in the Interpretation of Discourse Deixis." *Language and Cognitive Processes* 6: 107–135.

Weissenborn, J. 1988. "Von der demonstratio ad oculos zur Deixis am Phantasma: Die Entwicklung der lokalen Referenz bei Kindern." In *Karl Bühler's Theory of Language: Proceedings of the Conference held at Kirchberg, August 26, 1984 and Essen, November 21–24, 1984,* A. Eschenbach (ed.), 257–276. Amsterdam: John Benjamins.

Weissenborn, J. and Klein, W. (eds.) 1982. *Here and There: Cross-linguistic studies on deixis and demonstratives.* Amsterdam: John Benjamins.

Wilkins, D. P. 1992. "Interjections as Deictics." *Journal of Pragmatics* 18: 119–158.

Williams, M. M. 1976. *A Grammar of Tuscarora.* New York: Garland.

Wilson, P. R. 1980. *Ambulas Grammar.* Ukarumpa, Papua New Guinea: Summer Institute of Linguistics.

Woodworth, N. L. 1991. "Sound Symbolism in Proximal and Distal Forms." *Linguistics* 29: 273–299.

Wright, S. and Givón, T. 1987. "The Pragmatics of Indefinite Reference: Quantified text-based studies." *Studies in Language* 11: 1–33.

Zaharlick, A. M. 1977. Picurís Syntax. Washington D. C.: American University dissertation.

Ziervogel, D. 1952. *A Grammar of Swazi.* Johannesburg: Witwatersrand University Press.

Zigmond, M. L., Booth, C. G. and Munro, P. 1991. *Kawaiisu. A grammar and dictionary with texts*, P. Munro (ed.). Berkeley: University of California Press.

Zwicky, A. M. 1977. *On Clitics*. Bloomington: Indiana University Linguistics Club.

Zwicky, A. M. 1985. "Heads." *Journal of Linguistics* 21: 1–29.

Zwicky, A. M. 1993. "Heads, Bases and Functors." In *Heads in Grammatical Theory*, G. G. Corbett, N. M. Fraser and S. McGlashan (eds.), 292–315. Cambridge: Cambridge University Press.

Language Index

Name Index

Subject Index

In the series TYPOLOGICAL STUDIES IN LANGUAGE (TSL) the following titles have been published thus far:

1. HOPPER, Paul J. (ed.): *Tense-Aspect: Between semantics & pragmatics*. 1982.
2. HAIMAN, John & Pamela MUNRO (eds): *Switch Reference and Universal Grammar. Proceedings of a symposium on switch reference and universal grammar, Winnipeg, May 1981*. 1983.
3. GIVÓN, T.: *Topic Continuity in Discourse. A quantitative cross-language study*. 1983.
4. CHISHOLM, William, Louis T. MILIC & John A.C. GREPPIN (eds): *Interrogativity: A colloquium on the grammar, typology and pragmatics of questions in seven diverse languages, Cleveland, Ohio, October 5th 1981-May 3rd 1982*. 1984.
5. RUTHERFORD, William E. (ed.): *Language Universals and Second Language Acquisition*. 1984 (2nd ed. 1987).
6. HAIMAN, John (Ed.): *Iconicity in Syntax. Proceedings of a symposium on iconicity in syntax, Stanford, June 24-26, 1983*. 1985.
7. CRAIG, Colette (ed.): *Noun Classes and Categorization. Proceedings of a symposium on categorization and noun classification, Eugene, Oregon, October 1983*. 1986.
8. SLOBIN, Dan I. & Karl ZIMMER (eds): *Studies in Turkish Linguistics*. 1986.
9. BYBEE, Joan L.: *Morphology. A Study of the Relation between Meaning and Form*. 1985.
10. RANSOM, Evelyn: *Complementation: its Meaning and Forms*. 1986.
11. TOMLIN, Russel S.: *Coherence and Grounding in Discourse. Outcome of a Symposium, Eugene, Oregon, June 1984*. 1987.
12. NEDJALKOV, Vladimir (ed.): *Typology of Resultative Constructions. Translated from the original Russian edition (1983). English translation edited by Bernard Comrie*. 1988.
14. HINDS, John, Shoichi IWASAKI & Senko K. MAYNARD (eds): *Perspectives on Topicalization. The case of Japanese WA*. 1987.
15. AUSTIN, Peter (ed.): *Complex Sentence Constructions in Australian Languages*. 1988.
16. SHIBATANI, Masayoshi (ed.): *Passive and Voice*. 1988.
17. HAMMOND, Michael, Edith A. MORAVCSIK and Jessica WIRTH (eds): *Studies in Syntactic Typology*. 1988.
18. HAIMAN, John & Sandra A. THOMPSON (eds): *Clause Combining in Grammar and Discourse*. 1988.
19. TRAUGOTT, Elizabeth C. and Bernd HEINE (eds): *Approaches to Grammaticalization, 2 volumes (set)* 1991
20. CROFT, William, Suzanne KEMMER and Keith DENNING (eds): *Studies in Typology and Diachrony. Papers presented to Joseph H. Greenberg on his 75th birthday*. 1990.
21. DOWNING, Pamela, Susan D. LIMA and Michael NOONAN (eds): *The Linguistics of Literacy*. 1992.
22. PAYNE, Doris (ed.): *Pragmatics of Word Order Flexibility*. 1992.
23. KEMMER, Suzanne: *The Middle Voice*. 1993.
24. PERKINS, Revere D.: *Deixis, Grammar, and Culture*. 1992.
25. SVOROU, Soteria: *The Grammar of Space*. 1994.
26. LORD, Carol: *Historical Change in Serial Verb Constructions*. 1993.
27. FOX, Barbara and Paul J. Hopper (eds): *Voice: Form and Function*. 1994.
28. GIVÓN, T. (ed.) : *Voice and Inversion*. 1994.
29. KAHREL, Peter and René van den BERG (eds): *Typological Studies in Negation*. 1994.

30. DOWNING, Pamela and Michael NOONAN: *Word Order in Discourse.* 1995.
31. GERNSBACHER, M. A. and T. GIVÓN (eds): *Coherence in Spontaneous Text.* 1995.
32. BYBEE, Joan and Suzanne FLEISCHMAN (eds): *Modality in Grammar and Discourse.* 1995.
33. FOX, Barbara (ed.): *Studies in Anaphora.* 1996.
34. GIVÓN, T. (ed.): *Conversation. Cognitive, communicative and social perspectives.* 1997.
35. GIVÓN, T. (ed.): *Grammatical Relations. A functionalist perspective.* 1997.
36. NEWMAN, John (ed.): *The Linguistics of Giving.* 1998.
37. RAMAT, Anna Giacalone and Paul J. HOPPER (eds): *The Limits of Grammaticalization.* 1998.
38. SIEWIERSKA, Anna and Jae Jung SONG (eds): *Case, Typology and Grammar. In honor of Barry J. Blake.* 1998.
39. PAYNE, Doris L. and Immanuel BARSHI (eds.): *External Possession.* 1999.
40. FRAJZYNGIER, Zygmunt and Traci S. CURL (eds.): *Reflexives. Forms and functions.* n.y.p.
41. FRAJZYNGIER, Zygmunt and Traci S. CURL (eds): *Reciprocals. Forms and functions.* n.y.p.
42. DIESSEL, Holger: *Demonstratives. Form, function and grammaticalization.* 1999.
43. GILDEA, Spike (ed.): *Reconstructing Grammar. Comparative Linguistics and Grammaticalization.* n.y.p.